Journey to the Centre of my Being

Journey to the Centre of my Being

Jim Wilson

A Division of Maoli Media Private Limited

Journey to the Centre of my Being

First Edition: October 2019

PUBLISHED BY
ZEN PUBLICATIONS
A Division of Maoli Media Private Limited
60, Juhu Supreme Shopping Centre,
Gulmohar Cross Road No. 9, JVPD Scheme,
Juhu, Mumbai 400 049. India.
Tel: +91 9022208074
eMail: info@zenpublications.com
Website: www.zenpublications.com

Book Design: Red Sky Designs, Mumbai
Cover photo: Mal Clarbrough

ISBN 978-93-87242-64-7

To Mum and Dad who, by loving and trusting me,
gave me the confidence to leave their way
and seek my own.

CONTENTS

Foreword

I am happy to contribute this foreword to the story of Jim Wilson's rich and many-sided life, for I have had a long and personal connection with him. My first wife Nancy was his teacher for a short time when he started school inTimaru in 1942, and in the years 1960–2 I lectured to him on Old Testament Studies in his theological training at Knox College Theological Hall, Dunedin, where I tried, with only limited success, to teach him Hebrew. Later, during 1972–83, we were colleagues in Religious Studies.

As a young and inexperienced Presbyterian minister, I was a great admirer of Jim's father, Mac Wilson, whose preaching and pastoral concern at Chalmers Church, Timaru, became a model for me. So I was not surprised when Jim opted to follow him into the ministry. But neither was I surprised when, at the end of his training, Jim chose not to proceed to ordination. In 1963 my colleagues and I at Knox College joked about his decision to accept a postgraduate scholarship to study religion at Banaras Hindu University in India, for we knew his real intention was to use the opportunity to do some mountain-climbing in the Himalayas. Nevertheless, what he studied in Banaras was to prove very relevant and helpful when he later returned to Christchurch to take up a lectureship in the Department of Philosophy and Religious Studies at Canterbury University, where he spent the rest of his working career.

All New Zealanders have heard of Ed Hillary, but few know of the Jim Wilson who accompanied him on the epic journey up the Ganges from its mouth to its source in the Himalayan mountains. This is partly due to Jim's modesty for he has never been one to boast of his many exploits.

These pages reveal to us the chief passions that shaped Jim's life, such as mountain-climbing and other outdoor pursuits, philosophy, loyal and supportive friendships and, by no means least, his love for his wife Ann and their family of three boys.

This books tells the story of Jim's personal journey of faith... from being a conventional but not wholly convinced Christian, to being a very well-informed humanist with a positive appreciation of the major faiths by which humans live. While not solely autobiographical, the four Parts of the book do follow the successive stages in Jim's activities, beliefs and intellectual interests. Some additions by his wife Ann help to complete his story.

Part I contains some insights into his early years, told with frank and boyish enthusiasm. But, strangely, his account of his theological education follows after long and deep philosophical discussions of arguments for and against the existence of God, which he wrestled with during the course of his Arts degree, and which should have been enough to deflect him from proceeding to his theological education but did not do so until the latter was completed.

In Part II Jim provides some detailed discussions of the Buddhist and Hindu philosophies that he encountered in his postgraduate days in India and Nepal. Part III tells of his encounters with various religions during his years teaching Religious Studies, including times back in India, and in Fiji whilst on study leave. And in Part IV Jim describes how he has developed a physically based framework for living to replace his abandoned metaphysical Christian framework.

This book gives Jim's perspective on the many religious traditions that caught his imagination during the course of his life and engaged his academic attention throughout his teaching career. Being the kind of person he is, Jim was engaged with each of these traditions emotionally just as much as he understands them objectively and academically. This fact enables the reader to get a 'feel' for them as living cultural traditions, rather than being led to regard them, as is too often done, as sets of fixed and unchangeable doctrines.

Lloyd Geering

Acknowledgements

This tale was originally told for family and friends, and I received helpful feedback from family, and great encouragement to publish from Betty and Colin Monteath, and from Ros Henry and David Elworthy. Quentin Wilson did an excellent job on production and layout for a private printing of a small number of copies of an earlier version. Bob Stoothoff was tireless in helping me revise and edit this present version for publication. And Lloyd Geering has kindly written a foreword for this book. To all of these, especially Quentin and Bob and Lloyd, and for encouragement from readers of the earlier print version, my heartfelt thanks. My thanks also to the many – teachers, colleagues, students and friends – who have helped me on my journey, and made it so enjoyable.

My wife, Ann, who was with me for most of the journey, not only provided feedback and support, but also contributed to the text her own thoughts and reactions to some of our adventures together. She was particularly happy when I decided not to become a Presbyterian minister, because that saved her from becoming a minister's wife.

PART I

Faith Flowers, then Fades

1. When I Was A Child

My childhood memories contain no deep feelings about God. I suspect I took for granted that there is a Christian God as naturally as I took for granted the air I breathed and the sun that warmed me on long happy days on the hills and in the sea and rivers of South Canterbury, New Zealand.

We were, however, very much a Christian family. Dad was at that time – 1938–1951 – minister of Chalmers Presbyterian Church, Timaru. He was – and this is not just my loyal view – a very good preacher and a much-loved pastor. A constant factor in my later life has been meeting people who tell me, with deep emotion, how much Dad meant to them, how much he had helped them at critical stages of their lives.

And Mum was almost the perfect minister's wife. I say "almost" – her only flaw in church eyes, a source of great pride to us later, was that she took umbrage at St. Paul's sexist views about women's hair [1] and refused to wear a hat to church. She was very active in church affairs, and very supportive of Dad's visiting and counseling parishioners, I'm sure often contributing her woman's perspective to that counseling. Again, constantly throughout my life, I have been told warmly by people how much they owe to Mum. And she had incredible energy, which she put unreservedly at the service of church committees and organizations, with more than enough over for her growing and rather energetic children.

A little ditty, from the Presbyterian magazine of the day, always summed up for us kids the church side of Mum's life: "I'm late, I'm late, I'm late, for a most important date, I'm President of PWMU, I simply must be there by two, and I've had such a terrible lot to do, I'm late, I'm late, I'm late." [Presbyterian Women's Missionary Union] The best description of Mum was "a whirlwind". Much later, when she was teaching at St. Margaret's College in Christchurch and still coming home on her bike to prepare mid-day dinner for us all, Dad would put his hand to his ear as a sound like a jet plane, he claimed, drew nearer, and say "Here comes your mother". Next moment there'd be a crash as her bike was hurled against the house, and the whirlwind would whirl into the kitchen and whirl dinner onto the table.

Mum's and Dad's Christianity was, in my view, of the best possible sort. For them, the heart of the New Testament was Jesus' teachings of unlimited love and forgiveness, and his urgings to help the poor and the needy. The heart of the Old Testament was the very similar social and moral message of the prophets, about which Dad preached frequently. The prophets, speaking for Yahweh (the ancient Hebrew name for their God), castigated the people of Israel for putting outward religious observances ahead of care of others – observing the religious fasts and feasts while cheating in their businesses and ill-treating orphans and widows. Dad passionately believed that how you lived, and above all how you cared for others, was of infinitely more importance in the sight of God than what you believed, or whether you went to church (though he also strongly believed that constant worship of God in church, and constant exposure to Jesus' message of love, was of huge assistance in living lovingly.)

This passionate belief got him in trouble, theologically, with hard-line Presbyterian colleagues, ministers and lay people alike. There is a very strong theme in Protestantism, and especially in Presbyterianism – in my view a totally pernicious theme – the catch-cry of which is "justification by faith alone". The belief is that we are saved not by what we do – for we are hopelessly mired in original sin and can do nothing good by our own strength – but solely by our faith in God's redeeming act through Jesus Christ. It comes especially from the early Christian theologian Augustine, though with prompting from Paul, whose letters form part of the New Testament of the Christian Bible. Dad would have none of this. Like the prophets, including Jesus, he was frustrated by religiously pious people who were cold and judgemental in their dealings with others. He sided with a chap called Pelagius, who disputed Augustine's views and suggested works – i.e. what we do, how we live – are important as well as faith. For his pains Pelagius was declared a heretic, and Augustine's baneful influence has blighted the course of Christianity, and thus of the much of the world, ever since. At theological gatherings Dad, I've been told by his friends, used to delight in creeping up beside conservative Augustinian colleagues and whispering in their ears "What if, after all, Pelagius was right?"

Mum, probably not so worried about the theological intricacies, simply lived this Christianity of loving and caring for less fortunate people. There is a story told by Jesus of a rich man giving a feast and inviting all his rich friends who, one by one, sent paltry excuses and failed to turn up. Undaunted, the man sent his servants out into the highways and byways of the city and had them gather in all the beggars and widows and orphans to sit down at his feast.[2] Mum went one better. She didn't bother with the initial invitation to the well-to-do, she simply gathered in all the lame ducks she could find and fed them, physically and emotionally. Sunday dinner at the manse was frequently swelled well beyond the size of our normal family with the addition of all Mum's waifs and strays – refugees from war-torn countries, shy and/or psychologically disturbed people who had no other friends, members of Dad's congregation who were single, or bereaved – on and on. I vividly remember poor Dad carving away at the huge forequarter of cheap mutton Mum used to buy and, just as he filled the last plate bar his own, one of us fast-eating kids would be handing up our plate for more.

I don't remember resenting all these extras at Sunday and Christmas dinners – I don't remember thinking or feeling about it at all. This was just the way things were. And though we were so very much a church family, possibly from the outside seemingly hemmed in and nearly suffocated by all these church people and churchiness, and by such deeply religious parents, I can recall no feeling of restraint or hindrance at all. I felt gloriously free to pursue my own interests and life, and confident enough to do so because, I feel sure now, I was so certain that I was loved and trusted by Mum and Dad. If some of our wilder exploits caused consternation to conservative members of the Church, and if such consternation was expressed to Mum and Dad, no dampening hint of it ever reached my feelings. Years later I realized there was one inhibiting influence from which I am still not – and never want to be – free. My only lasting recollection of Mum's disapproval – for inevitable momentary clashes with Mum or Dad over minor matters like home chores have left no trace in my psyche – is of occasions when I could have helped someone in need, and didn't.

So though I came to hate the judgemental and 'one way only' aspects of Christianity with an intense hatred, from which I am not yet completely free, it was and is most certainly not Mum's and Dad's Christianity that I hated, ever. I still feel their faith was wholly admirable and good, because it was centred on love not on judgement. The most remarkable proof of this came many years after our childhood, when Mum learned that my brothers, John and Hugh, are gay. At the time most Christians, and many dreadful passages in the Bible, Old and New Testament alike, portrayed God as dead against homosexuality.[3] So Mum's Christian-influenced judgement came into direct conflict with her Christian-influenced, and maternal, love. Love won hands down.

In writing of my childhood I have written of my parents' religious feelings, beliefs and actions, not my own. I think I have done this for the simple reason that then I had none. I cannot recall awe at being in church. I cannot recall being comforted by – or needing comfort from – assurances repeated in hymn and sermon that Jesus loved me. I cannot recall being afraid of God when I was naughty – significantly, perhaps, neither can I recall being afraid of Mum or Dad, or of school teachers, when I was naughty. I cannot recall being moved to anguish or gratitude at the annual repetition of the macabre and then triumphant Easter story. And the annual celebration of the birth of Jesus was for me purely presents and stuffing myself to bursting point with Christmas dinner. I cannot even recall being grateful to God for creating the beautiful South Canterbury sea and hills and rivers amongst which we lived – though having no person to thank for the beautiful planet I live on is now one of my few regrets about not believing in a creator God.

But I am sure that the beautiful hills and seas and rivers, and Mum's and Dad's love of the outdoors, were a vital factor in us not being suffocated by churchiness, and that they had as important a part in my early development as did church and Christianity. Perhaps I romanticize my childhood: but what I do recall, and in many instances can relive still, are my intense feelings of excitement and happiness, and on occasions of trepidation, even fear and trembling, when in wild and beautiful surroundings. Judging by my recollections now of my feelings then, I was already feeling intensely towards nature those emotions Christianity would have me feel towards God, the creator of nature. I suspect my determined efforts to be a faithful servant of the Christian God were doomed from day one because I am, at heart, a naturalistic pagan.

2. God 'Calls'

Some time after Dad moved to Knox Church, Christchurch, in 1951, I ceased taking my parents' God for granted and began actively to believe in him. I was in my mid-teens.

The Hound of Heaven

It is possible that my move from passive to active faith was sparked by a curious episode during the summer after our family left Timaru. I was desperately lonely and homesick in Christchurch for my Timaru life and friends, so I enticed my Timaru school friend Rob McCullough to camp with me at the foot of Porter's Pass, and go scrambling on the Torlesse Range. All went well for two or three days, after Dad and my sister Margaret had dropped us off. We discovered the thrill of running down shingle slides. We climbed from the pass to the summit of Fog Peak. Then, feeling greatly daring, we climbed Castle Hill Peak from the Kowai Valley.

But then we ran out of energy and hung around camp for a day in brilliantly fine weather. A really dreadful depression enveloped and threatened to crush us both. Life seemed utterly and completely pointless. To do anything was impossible – we were absolutely energyless – and to hang round doing nothing was even worse. It must seem laughable to anyone else – one day doing nothing reduced two healthy lads to trembling wrecks. But I can still vividly recall the terror I felt, which Rob shared and also remembers, and it was no laughing matter to us. That night went on forever. As first light dawned – proving the previous sentence a literal lie but leaving its essential truth untarnished – we madly packed our tent and belongings and fled the brooding hills as if the Hound of Heaven was at our heels.

Was it the Hound of Heaven? Was this felt terror at nothingness, at the pointlessness of existence, part of what sent me flying into the arms of God? It is surely possible. But I cannot now recall any direct connection. We fled to home and family and other human company and, for me at least, the terror retreated back into some small dark void in the centre of my being, not gone, never forgotten completely, but quiescent, biding its time.

Be that as it may, as I advanced through my teens, and deeper into the uncharted and turbulent waters of rampant sexuality, I also advanced more and more into active commitment to the Christian God my Dad was preaching about each Sunday. The details are gone from the accessible layers of my memory. But two dramatic incidents are very accessible, unforgettable indeed.

God's 'call'

The first occurred at a Student Christian Movement retreat.There is a sexual memory from there also. All through one, no doubt pious, lecture, a girl called Lynne and I coyly held hands! Not much of a sexual adventure by the standards of today's youth I admit. But I was an incredibly naive and good little Christian boy in those days – never even been drunk let alone made love – and this was, to that point in time, the intensely exciting apex of my sexual career. But I digress from religious to sexual matters, a constant tendency of mine.

At some stage during the retreat I must have let go of Lynne's hand, for my important religious event took place when I was alone on the toilet. God 'spoke' to me. He didn't say anything about holding Lynne's hand, so presumably that wasn't a sin, or at any rate not a serious enough one to rule me out of the running. And it wasn't an audible voice in my physical ears. But it was such a tremendously intense conviction that God wanted me to become a minister that it was certainly as if a voice spoke to me. I don't remember any build-up to this moment of utter conviction. But I vividly recall my response: "Yes God, I will." I sat stunned and elated, suffused with happiness and purpose (which so often go hand in hand).

I'd like to say I burst out of the toilet shouting God's 'call' and my acceptance to all and sundry. But we Presbyterians are a dour reserved lot, and excess of emotion, even if religious, is more an embarrassment to us than a virtue. I told no-one at the retreat, nor did anyone remark on my changed demeanour and glowing eyes, so presumably there was no outward and visible sign of my inward change. But the change, and the vow, were serious and reasonably long-lasting. Cautious wee man that I am I probably waited a while to make sure this was so, and then I told Dad about it. I'm sure he was thrilled, but, probably because I was then self-centred as many teenagers are, I don't recall.

In the Presbyterian Church of New Zealand, when people believe they are 'called' by God to His Holy Ministry, they apply to their local Presbytery and, if accepted, become a Divinity Student of that Presbytery. I was accepted by Christchurch Presbytery. My credentials were not far short of impeccable. My grandfather on Dad's side had been a Presbyterian Minister, first in Scotland then in New Zealand. My father was a Presbyterian minister, highly respected by all save those in whose ears he whispered "What if, after all, Pelagius was right?" My grandfather on Mum's side had been an elder in the Presbyterian Church of England, and one of Mum's brothers was a Presbyterian minister. Better yet, Mum's sister was a Presbyterian missionary, first in China till Mao took over and kicked her out, then in Malaya. Mum was a Presbyterian minister's wife and was highly respected by all save those who thought she should wear a hat to church. As for me, I was getting good marks at a Presbyterian school, including a prize for scripture (taught by Dad!), and Presbytery were not to know this was on account of my good short-term memory and good exam technique, and that most of my time and energy at this good Presbyterian school was expended on gymnastics and cricket and rugby and basketball and swimming and arguing with the masters. Also, as a virgin, I was pure in deed (though not in thought). Of course they didn't know that either.

So in my sixth form year I was a divinity student. This committed me to getting a university degree, for the training at Knox Theological Hall, in Dunedin, was post-graduate, save for a few exceptions for people accepted later in their lives. We divinity students were encouraged to include philosophy in our degrees. When, after my first year at university, I decided to major in philosophy it was more fateful than my decision to train for the ministry, and had longer lasting effects.

I have now no detailed memories of my early active Christian days. But that I was an earnest and enthusiastic Christian I cannot doubt. I was active in the university Student Christian Movement, active in Knox Church's Youth Fellowship, taught Sunday School, and sang in the church choir. And, though nervously and not often, I 'witnessed' for Jesus. During my 10 weeks' Compulsory Military Training, at Burnham Military Camp, I would kneel beside my bed and say my prayers each night before lights out in our dormitory. I also, when writing an article on one of our mountain trips, mentioned that we had used bad weather for Bible discussions, and had left a copy of St. John's gospel in the hut for others to do likewise. This article was published in the journal of the Canterbury Mountaineering Club, then a very hard-core all-male group not given to theological discussions. I scarcely know whether to wince at these embarrassing displays by my former self, or to admire my courage.

I 'crucify Jesus'

However, by far my most intense religious experience in those university student days was of a more serious nature. It was a dark and anguished counterpoint to the light and bliss of my believing I was 'called' by God, and it stemmed from a terrible tension at the core of Christianity. On the one hand God is presented as loving, merciful, forgiving, pleading with us to love one another, to act justly, to love kindness. Indeed, "God so loved the world that He gave His only begotten Son…". But, on the other hand, why did he need to give His only begotten Son? – "that men might not perish, but have everlasting life."[1] Perish? How and why should we perish if God our Father is all-loving and all-powerful? Because he is also presented as a jealous and vengeful God: "You shall have no other gods before me".[2] "I Yahweh your God am a jealous God … visiting the iniquity of the fathers upon the children to the third and fourth generation of those who hate me …".[3] It is to turn away this wrath of God that his Son is sacrificed: "There was no other good enough to pay the price of sin" says a hymn we used to sing. Nor is God presented thus only in the Old Testament. In the New Testament Jesus is reported as saying that on the day of judgement "The angels will come out and separate the evil from the righteous, and throw them into the fire of the furnace; there men will weep and gnash their teeth".[4] Tragically, in my view, even the Son believed to have given his life for our redemption is, in Medieval European Christianity, turned into a stern and terrifying Judge, who condemns to everlasting hell those who do not believe in him. Small wonder that popular piety in the Roman Catholic Church takes its pleas for forgiveness or health or food to Mary, the Holy Mother of God, whose mother's heart remains inclined to love rather than to judgement; and to saints, who seem closer to suffering humanity, and more likely to have mercy on us than the stern God the Father or God the Son.

It was above all the presentation of God as a jealous God – "You shall have no other gods before me" – that led to my most miserable religious trauma. Though it was not part of Mum's and Dad's Christianity, there is a strong strain in Presbyterianism which stresses that intense involvement, and especially intense pleasure, in any activities other than God-centred ones is a direct threat to the supremacy God ought to have in all aspects of our life. This, I'm sure, is one of the many reasons why sexual love and activity is viewed so negatively by many religions, not just Christianity. So intense an involvement and ecstasy is seen as a dangerous rival to religious involvement and religious ecstasy.

But at this time it was not sex that caused my problem but mountaineering. For there was no doubt that next to, perhaps greater than, my involvement and pleasure in Christianity was my involvement and intense pleasure in moving and living amongst, and climbing, mountains. Almost every weekend, with Mike White especially, but also many other companions, I would be climbing in ranges close to Christchurch. And all year Mike, Barry Smith, Dave Elphick and I would plan and prepare for our three or four week summer trip, the anticipation and planning and preparation almost as exciting as the trip itself. If indeed God be a jealous God, demanding my whole and undivided heart and soul and mind, he was right to be worried, for I was consumed a great deal of the time, heart, soul, mind and body, by mountaineering.

This, then, is the background to my trauma. The foreground is the Edwards Valley in Arthur's Pass National Park, on a cold wet Easter night. Easter, when Christians remember Jesus dying in agony on the Cross for us. Easter, when God had been putting the finger on me for weeks to forgo mountaineering in favour of attendance at Church. Easter, when I tried to fob him off with a compromise, a shifty bit of bargaining, and he was not having a bar of it. Of course I am talking of how it seemed to me at the time, not of how any real god or spiritual energy might or might not be.

In those days New Zealand Railways ran a peculiar but priceless train known as the Perishable. It was a goods train taking, presumably, mainly perishable foodstuffs between Christchurch and Greymouth. I think there must have been one each way every night, at least at weekends. The one from Christchurch left about 6 pm, but, as every other bit of traffic on the line had priority, it spent much of its time shunting off the main line and waiting – and much time also, for reasons we never fathomed, going backwards. If you missed it at Christchurch station you could catch it at Hornby, along with Barry Smith, an hour or more later; often by eight or nine o'clock it was still puffing quietly away at Rolleston. Not till midnight or later did it reach the Bealey railway bridge, near Klondyke Corner, where, by arrangement with guard or driver when you got on, it would stop to disgorge a gaggle of sleepy mountaineers; as it would again shortly after at Arthur's Pass, Otira or Jacksons. For along with the many goods wagons the Perishables always had one, usually elderly, passenger carriage. Despite this we often travelled in the guards van and even, on one memorable occasion, in the engine cab.

You staggered out and did your climb; then about 24 hours later, or 48 hours later if you had both weekend days to spare, and if your alarm clock woke you, you staggered onto the Perishable coming from Greymouth and going to Christchurch. Many and varied were the grand feats of climbing and endurance achieved “between Perishables”, for we were young and eager and fit in those days.

My proffered compromise to God was made possible by the Perishable. Mike White and I were keen to do a climb at Easter, a great holiday for mountaineering. God wanted me, I felt, to go to church at Easter, a great holy day when all good Christians should be at church recalling Christ’s death and resurrection. “So,” I said to God, “I’ll go to Church on Good Friday, then catch the Perishable that evening and go climbing Saturday”. I realize as I write now that this should have enabled me to catch the return Perishable Saturday midnight, and go to church on Resurrection Sunday as well – two for God and only one for mountaineering. But I don’t recall that being in the bargain I offered God.

Mike would no doubt have preferred to take the whole five days of holiday for climbing. Though he was also at that time a Christian, he was an Anglican one, and they’re generally not so anguished and guilt-ridden as Presbyterians. But he respected my religious scruples and waited for me till Friday evening.

I knew before I got on the train that this wasn’t going to work for me. But a mixture of not wanting to let Mike down after he had waited patiently for me, and an intense desire to go climbing, mingled with the thought “surely I’ve done enough for God already”, saw me onto the train and away. Six hours in a train stopping, starting, going backwards, is a long time to brood over a sin, imagined or real. I became more and more anguished with every passing mile. Then we were out in the pouring rain and crossing the Bealey River and climbing up the gloomy track through the deep gorge of the Edwards River. The fossicking through the dark dripping trees, slipping in the mud and tripping over unseen roots, the relentless rain soaking through parka and clothes to skin, the looming awesome presence of unseen mountains above us, all combined into a chillingly apt setting for the torment building to a crescendo inside me. I was disobeying a clear command from God. I felt with terrifying intensity that with every step I took I was hammering nails into the hands and feet of Jesus, crucifying him again. And yet – on and on I went. I could have told Mike what I was feeling, told him I had to turn back, had to stop crucifying Jesus. I didn’t. On and on I went.

Dawn came at last, the rain cleared, my torment eased. After breakfast at the Edwards Hut we climbed out of the valley onto the ridge of Mt. Oates, then up towards the summit. Mike stood on top. I couldn't bring myself to do so. Hoping Mike wouldn't notice, but that God would, I skirted round a few feet below. We carried on down the other side to Goat Pass, and thence down the Mingha River and back to Arthur's Pass and the Perishable. I returned to my studies, shaken and chastened, and presumably made my peace with God, though not by giving up mountaineering. Perhaps some kindly soul crept up beside me and whispered in my ear: "What if, after all, a loving God created this beautiful world; surely then it would not be a sin to enjoy it?" Maybe I even worked this out for myself.

3. Philosophy

Perhaps I took to philosophy because I already loved arguing. Or maybe philosophy gave me my love of arguing.

Arthur Prior

I was very lucky that the professor of philosophy at Canterbury University in my time as a student there was Arthur Prior. Arthur had started training to be a Presbyterian minister, but had then moved to an academic career. He was already a world-renowned logician, with influential publications to his name. He was a brilliant and very endearing lecturer. He lectured with no notes, so easily it seemed to flow like a river, yet when I checked my notes later I found each lecture was beautifully structured as well as crisp and clear.

Nor were the sessions just him talking; he would ask us questions, present us with arguments and ask if we could find flaws in them, tease us by 'proving' things patently false, and take our contributions, always with respect, and weave them into his structured whole.

But above all he was a wonderfully warm and friendly human being. While he put up with being called "professor" by Stage I students, from then on he insisted we call him Arthur, which was most unusual in the stuffy academic circles of those days. He would invite us to evenings at his place, where we were equally warmly welcomed by his wife Mary. I especially remember one such occasion when he greeted us excitedly at his door and urged us to come inside and listen to an ethical argument. It proved to be part of a very funny record by Flanders and Swann, two British piano-playing and singing comedians, about a cannibal chief's son and heir who decided it was wrong to eat people. "What," said his father, aghast, "not eat people?" "Yes," said his son. "But son, we've always eaten people." "I will not let another person pass my lips," came the staunch reply. "But you'll ruin our entire internal economy," wailed the chief. "Eating people is wrong," came the reply. The chief was desperate. "But you might as well say 'don't kill people'". The son was stunned. "Don't kill people?" he spluttered.

"Don't kill people!!!" He and his father burst into laughter. "Don't kill people? – ridiculous."

So I might have chosen philosophy as my major for the man rather than the subject. But I didn't. The subject quickly enthralled and excited me. Philosophy started its long and illustrious career in the West as, literally, love of wisdom (Greek *philo* = loving, *sophia* = wisdom). At first it encompassed all of what became scientific enquiry as well as ethics and the meaning of life – indeed anything other than literature and drama. But by my time it was, in English-speaking countries, a narrower but still fascinating field, concerned mostly with enquiring into the basis on which we claim to know things. It examined and challenged things which the science of the day took for granted; for example, that we can be sure of the connection between events which we call cause and effect; or even that there is a real physical world external to our minds.

For me it was intensely stimulating. It provided a disciplined way of assessing arguments and evidence for and against various viewpoints that was both exciting and frightening. It greatly changed my life for the better. In many ways it was to me in the mental realm what mountaineering was in the physical – an adventure, a challenge, all the more intense for its spice of danger. Danger? Frightening? Yes, of course. To have things I had taken for granted challenged and often overturned was deeply disturbing. Crucially, for my present story, to have my Christian beliefs put under the microscope and dissected with philosophical skill was to have my whole life's plan and purpose challenged, not to mention my whole framework for making sense of this vast and mind-boggling universe. I am profoundly thankful that for some fortunate reason – genetic? my parents' love and trust? – for me the excitement far outstripped the fear, the danger was stimulating, not inhibiting.

Jim Thornton

I was very fortunate also that the lecturer taking Philosophy of Religion was a young ex-Anglican clergyman, Jim Thornton. Jim had spent time as curate and then vicar, but found it increasingly difficult to accept the Christian beliefs his position required him to commend. So he returned to Canterbury University to teach philosophy. For five fascinating years his mind and mine engaged in intense intellectual tussles as he, not in an adversarial way but objectively and fairly, introduced me to a raft of philosophical difficulties facing belief in a loving Christian God. He was not trying to persuade me out of my beliefs. But his duty as a philosopher was to explore with me arguments for and against the existence of God; and I engaged with him wholeheartedly in a long and exciting battle to defend my beliefs in the face of my increasing doubts about their validity.

I cannnot hope to reproduce in detail all the nuances, the advances and retreats, the yielding here and staunchly defending there, of this five-year adventure. The best I can hope for is a summary of the main moves, and a little of the flavour of it all.

It is convenient to divide this into two stages, though I did not progress chronologically through each stage in turn. The first stage was the examination of traditional Christian arguments for the existence of God – an examination during which I came to believe all are fatally flawed. The second stage was an examination of arguments against the existence of a loving Christian God, during which I fought tooth and nail to hold on to my faith, with some success, albeit, as it turned out, temporary.

4. Arguments for the Existence of God

Jim Thornton, in his philosophy of religion course, introduced me to arguments claiming to prove the existence of the Christian God. Three of them exercised my mind considerably at that stage of my journey: the arguments from design, first cause, and religious experience.

Argument from design

This argument is one of the easiest to understand and most commonly advanced. Perhaps the most famous of the many versions of it was devised by the English bishop William Paley,[1] and ran something like this. Suppose, strolling across a moor, you come across a watch. Picking it up and examining it, removing its back and looking at the intricate workings inside, and realizing sooner or later that it accurately marks the passage of time divided into seconds, minutes and hours, what would be your thoughts about its origin? Paley was in no doubt. You would conclude, he said, that so intricate and marvellous a device could not have happened by chance, or by unconscious natural processes. It must have been designed and made by an intelligent being for a particular purpose. How much more certainly, then, when you contemplate the intricate and amazing workings of the world we live in, and of the human mind and body and senses through which we experience it, must your conclusion be that this world was designed and made by an intelligent being; as we ourselves must also have been. Yet no human intelligence could be supposed great enough to design so mighty a project, nor could human powers be considered adequate to make it. This must have been done by an immensely intelligent and powerful superhuman being, namely God.

This seems a powerful argument. Prior to doing philosophy I had never spelt it out clearly like this. But I'm sure that in vague form it had been an important support for my belief in God. I'm also sure it is a major support for the belief of many, in many religions, to this day.

But as I examined it closely, with Jim Thornton's help, I came to believe it has two fatal flaws.

The first was most forcefully pointed out by the Scottish philosopher David Hume.[2] I came to like Hume very much, for the clarity of his arguments, his staunch character, and his humour. He lived in 18th century Scotland, where belief in God was almost universal, and questioning this belief almost a crime. But David, with wit and elegance, followed the truth as his mind led him, regardless of the horror of his contemporaries. And the truth, as he saw it, was that belief in God could not be rationally justified. In an age of faith he was an avowed agnostic[3] (did not know if God exists), if not an atheist[4](believed God does not exist). The story I love best about him – I hope a true one, but I've not been able to find a source – is that when he was on his death bed his friends gathered round him earnestly pleading with him to repent and believe before it was too late and he would be condemned to hell by the God he didn't believe in. "If there is a God," David responded wryly, "I think he will be big enough to put up with being laughed at by David Hume."

Hume pointed out that in order for the argument from design to hold even for a watch found on a moor, two things have to be true: 1) we must have had repeated experiences of things like watches, and 2) in the vast majority of previous cases we must have seen, or known in some way, that they have been made for a purpose by an intelligent being.[5] And for many of the things we see or use everyday – watches, cell phones, cars, bikes, houses, roads – both these things are true. So we are seldom led astray when we use the argument from design in such cases, even if we have not seen a particular type of artifact before. But we do not normally look at a tree, or the wonderfully intricate patterns on sand left by a retreating tide, or the exquisite symmetry and beauty of living coral, or a cauliflower, or a puppy, or a dolphin … and say, "Ah, this must have been made by an intelligent being for a purpose".

This is because most things we experience, even in a city, are not at all like watches, nor in our experience are they made by intelligent beings. If they are living beings they emerge from complex clusters of dividing cells under the influence of genes, plants from seeds and birds and animals from eggs or wombs. If they are inorganic, for example hills or rocks or rivers, they are formed by geological and/or climatic forces. Hume gently teases his religious readers at this point. If you think there is a Supreme Being from which all this comes, he says, and claim "most things in my experience come from It", then the most plausible conclusion is that this Supreme Being – God – is a giant vegetable, or a couple of copulating mammals.[6] More seriously, he points out the flaw in assuming the whole world, let alone the whole universe, can be assumed on the basis of our experience to be created by an intelligent being, like a watch by a human. We assume this in the case of the watch because we have previously seen many things like watches being made. But we have never seen even one world or one universe being made. Far from having numerous previous experiences to guide us we have none at all.[7]

The second flaw is even more fundamental.[8] The argument from design depends for its apparent plausibility on our tendency to want an explanation for the origin of complex things. But it postulates as origin something infinitely more complex and mysterious than that which we are trying to explain. God, if she or he exists and created this universe, must be far more complex than even the most complex things we know of, the brains of primates and dolphins. Since we want explanations for things like brains, it is impossible not to want an explanation for this most complex thing of all, God. So rather than providing a final explanation for all things, the notion of God creates a new and even more difficult question to answer – who created, or what caused, God?

Despite these logical flaws the argument from complexity and seeming purpose in this world to an intelligent designer of this world had great force in earlier ages. Such a designer seemed an obvious way to account for this complexity, and especially for extremely complex things which seem to serve some purpose perfectly. And, of course, the argument is still very much in vogue amongst conservative Christians, particularly those that label themselves creationists. An example often given is the eyes of humans and other animals. They are astonishing, even if a little less than perfect now in my case as age creeps on apace. They focus light reflected from myriads of shaped and moving surfaces, like shiny leaves on wet beech trees outside the window, and send electric signals along optic nerves to the brain where they are constructed into the objects and processes we experience. To suppose eyes are the fortunate result of unconscious natural processes seems, to quote a common creationist quip, about as idiotic as supposing that a cartload of monkeys, set before a bank of typewriters and persuaded to bang at random on the keys, could produce the complete works of Shakespeare.

So till recently there seemed in the western world no plausible alternative to some version of creationist theory to explain how this world, and we, came about. This has now altered. Physics and astronomy give increasingly detailed and plausible accounts of how inorganic aspects of the physical universe may have got to their present stage of complexity by natural means. Biology has plausible theories about how living cells may have arisen from inorganic matter. And, since Darwin's *Origin of Species*, there is a plausible explanation of how these living cells may have evolved into the amazing variety of life forms past and present. These alternative explanations certainly weaken the force of the argument from design.

Moreover, acceptance of these scientific explanations is much more rational than accepting theistic ones. Scientific theories are far more detailed and comprehensive, and are tested repeatedly by thousands of independent researchers through carefully controlled and repeatable experiments and observations. And on the basis of these theories astonishing and repeatable and verifiable results can be achieved, from sending spacecraft to the moon and other planets, to building computers, to curing illnesses, … the list could go on and on. By contrast, theistic claims about the power of prayer, or faith healing, are never rigourously tested or, if they are, fail the tests; nor do they ever give rise to repeatable practical consequences. So for me, modern science does not merely weaken the force of the argument from design, it removes its force altogether.

There is another very serious difficulty in accepting that complexity and apparent purpose in the world prove the existence of a creator god if, like Christians and others, you add that he is a loving and all powerful god. For, marvellous though many aspects of this world are, many other aspects are heartbreakingly less than perfect. Eyes, those amazing tools for seeing, often suffer cataracts and glaucoma and for many do not work at all from birth onwards. Kidneys, brilliantly filtering out poisons from our systems, contract cancer and people like my sister Ali die prematurely as a result. Hume, tongue in cheek again, suggests that, if we take these aspects into account when considering what the argument from design proves, we might well conclude this world was designed and made by a young and inexperienced or an old and doddery god, or, most likely, by a committee of gods![9] But for me these aspects were more powerful as an argument against the existence of the Christian God than as a flaw in the design argument for the existence of God, so they belong in the next chapter.

I came to believe that the argument from design has no force. But of course showing this argument is flawed doesn't disprove the existence of a Supreme Intelligent Creator God. It simply removes one reason for believing that such a being exists. And Hume can't resist yet another dig at the religion of his day. If arguments for God's existence were valid, he points out, then every thinking person would have to acknowledge God's existence by virtue of reason. There would then be no need for, and no virtue in having, faith. Many Christians put great emphasis on faith – justification by faith alone was Paul's and Augustine's cry. So I've really done you a favour, Hume says. By showing reason cannot establish God's existence I have left faith the sole victor on the field of belief.[10]

Nor is his joke without foundation; there is a strand in Christianity which does welcome the failure of reason to establish God's existence; indeed which glories in the irrationality, the going against the evidence, that is involved in believing in God, precisely because it underlines the brave leap beyond reason, namely the leap of faith. Tertullian, a 3rd century Christian theologian, wrote: "The Son of God is dead; this is to be believed because it is absurd. Having been buried, he rose again; this is certain, since it is impossible."[11]

First cause argument

This argument is more abstract, but a fascinating one nonetheless, and one which requires facing whether one is a fundamentalist Christian/ Muslim or an atheistic scientist. It takes one of our most familiar intellectual processes – one strong already in children with their endless chanting "Why?" – and extends it. Take a simple example, appropriate to my present situation writing in a mountain hut as rain rattles on the roof and slants across trees and mountains outside the window. Why does it rain so much at Arthur's Pass? Because warm winds from Australia gather moisture from the Tasman Sea as they race towards New Zealand. Why drop it here? Because the Southern Alps force the moisture-laden air higher and cool it, thereby reducing its capacity to hold water aloft. Probably at this point many adults would be satisfied, but not a child or a childlike adult – and certainly not our grandchildren! Why does the wind gather moisture from the sea? Because its warmth turns some of the water into vapour, which the air is dense enough to support and carry along. Why can't it support it when it is forced higher and cools? Because as it cools water vapour turns into heavier drops of liquid. Why are air and water like this? Oh please, I don't know, they just are. But of course we don't have to stop here, and it would be wrong to stop a child here. We can go on to become scientists and try to understand, on the subtle level of atoms and molecules, why air and water are as they are. And so on, and so on, and so on.

The first cause argument for the existence of God depends on this most common of human intellectual activities – explaining the existence or activity of something by pointing to the cause of which it is an effect. For there seems to be in the human mind a profound distrust of an endless regression, explaining one thing with a prior thing or cause, and that thing or cause with a more basic one, on and on for ever. This cannot be, the argument claims. Eventually we must reach a first cause which, if it is to be accepted as the end of the otherwise endless regression, must be causeless or self-caused. And that, the argument concludes, is God. Those who accept the argument are convinced by this that there is a God who is the cause of all else – a creator God such as Jews and Christians and Muslims believe in.

There are two ways the plausibility of this argument can be weakened. But as both, like the idea of God, are beyond the furthest limits of human understanding, neither can be put simply or compellingly.

The first is to query what's wrong with the idea of an infinite regression of effect and cause. In some of the deeper forms of Hindu and Buddhist philosophy and religion this is in effect, though not explicitly, a counter to the first cause argument. These philosophies present the universe as beginningless and endless – infinite in time and space – though repeating vast cycles of formation, preservation and destruction which can be said to have relative beginnings and ends. On this view there is always a previous cause no matter how far back you probe, because there is no absolute beginning to the incomprehensible processes of the universe. An infinite regression and an infinite progression, of effect and cause, cause and effect, is just what we have.

I find this neither more nor less mind-boggling than the idea of a first and uncaused cause. It's easier for me to express this in spatial than in temporal terms. As I gaze at the stars on clear frosty mountain nights I contemplate the milky way, my end-on view of the rest of our galaxy, and then the clouds of Magellan, two other 'nearby' galaxies. I then meditate on what modern astronomy tells me, that there are millions of other galaxies out there in space. And my mind finds it equally impossible to imagine either a boundary to all this (I would want to know what lies beyond this boundary) or space going on for ever. In similar fashion, with the first cause argument, I find it impossible to imagine either an end to the regression of effect/cause (I'd want to ask what caused the first cause, and calling it "self-caused" doesn't satisfactorily answer that for me) or the process going on forever. Though immersion in Hinduism has made the latter a little more emotionally acceptable to me, I don't pretend it has made it any more imaginatively comprehensible.

The second query about the first cause argument is along the lines of "Why not stop one step earlier?" If I follow the argument through to a creator God I'd still want to ask "Who or what created/caused God?" Similarly, of course, if I was able to follow the brilliant unravelling of ever tinier particles and processes which is modern physics, and which explains why air and water are the way they are by reference to differing characteristics and combinations of quarks and bosons and mesons and photons and …, I would still, at whatever level they have currently reached, want to ask "But what causes them to have those characteristics?" And at some level, I believe, scientists with their sub-nuclear particles or wavicles as the basis of physical energy and matter, and theists with their Creator God, have to resort to the answer I frivolously imagined giving to the importuning why-asking child: "Oh please, I don't know, they just are – they just have these characteristics."

Now if atheistic scientist and theistic believer are both in the same boat when it comes to accounting for their basic reality, then Occam's Razor can be invoked. William of Occam was a philosopher who suggested that we should not postulate additional entities unnecessarily. I would prefer to stop, mind- boggled, at ultimately inexplicable physical energy, some manifestations of which can be seen and heard with our physical senses, rather than going a step further and postulating a God who created this physical energy but who himself cannot be seen or heard with physical senses. I can understand a theist's response: "But I can see and hear God with my inner senses, my spiritual senses"; after all, on the toilet at that Christchurch retreat I was certain I heard God 'call' me to be a minister. But this response is more relevant to the argument from religious experience than to the design or first cause arguments.

One general point about design and first cause arguments warrants mention. Even if the arguments were sound the God whose existence they prove would be far less than the loving God most Jews, Christians and Muslims believe in. This philosophical God would simply be a designer/creator or first cause – in the latter case not even necessarily an intelligent purposive being. Her, his or its further characteristics, and in particular moral characteristics – whether loving or malevolent or indifferent, trustworthy or unreliable – are not touched on by these arguments. They would need to be ascertained either from the nature of the universe created or caused, or by revelation through holy books, or by religious experiences. To this latter we now turn.

Argument from religious experience

I am not sure this can properly be called an argument. If I doubt the existence of giraffes, and you take me to Africa to see one with my own eyes, I will probably then believe in them. But you have not argued me into this belief. You have enabled me to directly experience giraffes. And, significantly, even this is not always convincing. The story goes that when a Cockney first laid eyes on a giraffe brought to London he exclaimed "There bain't no such animal!" But the 'argument' from religious experience to the existence of God deserves examination because for most devout believers by far the most compelling evidence of God's existence is their own experience. Certainly this was the case for me during my devout period, initially with the 'call' by God, but also subsequently through 'feeling' his presence or, in my Edwards valley trauma, feeling myself in conflict with what (I thought) he wanted.

It is an embarrassing 'argument' to respond to. It is utterly convincing to people who 'experience' God, and, of course, fundamentally important to them. So to refuse to accept that their experience should compel you also to believe seems insultingly to doubt their truthfulness by refusing to accept that they have experienced God just because you haven't. After all, if you return from Africa to tell me you had a giraffe eat leaves from your hand, I seem on weak ground if I refuse to believe there are such animals simply because I haven't seen one myself.

However the comparison between experiencing giraffes and experiencing God is a dubious one. If giraffes do exist they exist as physical animals. If it is important for us to get agreement on our giraffe/no giraffe debate you can take me to see one. End of story, unless I'm a Cockney. But God, if she or he exists, is not believed to be a physical being, and therefore there is no exact parallel to taking me to see a giraffe. "Ah but," the believer can respond, "there is a parallel. Come to church, hand over your life to Jesus, and you will experience God. It is just that you haven't travelled the path to where God can be experienced."

There are least three problems with this response. First, many try the path the believer prescribes but fail to experience God. It is certainly not as clear-cut as seeing a giraffe. Second, religious believers differ alarmingly, and often violently, in their descriptions of what they experience, even within Christianity let alone between different religions. In Italy visions of Jesus and Mary abound, but in India visions of Krishna and Kali. And third, alternative explanations are possible, even for repeated 'experiences' of God. For example, later on I came to explain both my initial 'call' and my subsequent 'experiences' of God in psychological terms. I grew up in a family where belief in God was taken for granted. My parents lived their lives in the light of this belief, and my father preached it powerfully every Sunday. I was an impressionable youth wondering what I should do with my life. Little wonder that I felt strongly that this heavenly Father wanted me to follow in my earthly father's footsteps, and that, once committed to this idea, I 'felt' God's presence, and his guidance and his condemnation, frequently thereafter.

This explanation would not convince everyone. But that there are alternative explanations for 'experiences' of God does weaken the claim that such 'experiences' are compelling evidence for God's existence.

However, religious experiences remain a tricky subject. And much later, when trying to enliven a discussion on the argument from religious experience while teaching a philosophy of religion course, I landed myself in trouble. I burst into the class feigning joyful excitement and told the startled students that as I biked to work that winter morning, with the rising sun spectacular on towering cumulus clouds, I suddenly 'saw' Kali, the great Hindu goddess, awesomely hovering above me. I gazed amazed, miraculously meanwhile not run over by cars, and biked on in bliss at being vouchsafed a vision of the Mother. "Now then," I concluded, "what do you make of this? Surely it is convincing evidence for the existence of Kali. I saw her with my own eyes."

As a ploy to spark discussion this worked admirably. Some agreed this was convincing evidence, at least for some supernatural being or energy. Others raised queries and objections along the lines I've discussed above, thereby saving me from having to do so in a laboured theoretical manner.

Unfortunately there was in the class that year a lovely spiritual person who, during Stage I lectures, was convinced I was deeply religious, but was now distressed as I seemed so sceptical during this Stage II philosophy of religion course. I thought I had put sufficient hints into my Kali story – morning sun on cloud, etc. – to make clear it was made up to encourage discussion. And so most of the class had taken it. But I had underestimated the effect my power of persuasion would have when coupled with Tania's desire for me to have a spiritual experience. She was overjoyed for me during and immediately after the class, and then doubly distressed when others later convinced her I was only joking.

Exploring these arguments for the existence of the Christian God was the stimulating beginning of my intellectual examination of my faith. This examination became eventually more important for my journey than my intensely emotional 'experiences' of God. However, coming to believe that none of the arguments are valid was not a huge blow to my faith. Though design and first cause arguments had probably in vague form supported my belief, they had not been crucial to it. And disproving 'proofs' of God's existence doesn't disprove God's existence; it merely removes some reasons for believing. The real intellectual test of my faith came when examining arguments against the existence of the Christian God.

5. Arguments Against the Existence of the Christian God

The problem of suffering

Most Christians believe, and I was brought up to believe, in a God who is all-loving and all-powerful. This God is frequently thought of on the analogy of a human parent – "Our Father which art in heaven …." If we take this analogy seriously it is relevant to point out what we would expect from loving human fathers and mothers, especially when their children are enduring pain or threatened by death. They would do everything in their power to prevent such suffering. As we human parents know all too well it is often not within our power to do so. We look on, anguished but helpless, as incurable disease and lunatic driving claim our children or, in war and other forms of terror, as evil men restrain us while they torture and kill our children. For our power to help is limited, often severely so. But the Divine Parent is not so hampered. He, theology insists, is all-powerful as well as all-loving. So there is nothing he cannot do.

Why, then, is there so much suffering in the world – children with incurable diseases or ghastly birth defects, children and adults overwhelmed by tsunamis, children and adults tortured and killed by evil men – let alone all other living beings on this planet locked in a cycle of eat or be eaten? Doesn't God care? If he is all-loving, he must care. Is he unable to help? He is all-powerful, so of course he is able to help. Here, then, is the problem for believers in an all-loving all-powerful God, and it can be put in logical form:

If God is all-loving, he would end suffering if he could.
If God is all-powerful, he could.
But suffering exists.
Therefore either God is not all-loving, or he is not is not all-powerful; or he is neither all-loving nor all-powerful.

Note the difference from arguments for the existence of God. If they were valid they would establish the existence of a creator or sustainer, but would not indicate anything directly about her or his moral nature or degree of power. This argument takes a belief in the existence of a creator God characterised as all-loving and all-powerful, and points out the apparent contradiction between this belief and the existence of suffering and evil.

The most common theistic response to this dilemma is, in my view, a complete cop-out. It simply insists that God's ways are inscrutable to us humans. "For as the heavens are higher than the earth, so are my ways higher than your ways, and my thoughts than your thoughts," Yahweh is depicted as saying in the Old Testament.[1] In the most moving discussion of the problem of suffering in the Bible, the book of Job, Yahweh is portrayed as falling back on this cop-out at the end, in response to Job's anguished questionings. "Where were you when I laid the foundations of the earth?"[2] he asks Job, and carries on in like vein for the next four chapters – in other words, you know diddly-squat about things, you human insect you, so how dare you question or complain?

Thanks a lot, Yahweh! To my lasting sorrow Job capitulates to this bullying after being so staunch through all his ghastly suffering. In a suspect move, which biblical scholars perhaps too frequently employ, I convinced myself that the conclusion to the book of Job is a later addition by a pious scribe appalled at Job's temerity in questioning the almighty. But I digress.

Two other counters have more substance. The first argues that though the case against God looks convincing if we take only this world into account, we are then attending to less than half the story. In Christian belief there is not only this world but also the next, i.e. heaven and hell. So long as we can see only what happens in this world we have good grounds for doubting God can be all-loving and all-powerful. We see not only that the innocent suffer but often also that the evil prosper, even the very ones causing the suffering of innocents. But in the after-life God redresses the balance. The innocent sufferers shine in glory and bathe in bliss in heaven, forever, and the evil get their come-uppance in hell. In one of the less edifying Christian depictions of this redress, part of the bliss of the saved in heaven is that they can look down on their erstwhile oppressors suffering the torments of hell – which is hardly consonant with the admonition of Jesus to "love your enemies and pray for those who persecute you".[3] And part of the torment of the damned is that they can see all those they oppressed on earth swanning around happy in heaven – again a vindictive rather than a compassionate picture.

I can see how if you believe in an after-life, heaven at least with or without its dark counterpoint hell, this argument might help preserve your belief in an all-loving all-powerful God. It is of course circular in that it depends for its effectiveness on what it is attempting to defend, belief in an all-loving all-powerful God who controls heaven and hell and will redress the balance. For me, however, by far the most telling rejection of this argument is a literary one, based more on an emotional appeal to our fundamental values and sense of right and wrong than on reason.

It occurs in Dostoevsky's *The Brothers Karamazov.*[4] Ivan, with whom I identify strongly, is telling his brother Alyosha why he has difficulty believing in a loving God. Like me it was because of suffering, and there was plenty of that around in Dostoevsky's Russia. Alyosha had invoked the argument we've just looked at: "I know it looks bad here, at times, Ivan; but eventually God will redress the balance that is upsetting you, and the innocent sufferers will be blessed and the wicked cursed." (My paraphrase, not an accurate quotation.) In response, Ivan tells one of the most terrible tales in all literature. A Russian aristocrat had hundreds of hunting hounds of which he was inordinately proud. One day an eight-year old serf boy playfully threw a stone which inadvertently injured a paw of this man's favourite hound. Enraged, the aristocrat had the boy seized and stripped, then, forcing the mother to watch, made the boy run off down a meadow and sent the whole pack of hounds baying and slavering after to tear the terrified child to pieces. Passionately Ivan declares that he could never accept divine harmony and justice after death if it was built on the suffering of even one such innocent child, and even Alyosha in horror admits he couldn't consent to this either. I read *The Brothers Karamazov* during my first stint in the Antarctic. It is a big daunting book and I thought it would last me the three months. At grave risk to my ability to stay awake for what I was there to do, I read it inside the first week. And I suspect Ivan's anguished cry over innocent suffering did as much to doom my faith to eventual extinction as did all the years of careful philosophy before and after.

Then there is the 'free will' counter. God is all-loving and all-powerful. He could have created a world of automatons inevitably doing only good and never causing any suffering. He chose not to, because he saw in his infinite wisdom that automatons who had no choice but to do good would have no merit in so doing. He judged – and since, in Christian theology, he is all-knowing as well as all-powerful, he should know – that a world where we humans have free will, and in which therefore there is a possibility of evil, is more valuable, and better for us, his dearly loved children, than the automaton and no evil alternative. So precisely because he did love us – or would once he had created us – he chose this free will model. We humans then, of our own free will, choose to disobey this loving God and to be considerably less than loving to our fellow living beings. So suffering is our fault, not God's – he is cleared of the charge against him.

The sceptic here raises a query about the balance between temptation to do evil and desire to do good. Given the appalling amount of evil and suffering in the world, even just that which is caused by humans, couldn't God have made the balance a bit more weighted to good and compassion and against evil and cruelty, and still left us with sufficient real power of choice to preserve the value of his free will model? I find this point very slippery, a sort of moral calculus with no firm figures to work with. How much free will is enough to preserve the value of freely choosing good over evil? How fine must the balance be between the tendency to do good and the tendency to do evil for there to be meaningful free will but no descent into appalling evil and misery? To me these questions seem unanswerable, meaningless even. So for me this debate highlights how unlikely it is that a God, even an all-knowing one, resolved these issues and created this world accordingly.

Another interesting counter to this free will defence of God is to ask: "If God is all-powerful there is surely nothing he cannot do. So if he'd wanted to, he could have created a world in which we all freely choose to do only good. Since he didn't do this he must be either limited in power, or limited in love, or both."

This one seems to me to have a forceful theistic answer. To have free will and no possibility of choosing other than good is surely a logical impossibility. Not to be able to create something which is logically impossible is not a limitation on one's power. To give a simpler example, God could not create a round square, not because he is not all-powerful, but because there can be no such thing. The term is meaningless because one half of it – round – contradicts the other half – square, i.e. not round. Similarly, God could not create a world where we had free will and at the same time cause us always to choose good, not because he is not all-powerful, but because one half of the description, free will, contradicts the other half, cause always to choose good. The argument then gets slippery again. All that is required for genuine free will, argue God's opponents, is the possibility of choosing evil over good – no need to have anyone actually choosing it. But a possibility coming with a guarantee that no-one will ever choose it is surely close to no possibility at all.

The free will argument is, I think, the strongest defence of an all-loving and all-powerful God in the face of evil and suffering. Its weakest point, to me, lies in the endlessly troubled notion of free will itself, and its relation to a seemingly deterministic universe where effect follows cause with no room for human choice. My M.A. thesis was on this topic and wrung from its external assessor the comment "One hundred and thirteen pages without reaching a conclusion!" I have wondered since whether that was a compliment or criticism. But to explore this topic here would take us too far from my main theme. Suffice it to say that my inability to come to firm conclusions about whether we can really be said to have free will, combined with what seems to me the appalling amount of evil and suffering around us, meant that the free will defence of God against the problem of suffering, though probably the strongest available, was never convincing for me.

We need to note also that, even if it is accepted as effective, it clears God only of responsibility for human-created suffering – a big slice, true, but by no means the whole. It cannot absolve God from the charge that he allowed? – created? – in his world a ghastly range of illnesses and deformities which add horrendously to the sufferings of all sentient beings. Nor does it absolve God from responsibility when, for example, the sea he created rears in a tsunami, caused by the geology he built into his earth, which drowns thousands and leaves hundreds of thousands homeless – unless, of course, you choose to blame those poor people for living on low-lying coasts when they surely knew about tsunamis. This seems a trifle harsh, especially when you consider they probably had no option since in populous Indonesia and Sri Lanka, hit by a terrible tsunami a few years ago, all other habitable places were already occupied, mostly by the rich.

Logically, there are two other ways for a theist to escape the problem of suffering. Remember it can be phrased simply:

If God is all-loving, he would end suffering if he could.
If God is all-powerful, he could.
But suffering exists.
Therefore either God is not all-loving or he is not all- powerful, or he is neither all-loving nor all-powerful.

So a theist could abandon one or other (or both) of the initial premisses and concede that God is not all-loving and/or that he is not all-powerful.

Despite heavy emphasis in the Old and New Testaments that God is a stern judge, indeed often vengeful, I know of no Christian theologian who has conceded that God is not all-loving. Hinduism does to a considerable degree opt for this position, taking Ultimate Reality, and many of the personifications of it in goddesses and gods, to be complex and often terrifying mixtures of creation and destruction, of compassionate nurturing and terrifying wrath. As a result, the philosophical problem of suffering is not so acute in Hinduism. But of this more anon. At this stage it was belief in a loving Christian God that I was struggling to retain, and Hinduism's liberating influences were still in the future.

Some Christian philosophers have toyed with the concession that God is not all-powerful; either that he voluntarily surrendered some of his power to enable free will to be real, or that he is simply not all powerful, being challenged and constrained by an almost equally powerful force of evil. It is an interesting notion: a loving good god locked in a real life and death struggle with a hating evil devil. In general terms it is a powerful and very pervasive theme in all literatures I've come across with the possible exception of Māori and the deeper levels of Hinduism and Buddhism: the classic battle of good against evil that is as fundamental to *The Lord of the Rings* and the *Ramayana* and *Mahabharata* as it is to *Star Wars.* But it is a disquieting notion to most ordinary Christians, gnawing at their confidence that eventually all will be well, for their loving God is all-powerful and must at length triumph. So within Christianity this move has remained the preserve of a few philosophers and theologians. All power to their pens, I say, in trying every possibility. But I'm not surprised it hasn't proved popular with most Christians.

"God loves us" is meaningless

All of this, though very exciting and challenging for me, turned out to be preliminary to the most fundamental challenge to my belief in an all-loving all-powerful Christian God. This is the argument that the very notion of such a being is meaningless; or, more accurately, is reduced gradually to meaninglessness as a result of repeated qualifications to the notion in response to the sort of attacks we've been considering. A British philosopher, Antony Flew, wrote the most telling exposition of this argument. He borrowed from a chilling method of killing known as death by a thousand cuts, and coined the phrase "death by a thousand qualifications".

Flew's essay appears in the section headed 'Theology and Falsification' in *New Essays in Philosophical Theology.*[5] For me it was the more powerful for being only a brief sketch of the idea; there was plenty left for my mind to expand.

Flew tells a simple parable, which I shall re-tell in my own words. Two explorers come across a clearing in a jungle. It contains a mixture of flowers and weeds struggling for dominance. One explorer says "Ah, a garden, it must be tended by a gardener". The other demurs. "If this was ever a tended garden it certainly is not now – it has been abandoned." They debate the issue but cannot agree, so decide to wait and see if a gardener turns up. A year passes with no sign of one. "I told you so," says the sceptic. "This doesn't show there is no gardener," responds the believer, "it just shows that this is not an ordinary gardener, but an invisible one. He does come and tend the garden, but we can't see him". "OK," says the sceptic, "I just happen to have electric fence material in my pack. Let's string a fence round the garden; if the gardener comes he or she will get a shock and cry out, and we'll see the fence shake." Another year passes. No shouts, no trembling fence. "There" says the sceptic. "Ah no," says the believer, "this only shows the gardener is intangible as well as invisible, not that she is not coming and tending the garden". Exasperated, the sceptic points out that in the two years they've been watching no weeds have been pulled and no new flowers planted. "Ah," responds the believer, "you're making the mistake of assuming this gardener is like a human gardener, and pulls weeds, and plants flowers. This is not the case. There is a gardener, who comes and tends this garden, but he is a mysterious gardener who works in mysterious ways his gardening to perform." "Holy fertilizer," cries the scandalised sceptic, "in what way, pray, does your invisible intangible gardener, whose gardening produces no changes in the garden, differ from no gardener at all?"[6]

In the same way, Flew contends, believers in an all-loving all- powerful God respond to queries and criticisms by qualifying the nature of God again and again until nothing is left, no assertion is being made at all. "God loves us," it is claimed. "Then why don't we see him helping the suffering and restraining those causing suffering?" "Ah, because God is invisible." "Why don't we feel his hands helping us?" "He is intangible." "Then why don't we at least see or feel his effects in lessening suffering? – after all a loving human father would be doing everything in his power to save his children from suffering." "Ah, but God's love is not like human love – he works in mysterious ways his wonders to perform."

Flew's argument depends on the fact that descriptive statements are meaningful only in so far as we can specify what would count against them, that is falsify them. Let me give a simple example, again appropriate to Arthur's Pass where I am writing this. Suppose that yesterday, with drops of water falling from clouds in the sky and pattering on the roof, I said to Ann "It's raining". Understanding easily what I meant, and probably with effort restraining a smile that I should bother to make so obvious a statement, she would agree with me. But then this afternoon, clouds largely cleared away, mist and sun vying for dominance on the mountains, no more than a hint of dampness in the air, to Ann's astonishment I say again "It's raining". "No it's not," she'd say patiently, "it's not even drizzling – only a bit of mist about." "No, you don't understand," I say. "It's raining." Then tomorrow, a cloudless day with sun pouring through the trees and windows, I look outside and again say "It"s raining". "No it's not," laughs Ann, "come outside, feel and see." I go outside, stretch my hands sideways and my eyes skyward. "See?" says Ann hopefully. "No I don't" I reply stubbornly. "What's this got to do with whether it's raining or not? It's raining. It's an invisible non-wetting non- puddle-forming rain, but it's raining."

It's easy to see I would have emptied the phrase "it's raining" not just of its normal meaning but of all meaning. Ann simply would not be able to understand what I was trying to assert. And the reason for this is that I would be steadfastly refusing to let anything count against my apparent statement "it's raining".

So too, says Flew, with the statement "God loves us". In order for it to have meaning it must be possible to say what would falsify it. If no conceivable state of affairs would falsify it then the statement is meaningless. And Flew thinks his parable of the garden and the invisible intangible no-perceivable effect gardener, and its application to what theists do when their belief in a loving god is challenged, shows that such theists have indeed emptied their apparent assertion of meaning. When examined carefully, "God loves us" is seen to be neither true nor false, because it is meaningless.

When I encountered this alarming argument, during one of Jim Thornton's philosophy of religion courses, I fought hard to save my notion of god from this charge that it was meaningless. Along with other theistic philosophers, who responded to Flew's essay in the same publication, I suggested that we could specify what would falsify our assertion "God loves us": widespread or universal, and utterly irredeemable, suffering, and/or an overwhelming predominance of evil over good. This is not what we encounter. Much suffering has point – for example to warn us something is wrong with our bodies. And much is redeemable – many have coped with and risen above appalling suffering, and not only emerged stronger themselves but have also inspired others to do likewise. The meaning of

"God loves us" is thus assured for it can conceivably be falsified. And theists can claim it is not in fact falsified for irredeemable suffering and overwhelming evil is not what we find.

So at that time I fought out from under the force of Flew's argument with faith still (just) firm enough to proceed to theological studies. But I now find that argument unconvincing. For me redeemable suffering and good has predominated: I have experienced so much love and kindness, and virtually no hate or cruelty; and so much beauty and so little ugliness. But for many the balance must seem overwhelmingly the other way: crushing suffering and poverty, horrendous predominance of hatred and cruelty over love and kindness, and a crowded world of urban ugliness. To me, if the statement "God loves us" is not rendered meaningless by repeated qualifications, the amount of suffering in the world clearly indicates that it is false.

6. Theology

Despite philosophy raising in me so many doubts about my Christian faith I did not at this stage give up my intent to be a Christian minister. Since I had embarked on this road I had built up considerable momentum, and it would have taken a lot of courage and determination to change course. In addition, perhaps even more influential, it has always seemed important to me to have a framework within which to adjust to life's challenges and mysteries. Though by no means all aspects of the Christian framework are comforting ones – hellfire and damnation come to mind – the ones my parents lived by were both comforting and inspiring.

But before I proceeded to the next stage – three years' study at Knox Theological Hall, Dunedin – a vastly more important and life-changing event took place. Ann and I got married. So Ann and I went together to Dunedin.

For me, the three years there, 1960-62, were great: intellectually stimulating, and a lot of sailing and climbing in new areas. For Ann, it wasn't quite so good. She enjoyed the sailing and climbing. But it fell to her to work to give us enough money to live on. She worked in several jobs: first District Nursing, then staff nursing in a private hospital, then sub-matron at a student hostel, and, finally, night duty in Dunedin Women's Prison. In those days I wasn't even a halfway enlightened new age guy taking a fair share of household chores and meal preparation. So poor Ann would rise early to go to work along with the other wives while we boys would sleep in and then walk leisurely to classes. Ann would then come home to find me and the other students lounging about talking arcane theology, after doing ditto all day at the Theological Hall, with the washing and vacuuming undone, and the meal yet to cook.

At the Theological Hall in those days three of the four academic staff were superb: Wee John Allen, Principal and Professor of New Testament; Cappy Rex, Professor of Church History; and Lloyd Geering, Professor of Old Testament.

Wee John Allen and the New Testament.

Wee John (to distinguish him from Long John, Professor of Theology) introduced us to biblical criticism in relation to the New Testament, and I lapped it up. It involved careful examination and comparison of, especially, the four gospels, Matthew, Mark, Luke and John. Uncritical Christians had for nearly two millenia accepted that these gospels all told the gospel truth about the life and teachings and death and resurrection of Jesus of Nazareth, whom Christians believe is the Christ, the Son of God. Discrepancies between the gospels, if noticed at all, were explained away with varying degrees of ingenuity. If, however, you accept the findings of modern critical examination, a very different picture emerges.

I'm not now accurate on all the details, but I remember the general outline. For perhaps thirty years after Jesus was executed, purportedly for treason against the Roman State, the stories about him and his teachings circulated orally amongst his followers. It is believed that then there was a written document, known as Q, though no copies of this have been discovered. The three earliest written gospels we have now, Mark and Luke and Matthew, often tell the same story almost word for word, probably because they were copied from Q. Mark is believed to be earlier than Luke, with Matthew the third to reach its present form and John the last. I think Mark's final written form is dated about 60 AD, John's not till about 100 AD, and Luke's and Matthew's somewhere in between.

Once you have an order for the composition of the four gospels, and then compare them carefully, an interesting trend emerges. In the earliest, Mark, Jesus mostly seems a human figure, very much in the line of the Old Testament prophets. He is not often portrayed as claiming to be the Messiah/Christ that Israel was expecting, or the Son of God Christians came to believe he was. More often he referred to himself as the Son of Man, and as having authority to do and speak as he did, as if he had this authority from someone else, namely God.[1] Indeed, there is a saying attributed to Jesus in Mark, and in Luke, which suggests he thought of himself as a prophet, not as the Son of God or equal to God: "A young man came to him saying, 'Good teacher, what must I do to inherit eternal life?' Jesus said 'Why do you call me good? No one is good save God alone.'"[2]

I came to believe this passage is our best clue to how Jesus thought of himself. I could be charged with believing what I wanted to believe, since I was having increasing difficulty swallowing orthodox Christian belief in Jesus as the Son of God, indeed as God himself. But there is a good reason for my belief. Jesus' reply flies in the face of what Christians soon began to believe about him. That it was retained in Mark's and Luke's gospels, surviving all the early oral transmission and editing of stories about Jesus, suggests to me that it was deeply rooted in memories about the real Jesus, too deeply to be expunged; and that therefore, amidst all the difficulty of deciding what Jesus might actually have taught and said, and what, by contrast, was attributed to him later, it is very likely that Jesus did say this.

This is what New Testament biblical criticism is mainly about; trying to decide, by careful examination and comparison of passages and sayings, what Jesus actually did and said and was like, and what has been attributed to and said about him in the light of, and to substantiate, later beliefs.

The bulk of the material in Luke and Matthew gives the same impression as does that in Mark – not surprisingly, since much of it is the same material as is in Mark. But the beginnings and endings of these two gospels are very different. In Mark, Jesus appears as an adult, preaching, and at the end there is only the story of the empty tomb, hinting at his resurrection. Luke and Matthew begin with the miraculous virgin birth of Jesus; give a genealogy back through King David to Abraham; tell stories about his childhood and his temptation by Satan in the desert; and end with a full account of his resurrection and subsequent appearances to his disciples. In addition, in his handling of the main material, Matthew emphasises that Jesus is fulfilling earlier prophesies about the coming Messiah.[3]

Thus there is an increasing tendency to portray Jesus as more than a prophet, indeed as the expected Messiah, the Christ, the Son of God. This reaches its climax in John's gospel. This gospel is more a theological reflection on the nature and significance of Jesus than an account of his doings and sayings. Unfortunately it is presented as such an account, and, if you accept the predominant scholarly opinion, John's and the early Christian church's beliefs about Jesus are put into the mouth of Jesus as his own views.

The theological tone is set at the beginning with the famous passage identifying Jesus with the Word of God. In Hebrew thought this means the active power of God, for words were in the past believed to have direct power in their own right, not just via their meaning. In Genesis God is credited with creating the world by a series of words: "And God said, 'Let there be light', and there was light."[4] So it's potent stuff when John says: "In the beginning was the Word, and the Word was with God, and the Word was God,"[5] then goes on to say of Jesus, "And the Word became flesh and dwelt amongst us, full of grace and truth."[6]

It is against this background that John presents Jesus as making claims for himself that he is at least a unique mouthpiece for God, and sometimes that he is God in some sense. Most strikingly John has Jesus claiming "I am the way, and the truth and the life: no one comes to the Father but by me."[7] This is in remarkable contrast to Mark's (and Jesus'?) "Why call me good? There is none good but God." It has led me to think that Jesus saw himself as a prophet, pointing to God, reminding his fellows of what God requires (justice, mercy, compassion); and that Jesus as Messiah, Christ, Son of God, and eventually Dreadful Judge, are later Christian constructs.

For me, what emerges from this attempt to find the real historical Jesus doesn't confirm the Sunday School image of "gentle Jesus meek and mild". Instead a complex picture emerges of an itinerant preacher with a similar mixed message to that of the great Old Testament prophets. He urges a very radical moral stance of unlimited compassion and forgiveness,[8] and for all, not just for fellow Jews if we take the parable of the Good Samaritan seriously (in this parable it is a non-Jew who has compassion on a man robbed and wounded by robbers, and he is the one Jesus praises).[9] He backs up this moral message, however, with stern threats of punishment if one falls short of this ideal, and/or fails to repent and turn to God ("there men shall weep and gnash their teeth")[10]. He resorts to outraged and violent action when he sees God's temple being used for shady commercial transactions, overturning money-lenders' tables and driving them out of the temple: "It is said God's house shall be a house of prayer, but you have turned it into a den of thieves."[11] And, movingly, as he dies in agony on the cross, he is not the triumphant Son of God giving his life to avert his Father's wrath from the rest of us, but a bewildered man in mental as well as physical agony as he cries "My God, my God, why hast thou forsaken me?"[12]

But Wee John did far more for me than introduce me to biblical criticism. As we went through portions of the Greek New Testament together we engaged in wonderfully fierce but, I felt, equal and equally enjoyed, arguments about how the passages should be interpreted. I say equal because although he could have treated me as a brash disruptive philosophy student, holding up progress for the rest of the class, he always took my objections seriously and accorded them the greatest possible respect , i.e. an intense and passionate response.

Of course I can't remember all the jousts; and of course I exaggerate in presenting the whole three years as a continuous argument between Wee John and me. But we sure had some beauties. And by far the fiercest centred on the Augustine/ Pelagius controversy. Augustine's view is that we humans are so hopelessly mired in our sin and corruption that nothing we can do with our own strength could possibly save us from damnation by God. Only faith, throwing ourselves on God's mercy in complete trust in him, can save us. So works – the things we do – are irrelevant to salvation. "Justification by faith alone" is the catch cry. Pelagius, bless him, didn't try to overturn this completely, as I (and Jesus I think) had a tendency to do. He wasn't saying "Justification by works alone". But he couldn't help feeling, perhaps influenced by Jesus' parable of the Good Samaritan and stress on compassion rather than ritual purity, that what you did – whether you helped or cheated widows and orphans, for example, or loved and did good to, or hated and harmed, your enemies – did have some importance. And I was wholly on Pelagius' side, and vehemently opposed Augustine, and the passages in Paul's letters which gave Augustine a basis for his baneful beliefs.

Matters came to a head as we battled our way through the enormously influential letter of Paul to the Romans. It may have been Romans 9.16 that started us off once more: "So it depends not on man's will or exertion, but upon God's mercy." I was being especially obstreperous, I've no doubt, with no right to bring the matter up yet again since we were meant to be discussing what Paul meant, not what I thought he ought to have meant. But this seldom hampered Wee John or me. I passionately restated my position. Wee John flared up. When excited, an incipient stutter he had was exacerbated. "W-w-well if that's the case M-M-Mr Wilson, w-w-what it comes down to is this. A-A-Are you for God or for the Devil?" "Well if you put it like that, Sir," I responded heatedly, "I'm for the Devil." "I-I-I thought so Mr. Wilson"!

Such was our healthy relationship, teacher to student though we were, I never for a moment took this amiss, nor, I'm sure, did he intend it as a put-down. It was simply a wonderful illustration of how passionately involved in the argument we were, and I cherish the incident to this day.

All of this was in line with the Theological Hall's policy of getting students to examine their Christian faith, and the documents on which it was or should be based, seriously and critically. Since I came to believe the Christian faith, and its scriptures, cannot stand up to such rigorous examination and retain credibility and authority, I have wondered whether this policy hastened or delayed my exit from the faith. But on balance I think it delayed it. For one thing I agreed wholeheartedly with the policy. If you are sending out ministers to preach the gospel in an increasingly secular and educated and critical society, it certainly seems essential that such ministers have examined their own faith long and hard. If it results in some falling by the wayside – as I did in the end – well that is better than sending that person out with a shaky and unexamined faith, which would surely either fail later or be ineffectual because not well grounded. Moreover this rigorous examination held me longer in the faith because it took the faith seriously in an intellectual sense, and for me continued from a different angle the exhilarating examination of the faith I was living by, and was still intending to preach, which had occupied me so intensely during the philosophy years.

But spare a thought for my fundamentalist fellow students. To them all this was anathema. Their faith was that the Bible was literally true, every word of it. And they deeply feared that once you start on the slippery slope of examining the Bible critically, and trying to discern, for example, what Jesus might or might not have really said or done, you were doomed to slide at high speed into the abyss of no faith. If any of them heard of my subsequent defection I'm sure they would say "I told you so" – and with some justification. For while critical examination of the New Testament's portrayal of Jesus was not the sole assassin of my faith, it certainly played an important part in the murder. But I didn't see it as murder, but as liberation, freeing me from regarding Jesus as sole, or even pre-eminent, guide to moral and religious truth.

Cappy Rex, Church History and my trial for heresy

Then there was Professor Helmut Rex, fondly known as Cappy because his Christian name sounded like a hat.

Cappy had escaped from Nazi Germany but not before being gassed and I think tortured by Hitler's thugs, presumably because he voiced opposition to the Nazi regime. His health, as a result, was very poor, and worsened while we were at the Hall. His lectures were agonising affairs in one sense, for him and for us, for he breathed and therefore spoke with difficulty. Often there would be long pauses till he recovered sufficiently to continue. It speaks volumes for the brilliance and interest of what he was gasping out that his lectures never failed to grip me, and I think most of the others, intensely.

Cappy was Professor of Church History. With every three- year intake of students he fully intended a tour of the whole span, from nought AD to the present day. I believe he never got beyond about 500 AD. This was only partly because his health forced him to speak slowly. The main reason was that he was a perfectionist, determined to treat each phase of the developing Christian Church with the seriousness and in the detail it deserved. For me, not getting beyond 500 AD was of no consequence. These were the years I knew least about and, as I think Cappy believed and I came to believe, the most important for understanding what followed. Also, what I gained from Cappy was not just facts but a careful method for sorting fact from fiction. The details of events and creeds and councils to which Cappy introduced us have long since fled my memory. But the importance of ascertaining details in as careful and unbiased a way as possible has stayed with and influenced me ever since.

We got from Cappy an exhilarating struggle with Christian theology. For it was in these early centuries that Christian thinkers wrestled with their complex theological themes, and devised creeds and other forms of expression for these themes which survive and influence Christianity to this day.

There are two great problems in Christian theology distinct from the general problems for theistic belief which we looked at in philosophy. For me the distinction is this. In philosophy we are examining whether it is likely there is or is not a supernatural being with the attributes Christians ascribe to their God. In theology we are starting with the belief that there is such a being and then seeking to understand and express how these attributes relate to each other. Of course the two, philosophy and theology, overlap. In particular, if theology fails to express in a consistent way what this God is like, and how his attributes cohere in the one being, the philosopher would suspect there may be no such being. But they are very different disciplines. At the Hall we were doing theology, not philosophy; we believed God exists and were trying our best to understand him, or rather to understand what Christian theologians throughout Church History have said about him. The male pronoun is appropriate here because Christianity has until recently used only male terminology for God. Recently feminists have challenged this, most amusingly in the jibe "When God created man, She was only joking!".

The first problem is how Jesus can be both fully human and fully divine (the doctrine of the Incarnation). The second problem is how God can be three persons yet one God (the doctrine of the Trinity).

I have great difficulty, now, reaching back to these problems. Though I believe Jesus lived, and was human, I no longer believe Jesus is/was God, nor even that he thought he was. So the first is a problem for me no longer. Even less, then, the second; I don't believe God exists. But since these issues used to bother me considerably I shall try briefly to explain them, and my responses to them.

I still see why the first problem is important to Christianity. Belief that Jesus was fully human, and grew up like us, suffered and laughed like us, engenders great confidence that he, though now in heaven, nonetheless understands us in all our weakness and helplessness, and therefore is likely to care for and help us in a sympathetic way. As a children's hymn puts it; "...day by day like us he grew...tears and smiles like us he knew...". So for Jesus to be fully human is important. But for him to be able to help us it is important he is also fully God and hence all-powerful.

The most common Christian 'solution' to this problem is to repeat at frequent intervals "This is just how things are – Jesus was fully human and fully divine – he did indeed share all our human frailties but was still, at the same time, God, so all- knowing, all-powerful, all-loving."

Not surprisingly, this did not satisfy me. I can't now remember all the ways in which I tried to solve this problem and retain my Christian faith. But one move which I espoused with enthusiasm towards the end of our three years in Dunedin I remember very well, for it led to my being tried for heresy, a fitting fate for a friend of Pelagius.

There is a moving passage in Paul's letter to the Philippians: "Have this mind among yourselves, which you have in Christ Jesus, who, though he was in the form of God, did not count equality with God a thing to be grasped, but emptied himself, taking the form of a servant, being born in the likeness of men."[13] Some Christian theologians, presumably troubled, as I was, by this fully human/fully divine doctrine, seized on this to suggest that the divinity of Jesus lay in his self-sacrificial love, his emptying himself for the sake of humanity. This view became known as kenotic Christology, from a Greek word meaning empty. For my New Testament exit exercise, a sort of mini-thesis we had to do at the end of our course, I chose to comment on this passage, and on kenotic Christology. If I remember correctly my thesis was that Jesus was God as well as human in that he was 'Godlike' in this self-sacrificial emptying of himself in love for humanity, not that he was God in some mystical or supernatural sense. I liked the argument, and it probably helped prolong my faith in Jesus as divine for a little longer, though by this stage I had little such faith left.

The exercise gained me a pass from Wee John, who was doubtless relieved I hadn't exercised myself yet again about Paul's justification by faith. But it had then to be approved by the Christchurch Presbytery, since I was their divinity student. Unfortunately it was given to a very conservative minister to assess. He thought that my views didn't adequately preserve the 'fully God' part of the doctrine of God's Incarnation, and therefore raised serious doubts about my fitness to be licensed, let alone later ordained.

Even more unfortunately, he waited till the Presbytery gathered prior to the service to license me, then, with me before them and with Dad in the chair (for he was at that time moderator of the Presbytery), he launched his bombshell. "This candidate's New Testament exercise is clearly unbalanced, one-sided, heretical, and I recommend he be asked to reconsider his views, and that Presbytery seriously question his suitability to be licensed." There followed a very long debate, while family and friends waited in the church next door for the service of licencing to begin. Eventually, the verdict was in my favour, though to appease the conservatives it was coupled with an invitation to me to consider whether my views were heretical. I felt no animosity towards my accuser, even sympathy for him. For the views I expressed in the exercise were orthodoxy itself compared to my overall view of the Christian faith. I already knew beyond doubt that I was far too unorthodox to be inflicted on even the most liberal congregation; and far too uncertain of the faith to consider preaching it to others.

The second problem concerns the doctrine of the Trinity, one of the doctrines which make Muslims view Christians as heretical, as polytheistic indeed, worshipping not one but three gods: God, Jesus, and the Holy Spirit.

For what the Trinitarian doctrine says, or tries to say, is that God is three persons yet one God. I can see how this came about. First there was Yahweh, the God of Abraham and Isaac and Jacob, the God of the Jews, of whom Jesus was one. For Christianity is an offshoot of the religion of the ancient Israelites, as is, later, Islam. All would have remained simple, and acceptable to Muslims, if Jesus had been regarded by Christians, as I believe he was by himself, as a Prophet of Yahweh, like Amos and Hosea and Isaiah before him, and Muhammad after. This is the Muslim view of Jesus, and in a delicious passage in the Q'uran Jesus is portrayed as fronting up to God's Judgement Seat. God sternly asks Jesus whether he told men, "Take me and my mother as gods, apart from God." Jesus replies that he only said what God had commanded him: "Serve God, my Lord and your Lord."[14]

But, as we've seen, as early as Luke's and Matthew's gospels, and much more so in John's, Jesus is regarded as more – increasingly as much more – than a prophet. Firstly, he is regarded as the Messiah foretold in the Old Testament, a special and final messenger of God; then, in John, as the very Word (i.e. power) of God, and as the Son of God. In early creeds – for example the Apostles' Creed, still in use today – there is still a distinction between God and Jesus: "I believe in God the Father Almighty … and in Jesus Christ his only begotten Son … on the third day He rose again from the dead and ascended into Heaven to sit at the right hand of God." I'm sure Cappy took us excitingly through the stages whereby this distinction was narrowed to the point where Jesus was considered fully God (as well as fully human), but I can't now remember the details.

But it is not the doctrine of the duality, but of the trinity. There is a dramatic passage in the Acts of the Apostles where the disciples of Jesus are suddenly infused with the Holy Spirit of God, descending "like the rush of a mighty wind" and "tongues as of fire".[15] If Christians had interpreted this simply as the spirit/power of the one God, not as a separate entity, no problem. But – again the stages and details elude me, but certainly didn't elude Cappy – they felt impelled to speak of this inrush of energy as a distinct entity, a distinct person indeed. So the creed goes on "I believe in the Holy Ghost (or Spirit)". And, bingo, you have the Trinity: God the Father, God the Son and God the Holy Ghost, three persons, one God. My sympathy on this one is wholly with Muslims.

Lloyd Geering and the Old Testament

Wee John, Cappy – and the third, fated to become by far the most famous, for some the most notorious: Lloyd Geering. He and Arthur Prior are the best teachers I ever had. And curiously Lloyd, like Arthur, not only knew my father well but was also helped by Dad at a critical stage in courting his wife.

Even more curiously, given the controversy that raged about him later, Lloyd's teaching to me was much less controversial than that of Wee John or Cappy. Lloyd was Professor of Old Testament, and while conservative Christians, who lay great stress on the literal truth of the Bible, acknowledge the Old Testament as an important part of the Bible, their fiercest defence is of the teachings of and about Jesus that occur in the New Testament. Not till Lloyd published his views on the resurrection of Jesus (in an Easter article in the Presbyterian magazine *Outlook*) did the full force of fundamentalist fury fall upon his bewildered head. But this happened in 1976, well after my time at Theological Hall.

What Lloyd did was take us through selected parts of the Old Testament, in the original Hebrew language, filling us in on the historical background out of which these texts emerged. And he was superb at it: careful and accurate without being pedantic, respectful always of his students' views and questions, exciting in his ability to bring alive long dead people and events and teachings.

For me the highlights, as was the case with Dad's preaching, were when we were examining the sayings of some of the great prophets of the Old Testament – Amos, Hosea and Isaiah particularly. Perhaps because of Dad's preaching, but also by natural inclination, I found myself in complete agreement with the constant cry of these men: that what God required of us was not pious religious observance but active effort to promote social justice, to "do justice, and to love kindness, and to walk humbly with your God."[16] These prophets saw the pious religious people of their day laying great stress on formal ritual observances and ostentatious adherence to religious laws, while in their business and private lives they cheated their competitors and were indifferent to the plight of the poor and widows and orphans. The prophets believed they were messengers from Yahweh, his mouthpiece indeed, and spoke boldly the words they believed were those of Yàhweh himself: "I hate, I despise your feasts…".[17]

The similarity to Jesus and Muhammad is to me very striking indeed, both in the substance of their religious and social teaching, and in the way they delivered this substance as direct words from Yahweh/God/Allah. It still moves me profoundly – a very powerful yoking of religion and social ethics. When you care for others, love others, you are acting as your all-powerful all-loving creator wishes you to act, and are as a consequence coming into close communion with him – a far cry from later Christian justification by faith alone, and strong support for Pelagius. Even some purely religious passages in the prophets' teaching still have the power to move me: promises from God that he will not desert us in our times of trial and grief, but will lift us up and comfort us. I will always acknowledge the powerful appeal of this aspect of religion in a vast and seemingly indifferent universe. Sometimes, on occasions of stress or grief, I wish I still had this to comfort me.

Throughout this intellectually exciting three years of theological study my faith was not just changing but waning. Being stubborn once set on a path, and since a change in one's planned career is major and daunting, I had fought hard to stop my faith from fading away completely. But my moves were becoming increasingly desperate, I now realize – suspect even to me, let alone to conservative Christians.

This is obvious from an article I contributed to our divinity student magazine during my final year. Entitled "Acting As If Theology", it advanced the view that, even if it is damnably difficult in the modern world to believe in the Christian God, and the ongoing presence of Jesus, it is worthwhile to act as if the two exist and are as described in Christian theology. By this I meant acting in as loving a way as possible, using the stories about God and Jesus as role models and inspiration for life, even if unable to believe them true. It was a brave attempt to salvage something, and must have struck a chord with at least one of my fellow students who out of the blue rang and reminded me of it a few years ago. But it could hardly be rated a solid foundation on which to build a career as a Christian minister and preacher, nor an acceptable one to a congregation of Christians.

My time as trainee Presbyterian minister drew to a close. I no longer felt at ease in the Christian religion. But I was still intensely interested, indeed intensely involved emotionally and intellectually, in religious issues. Somehow I heard that India offered scholarships for New Zealanders to study there. India is the home of Hinduism and Buddhism, two of the major religions of the world. By a fortunate coincidence it also stretches south from the highest range of mountains in the world. Could anything be more obvious than that I should try to get a Government of India Commonwealth Scholarship/ Fellowship to study Indian Philosophy and Religion in India, and, if successful, combine it with a few sorties into the high Himal?

So by the time of my heresy trial all church matters were of scant significance to me. Though I was cleared of heresy and licensed, I had no intention of taking the next step and being called to a parish and ordained as a fully-fledged minister. Ann and I had our passage booked to India and were shortly to be off on the next stage of our life's adventure.

PART II

Nepal and India

7. Sherpas and their Buddhism

I had been successful in my application for a Government of India Commonwealth Fellowship to study Indian philosophy and religion at Banaras Hindu University. As a mountaineer, I had carefully selected this university as the nearest appropriate one to the Himalayas. It had the additional advantage of having English as its declared main teaching language, which was vital given my lack of linguistic ability.

Preliminary adventures

But we were not going only for study. Ed Hillary had invited me to join his 1963 Himalayan Schoolhouse Expedition[1], March to May, and Louise Hillary had invited Ann to accompany her when she joined the expedition in its later stages. The sensible course, of course, would have been for me to fly over with Ed and the other expedition members, and Ann to wait and fly over with Louise. But opting for the sensible course has never been our strong point. Besides, we had romantic notions about an ocean cruise, utterly mistaken ones as it turned out. So, in February 1963, we embarked on an ocean liner bound for India.

From Colombo, Sri Lanka, Ann carried on bravely on her own. Her introduction to India was traumatic, to put it mildly. She had to deal on her own with clearing our 13 pieces of luggage through customs and freighting them to friends in Chandigargh who had offered to store them till we settled into Banaras Hindu University in June. She then flew to Delhi, and had a frightening night there: "I remember being driven in a taxi through a dark and sordid Old Delhi, uncrowded at that hour, two a.m., but with shrouded sleeping bodies on the pavements. The driver and I had enormous trouble understanding each other, but he eventually found the mission home of St. Stephens, where a nursing sister on the ship had arranged for me to stay. But, alas, I found on arrival that they had never heard of me. Moreover, I'd been told there was no need to change currency, but now found I couldn't pay the taxi except in Indian rupees. However, a kind man paid the taxi and took me in, leaving me in a large room with a bed in the centre under a creaking fan, and assuring me I'd be fine as there were servants sleeping in the garden. All night Old Delhi played its endless cacophony of barking dogs, shouts, running feet, whistles, gunshots and screams, while I lay, purse under pillow, rigid with terror."

She survived all this and found her way to Mussorie, at 7,000 feet in the Himalayan foothills north of Delhi, where she nursed at a mission hospital for two months. "I had packed thinking everywhere in India would be hot and now found myself in sub-zero mountain temperatures. I ate – or rather on the whole didn't – with the Indian nurses, whose food seemed to consist largely of red-hot chillies. My inability to communicate with my fellow nurses and with patients was a nightmare. Also drugs were different from those I was used to.

"I was very lucky to have a small outer room to myself, with a tiny fire. Huddled over this with a storm raging outside, feeling cold and lonely and hungry, I'd mark off my diary like a prisoner counting the days to release, then crawl into bed with my legs in the arms of a jersey for warmth."

Eventually things improved. She became friendly with a lovely older married nurse who spoke good English. She was put to good use as a night supervisor, looking after very sick or post-operative patients, and deciding if a situation was serious enough to warrant calling the doctor, who then managed to get some much-needed sleep. The daughter of the English matron arrived for a visit and befriended Ann. And her walks up the hills behind the hospital were exhilarating and became almost a daily habit.

So towards the end of the two months she started really enjoying her life there. "All the same I was mighty relieved when I could leave and join Louise Hillary in Kathmandu, in May, 1963, and trek into the Khumbu to join Jim and Ed for the last month of their expedition."

Sherpa religion

I flew to Calcutta to join Ed and the rest of his expedition, and began my first real encounter with a religion other than Christianity. Sherpas are Tibetan Buddhists.[2] Intensity of belief and practice varies amongst them as it does amongst Christians. But their religion infused every aspect of their lives and thoughts in ways strikingly different from the society I had grown up in.

In New Zealand, in those days, people tended to be either religious, and dour and intense about it; or indifferent; or hostile to religion, and dour and intense about it. Here in the Solu Khumbu I was amongst people who were serious about their religion but in a wonderfully relaxed way.

Ceremonies were held, and lamas (monks) came and blessed proceedings and houses and people, for every important stage in the yearly cycle and every important milestone in people's lives. And instead of the fiercely quiet and reverent atmosphere I was used to in Presbyterian services, even Dad's comparatively relaxed ones, I found Sherpa religious occasions to be laid back noisy affairs. People came and went at will, and children were allowed to run around and talk freely, none of which disturbed the lamas or lay people in the slightest. And because they were not forced to be quiet and still, children and adults were far less fidgety than in a solemn ceremony in church. Nor did this make the ceremonies less impressive; on the contrary they enhanced them. I found this very liberating and revelled in it.

One of the many good things about Ed's Himalayan aid projects was that he always wanted them to fit into Sherpa or Nepali ways of doing things as much as possible. He combined Sherpa methods of building with New Zealand metal roofing and skylights, to make schools as dry and light as possible. And he always had lamas, and on special occasions the Rimpoche (Head Lama) of Thyangboche Gompa (Monastery), bless the building or bridge or water-supply. In this, as in all things, he was advised by Mingma Tsering, his Sirdar. Mingma was religious in a relaxed Sherpa way. I learnt not to talk to him for the first half hour or so each morning, when he was chanting mantras.

Ed also responded to requests from lamas and nuns to repair monasteries, or provide water supplies or build schools for them. So rather than prying into Sherpa religion from the outside I was part of it in the normal course of what we were doing. In subsequent years Ann and I got to work on many projects in and around monasteries and nunneries, with Ed or on his behalf.

One incident above all others, during this first encounter, has always for me typified the Sherpa attitude to religion. I was with fellow New Zealander Murray Ellis, and two of my closest Sherpa friends, Phu Dorje and Pemba Tarke. We were trying to increase the flow of a mountain spring preparatory to piping water from it to a holding tank we'd had built in the village of Khunde. With crowbars and shovels we prised and dug our way deep into the hillside, jousting with huge boulders as we dislodged them from above. Just before we finished for the day I spotted a small toad trembling at the back of our hole. I pointed him out to Phu Dorje and Pemba Tarke. "Na ramro (not good) Jim sahib, that is god of spring," they said solemnly.

All Sherpas love teasing but these two are the masters, so at first I was sure they were pulling my leg. But they kept perfectly straight faces as they said we must take the toad to Khunde Major (the elected head of the village council) and seek his advice on what to do, for if we had indeed disturbed the god of the spring he might stop the flow completely. I began to get alarmed, for what we'd done to the spring might do that anyway. So I picked up the poor wee cowering beastie and we trooped, as solemnly as Phu Dorje and Pemba Tarke ever troop which isn't very, to Khunde Major's house. We edged cautiously past his particularly ferocious Tibetan mastiff and in his door.

Khunde Major heard us out quietly, looked carefully at my friend the toad, and pronounced him indeed the god of Khunde spring. "Help!!! – what to do???" I asked aghast. "Ah," said Khunde Major, "you must take the god to your camp tonight, keep him warm, and tomorrow we will perform puja (religious ceremony) and put him back in his spring." If there was a twinkle in his eye, and/or a wink to him from the terrible two, I didn't catch it. I was so scared the toad would succumb to the fierce frost that I slept with him inside my sleeping bag, risking his death by fart-induced asphyxiation. To my intense relief he was alive next morning, and seemed even quite happy. Khunde Major and several other dignitaries and lamas, and of course Phu Dorje and Pemba Tarke, accompanied me and the toad back to the spring, which to my relief was still flowing strongly. In a ceremony as punctuated by laughter as by mantras we restored the god to his proper place.

As I walked back with Phu Dorje and Pemba Tarke, curiousity consumed me. Did they, and/or Khunde Major and the others, really believe the toad was the god of the spring, or were they playing an elaborate trick on me? What was all the laughter about? To me, their answer epitomizes the healthiest attitude to religion I have come across. "Ah, Jim sahib," they said, grinning engagingly, "this being god of spring, we no puja doing, spring drying, ekdam na ramro [very bad]. This not being god of spring, no harm puja doing, and good time having." Surely the best of win-win situations.

I remember only the gist of their replies, of course, not their exact words. And since I understood little Nepali and no Sherpa they spoke to me in Sherpa English. I became a great fan of Sherpa English, and used it not mockingly but admiringly, and for practical reasons, as did Ed when conversing with Mingma who I think was creator, and certainly was master, of this language. Practical as always, Mingma scorned tenses and irregularities of English English and reduced all verbs to present participles. "I yesterday coming" is just as precise in meaning as "I came yesterday", and the formula can easily and accurately be used in "I now coming" or "I tomorrow coming". Ed, who was as bad at languages as I am, quickly learned Sherpa English from Mingma, and it was a treat to hear the two of them conversing in a combination of it and mangled Nepali. It was equally a treat to see the looks of bewilderment on passing English speakers, who couldn't understand the interchanges but could see that Ed and Mingma understood each other perfectly.

Several weeks later two Sherpas we'd left guarding base camp on Mt. Taweche came hurtling into camp late at night, clothes torn and legs bruised from their reckless descent. "Yeti, yeti," they gasped, "Yeti hearing." Next day I consulted Phu Dorje and Pemba Tarke again. "Do you believe it was a yeti?" I asked. "Do you believe yetis exist?" I suspect they secretly sighed at this literal-minded simpleton worrying about what does or doesn't exist when, according to Buddhism, all life is an elaborate illusion anyway. But they answered, in similar vein to their god of the spring approach. "Ah, Jim sahib, yetis believing, very careful being not annoying them. No yetis being, no harm doing. Yetis not believing, one day corner coming and yeti seeing, ekdam na ramro."

I was delighted with both these answers. They helped release me from years of Christian-induced worries about what is true belief, and philosophy-induced worries about what exists and what doesn't, resonating with the approach I'd toyed with in my 'acting-as-if' theology. As time went on I was to become more and more immersed in the Hindu and Buddhist notions of maya which infused Phu Dorje's and Pemba Tarke's attitude to yetis and gods. Maya is the varied and fascinating, but not ultimately real, display of the underlying energy of the universe.

Rebirth and karma

It is hard to be sure what struck me this first time, and what I know now from 50 years of frequent visits to Sherpa land, and much study of and teaching about Buddhism and Hinduism. But certainly another aspect did strike me forcefully on this first visit. Again a particular incident highlights it. We were working on Pangboche school and a village elder who was helping us was wearing a particularly fine jersey. One of our expedition Sherpas recognized the jersey as belonging to a Swiss climber killed the previous year while descending from an ascent of Pumori. The climber and his Sherpa companion had been buried at the foot of the mountain. Our Sherpa, who had been at the burial, told Mingma and Ed about the jersey, clearly stolen from the grave, and together they alerted the other village elders.

Secretly I sympathized with the thief; after all, the jersey was no further use to its previous owner. But everyone else seemed appalled at what they regarded as sacrilege. They debated the appropriate punishment for the miscreant, and decided on a public telling-off by the elders. I have to admit the punishment completely broke the man up. He sobbed and clung to his wife. But it seemed to me very mild given how seriously the offence was viewed. Afterwards the man was accepted back into the community with no further consequences other than his own conscience and – and here's the rub – his beliefs about the consequences of his actions for the rest of this life, and for his future lives.

This was my first insight into the way belief in rebirth and karma affects every aspect of Buddhist and Hindu life. I came to understand it more deeply later. At this stage I saw only a simple but very powerful application of it. The community had to act, partly I think because we, and especially Ed, were there, and partly to redress the slur on their community that one of their members had incurred. But they felt no need to judge, or to punish harshly, because what the law of karma says is that every action, good or bad, has its own inevitable consequences. What the man had done would affect him in this life and, if serious enough, for many lives to come. So the community felt no need to add its punishment; and to a remarkable extent no need to make social or legal regulations and prohibitions and police them. The universal law of karma was far more effective than any human system could be.

Maybe I romanticize this aspect of Buddhist and Hindu societies. For belief in karma can and does have very harmful as well as positive effects. But I am sure that, by contrast with judgemental attitudes I'd encountered too often in Christian circles, I found Sherpa and Hindu societies much more tolerant. I thought then, and think now, that belief in karma has a lot to do with this. No need to worry about people getting away with bad deeds; the law of karma is inexorable, and the consequences of those deeds will be borne by the doers at some stage.

Colourful ceremonies

Yet another aspect of Sherpa religion that struck me forcibly during this time was the splendid colourful noisy whackiness of it all. The Presbyterian churches and ceremonies I was used to were austere and bare to put it mildly, part of a ferocious attempt to be as little like Roman Catholics as possible. Dad even ran into opposition when he changed the layout of Chalmers Church, Timaru, and later Knox Church, Christchurch. He removed the pulpit from its central place of dominance to a more modest position on the side, and moved the communion table into the central place, with a simple cross behind it. Not, mark you, a papist cross with an agonised figure of Christ crucified on it – just an empty cross, symbol of Jesus' sacrificial death but more so of his triumphant rising from the dead.

Nonetheless I guess this was radical given the Scottish Presbyterian background. The pulpit had been central because, to Presbyterians, the Word of God was central, not rituals. From the high dominant pulpit for generations stern Presbyterian ministers had thundered denunciations of sin and awesome prophesies of punishment. "Ye're all doomed." In an important and pervasive sense the Presbyterian way to God was through the mind, not through ritual actions and the feelings they arouse. Even Dad's way of reaffirming the importance of the Word – he had the Bible reverently carried in and placed on the pulpit lecturn – was perilously close to papist idolatry according to some diehards. For he ritualised it, recommending it directly by warmth of action and emotion rather than indirectly by cold words passing through our minds.

Suddenly now, at religious ceremonies, I was surrounded by astonishing masks and images and wall paintings and thanka (paintings on cloth) of the Buddha, of Bodhisattva (enlightened beings), of great Buddhist teachers and saints, and of innumerable goddesses and gods, some benign, some ferocious. Nor were my eyes only overwhelmed – all my senses were assaulted. The lamas, in their ochre robes and amazing headgear, swung incense burners to add to the fragrance of smoky clothes and human bodies. They chanted rhythmic mantras, punctuated by long thunder-blasts from huge copper and brass Tibetan horns, a high syncopated melody on clarinet-like reed instruments, and booming drums and clanging cymbals. I was touched on the head in blessing by lamas, and ran my fingers along the raised letters of huge copper prayer wheels. And morsels of chang (rice beer) and food, after being offered to the goddesses and gods, were placed in our hands and we sucked them into our mouths.

So much for the five senses. What of the mind? Aha! Buddhism, as I learned later, distrusts the mind. The mind creates illusory concepts and objects out of the furious flux of the universe's energy, most dangerously the concept of an enduring individual self. So best of all, for me, was that my mind was not given the tiniest toehold in all this. Even the chanted mantras, though using intelligible words, were not intelligible to me (and probably not to many other than the monks). They were for me pure sound, bypassing my troublesome mind and vibrating instead my whole being.

It was like hearing opera sung in Italian – the often banal meaning of the words doesn't come between me and the visceral impact of the music. Or like hearing a Roman Catholic mass in Latin – a deep feeling of the sacredness and importance of what is going on, without it being spoiled by the unbelievable meaning of the words.

I should add that because of, rather than despite, its distrust of the mind, Buddhism takes the mind very seriously. The monks chanting the mantras would not only have memorized them, they would have studied their meaning and history, and engaged in intricate intellectual debates about them and the beliefs underpinning them. And, as I was to discover later, and admire greatly, the Buddhist philosophical tradition that developed in India is amongst the greatest and most subtle intellectual achievements of humankind. But for me this initial and hugely influential contact with Buddhism mainly bypassed my mind and overwhelmed instead, and wonderfully, the rest of my being.

All this was enhanced by the way in which we were made welcome at all ceremonies. Nobody gave a thought to whether we believed or not. I doubt the notion that non-believers might somehow dilute or wreck a ceremony has ever entered a Sherpa head. Partly, I think, this is because they trust the power of their rituals so securely that it wouldn't occur to them that some people not believing in them as they do could have any effect. But, probably more importantly, in Buddhism and Hinduism what you believe or don't believe is really your business alone. Unless your beliefs lead to actions which adversely affect others, there is no need for others to try to change them. If, through the law of karma, they adversely affect you, that is your lookout. Moreover, against the vast background of countless deaths and rebirths, it is clearly understood that different people will be at different stages of spiritual progress, and therefore not only will have, but will need, different beliefs. This understanding encourages great tolerance of others' views, or, put another way, a strong inhibition against wanting to convert others to one's own way of thinking. The contrast with the missionary zeal of many Christians was very vivid.

So my new-found Sherpa friends, though happy to share their beliefs and rituals with me, had no desire whatever to convert me to Buddhism. If they thought about it at all I'm sure their thought would be "No doubt Jim has the beliefs and habits appropriate for him in this particular rebirth of his." They may also have thought "How nice that he seems to respect and enjoy participating in ours" – but only if they'd had unfortunate encounters with zealous Christians; I think otherwise they'd simply have taken this for granted.

Ritual protection on mountains?

Consequently we were not urged to join in any ceremonies, but were made to feel very welcome. Not only that, we could request, or have suggested to us, ceremonies specifically for us. I've already mentioned that Ed and Mingma would always get projects we worked on blessed by lamas, preferably the Head Lama of Thyangboche – deeply moving occasions when we would line up with Sherpas to file past and be blessed by the Rimpoche. But we also, on this first trip, had a special ceremony at Pangboche Gompa to placate the god of Taweche, the awesome mountain rearing above the village. This god was represented in the gompa by a mask as ferocious as ever I've seen, highly appropriate to the mountain as it turned out. With due ceremony, and with our natural trepidation at attempting so difficult a peak both heightened and somehow also eased by the solemn yet noisy and colourful ritual, we appeased this fearsome being with mantras and offerings. Subsequently, elated by our efforts but defeated by the last dangerous 150 feet of the summit ridge, I jokingly chided Phu Dorje and Pemba Tarke about the ritual failing to bring us success. They were never stumped for a reply. "Ah, Jim sahib," they grinned, "puja all safely back getting, not summit getting – that we doing, not doing."

I don't know what lasting effect this brief but very moving encounter with Buddhism would have had if it had remained a one-off. But, to my huge good fortune, it was but the opening round of the rest of my life. These impressions and feelings were to be expanded and deepened enormously over the next two years, by my immersion in India and Hinduism, and my repeated re-immersions in Sherpa Buddhism. Then for the next half century, and still on into the future, through studying and teaching, and through repeated returns to the living sources in India and Nepal and Fiji, the Indian religious tradition has continued to work its gentle magic on me, to my lasting benefit.

Meanwhile, back in Solu Khumbu in 1963, Ann and Louise, and Dorene (the girl friend of Tom Frost, an American climber on the expedition), were walking in from Kathmandu to join us. Ed and I went to meet them far down the Dudh Kosi (River). We were striding up a steep forested section of the track wholly absorbed in one of our many debates, possibly on whether there is a creative intelligence behind the universe which later became our favourite topic. Ed and I debated loudly, so Ann and Louise heard us coming from afar, hid behind trees, then leapt out on us as we came level. Near heart attacks at the ambush melted into heart-warming reunion.

Thami School was still to be completed and blessed, but Pangboche School was up and running, and water had been piped into Khumjung and Khunde, sparing women of the villages a three-quarter mile hike up to, and an 80lb load of wooden container and water back from, the springs. But we still had Mt. Kangtega to attempt. Mike Gill, one of the New Zealand climbers, had at that time a bachelor's jaundiced view of the effect wives and girlfriends had on otherwise brave mountaineers. He was gloomily convinced that Tom and I would opt out of Kangtega in favour of remaining with our women. He obviously hadn't met the likes of Ann and Dorene. They warmly encouraged us to go, and immediately planned to follow over the high pass into the Inukhu valley, and join us at Base Camp when we came down off the mountain. Which they did. This time we had no pre-assault ceremony; Kangtega, by the route by which we tackled it, is too far from any village or gompa to have a god in residence to placate. And this time not only did we all return safely from the mountain – just – we also succeeded in reaching the summit. What price ritual then? Get thee behind me, oh sceptical mind.

8. Ah, India!

So the Himalayan Schoolhouse Expedition drew to a close, and Ann and I set off on our own, in June 1963, on our two-year expedition to India.

Despite Ann's traumatic Indian initiation in Mussoorie, and my much milder initiation into Calcutta and then Nepal, we were still very naïve and ill-prepared for life in Varanasi, the most sacred city of India. A lot is made in the West of how Orientals hate to lose face, as if Westerners don't mind doing so. Bullshit: it is a universal human trait. And don't knock it. Pride, fear of losing face, stubborn reluctance to admit a mistake, call it what you will, during the first few months it was the only thing that kept me from crawling home, tail between my legs.

Early days

First there was the heat. Forty degrees centigrade in the shade was commonplace. If you sat stock still under a fan, if lucky enough to have one, you might kid yourself life was bearable. Without a fan you sweated even while sitting still. Wiggle a little finger and the drops of sweat coalesced into rivers. Get up and do something – look for food or drink, visit an office to sort out enrolment or accommodation – and you nearly drowned in your own sweat.

In cold temperatures you can keep warm by putting on more clothing or vigorously exercising. In hot you can't get cold, even by taking all your clothes off, which is not usually socially acceptable anyway. At one stage – though this was later, we weren't so clever at first – we wrapped sheets round our naked bodies, stood under a shower (alas it couldn't be called a cold one) until the sheets were soaked, then lay motionless under a ceiling fan. It got us cool for up to five minutes at a time, then the sheets were dry and hot and the process had to be repeated.

Then there was the problem of eating and drinking. For the first few weeks we stayed in a cheap hotel in the swarming centre of town. To our fevered eyes everything was swarming, not just with humans and cows and dogs and cycles and rickshaws and motorbikes and cars and buses and elephants and monkeys, but also with bugs of every kind. Ann's nursing knowledge and books didn't help, for every disease we looked up seemed to end in death. We felt the symptoms and feared the consequences of every disease described.

Nor were our fears wholly unfounded. We were laid low by periodic bouts of dysentery. And once Ann had vomiting and diarrhoea so severe we thought she would die. I scoured the streets for safe fluid to keep her from dehydration, returning only with bottled fizzy drink – no bottled water such as tourists use these days.

The wonder is we didn't starve. In time we came to realize that food eaten straight from bubbling oil at roadside stalls, and chai (tea) straight from a roaring primus, was as hygienic as could be. But in those early days everything looked fly- and bug-ridden. At length we were directed to the Ace Restaurant by other foreigners, and survived on a diet of potato chops and labelled fizzy drink. Unlabelled fizzy drink meant bottles refilled unhygienically, and resulted in instant diarrhoea.

Then there was the problem of accommodation. Banaras Hindu University was just beginning to host foreigners. It had an International House for single male students, and a hostel for single female students, but was completely thrown by the problem of accommodating a married couple, one of each sex. After many office visits we were finally given a room in the Women's Hostel, a room just big enough to take two single beds pushed together. Shower, and toilet complete with resident rat in bowl, were communal, across a blistering courtyard.

It was while we were existing here that Ann came down with hepatitis B. She became ill, gradually at first, then very seriously indeed. Weak and nauseated she lay in bed in the heat. Going to the toilet was a terrible ordeal, and coming back she frequently had to run and throw herself on the bed to avoid fainting in the courtyard. For weeks the only sustenance she could take was glucose dissolved in water. Fortunately the university water came from deep bores and was safe to drink, the greatest boon imaginable to New Zealanders in India. But eventually she was so weak she'd faint from the effort of sitting in a chair while I freshened up her bed. We both thought she might die.

At some stage Ann sent me off to find a doctor. First I went to the medical school's hospital and came back with a junior one. She examined Ann and prescribed an appetizer to build up her strength, having diagnosed a common cold! This failed to convince us. Ann urged me to go back to the medical school and get the most senior doctor I could find. To her surprise, and mine, I came back with the Professor of Medicine, no less. He took one look at Ann's yellow eyes and skin and diagnosed hepatitis. He prescribed cortisone pills and large vitamin tablets which, to our intense relief, slowly put Ann on the road to recovery.

Ann takes up the tale:

At first we also had problems with the way Indians stare intensely at other people, and especially at foreign women. Sometimes the staring became unbearable. Maybe we'd had a frustrating morning and were hot and tired. Some fellow would be blatantly staring and suddenly we'd find ourselves poking a nasty face. We weren't very proud of this and it often amusingly backfired on us. On another more cheerful day we'd be cruising along on a rickshaw enjoying the crazy sights of crowded Varanasi streets when suddenly we'd be startled by someone poking that nasty face right back at us.

It was worse on train journeys, forced to sit opposite a staring face, continuous and unblinking. Staring back didn't faze him. Covering one's head with a newspaper only drew more attention. We finally thought up a mean trick. We'd look at his feet, nudge each other, and begin to giggle. This finally worked. He'd shift his feet uncomfortably, then reluctantly drag his gaze away to see what we were laughing at.

"What is it with all this staring?" we asked ourselves. In New Zealand someone caught staring would quickly look away. Not here! Thinking it through we realized it was a question of privacy. India, with its dense population and crowded cities, has very little of it, and no-one expects it. People in fields squat together for morning bowel movements. We gazed astounded from train windows at these scenes. We were being so precious in our privacy needs which our privileged lives allowed us. With this in mind we learned to ignore gazes if we didn't like them, and eventually became so accustomed we hardly noticed.

It was of course essential that we adjusted to India; we could hardly expect India to adjust to us. And it was more difficult for me as a European-looking woman. So I tried to immerse myself in the crowd and become as invisible as possible. Look Indian, eat Indian, speak Indian. We were amongst only the second lot of foreign students to study at BHU, and many stood out like sore thumbs – white skin, blond hair, strange dress and language, not to mention women riding out into the city alone on bikes. Indian women students lived behind locked and guarded gates set in tall walls studded with broken glass. They walked out only by day in pairs or groups.

I had already begun to grow my hair in Nepal, and had salwar kameez, traditional Punjabi dress with long loose trousers and flowing gauze scarf, which I'd had made in Mussoorie. Dressed like this our

English friend Mary and I were walking the streets of Calcutta one time and overheard some Indians behind us commenting that we might be Kashmiris, which pleased us enormously. Another time, when walking the mountain tracks of Nepal, a group of Tibetans our Sherpas had stopped to talk to asked if I was Tibetan. This also pleased me enormously.

So dressed in the famous Varanasi gold-embroidered silk sari at night, and Punjabi pants and dress by day, with dark hair tied back, I could become reasonably merged in the crowd when on foot, but still had hassling problems on a bike. Within University grounds cycling male students would advance slowly ten-abreast towards me, parting at the last minute and not missing the opportunity to brush shoulders on the way. Chun, our wonderfully feisty Thai friend, had no patience with such frivolity. She was studying intensely so as to be able to support her fatherless family back home. One day a student knocked her off her bike. She leapt back on and gave chase, pulled him off his bike and beat him with her bike pump, then kicked in his spokes.

We adjust to India

But gradually we did adjust. An important step was moving into a university flat, at the urging of our German friend Eberhard Buser. Though the same age as me, Eberhard was a staff member, courtesy of a German exchange scheme, and had been assigned a flat in the Multi-Flat Building. We managed, after a number of office visits, to persuade the university to assign one to us.

Our flat was on the second (and top) storey of the building, with access to the flat rooftop. It had a bedroom, a sitting room, a shower and toilet, a tiny storage room we converted to a kitchen, and a balcony looking out to trees at tree-top level. To this haven we could retreat when India got too much for us, and from it, refreshed, we could sally forth to sample India again. It is impossible to overestimate the comfort and courage a secluded home of one's own gives to New Zealanders in a strange and crowded land. We were definitely on the way back up.

Eberhard also encouraged us to buy an Indian made Lambretta scooter by using our foreign currency, so we had motorized transport for picnics by remote rivers, as well as bikes for transport around town. Then winter came, warm sunny days and cool nights, months with no cloud in the sky, tennis on cow dung courts with eager Indian girls and boys chasing and returning balls, picnics in humanless though crocodile-inhabited river gorges – life was wonderful.

What a staggering change this was. During our first few months in Varanasi I hated India, and to my shame also Indians, with a dreadful intensity. No mean feat hating 600 million people, but emotionally exhausting and morally debilitating. Then, gradually at first but with ever increasing intensity, I came to love India and (most) Indians, an infinitely better state to be in emotionally and morally. Equally amazing, Varanasi in particular and India in general eventually became as familiar and commonplace to us as Christchurch. This led later to a weird and continuing dichotomy deep in our being. While in India she seemed the only reality, and Christchurch and New Zealand a distant and not really believable dream. But back in Christchurch the reverse was true, India a distant dream and New Zealand real. As for many years we alternated frequently between the two this produced in us an intense but rather pleasant split personality.

Just how normal Varanasi had become to us by our second year was brought home to me when a New Zealand friend, Max Pearl, stayed with us on his way home from Nepal. I picked him up from the airport on our trusty scooter. We weaved our way past the monkey temple on the outer road, dodging camels and elephants and monkeys as well as humans. Suddenly it occurred to me this might seem to Max a little different from his home town of Auckland, and said so. There was a stunned silence before Max replied, with deep feeling, “Yes, you could say that!”

Study

So far no mention of what we were supposedly there for, i.e. study. This is no coincidence. During our early months in India we were about 90% consumed by getting settled and adjusting to the place. However the other 10% had some results. I’d enrolled as a PhD student in the Department of Indian Philosophy and Religion, my supervisor being the head of this department, Dr. N.K. Devaraj. His chief interest was the sex life of Krishna, and his chief value to me as supervisor was his lack of interest in me. This enabled me to disappear from his ken for up to three months at a time, on expeditions to Nepal with Ed or on Ed’s behalf, without Dr Devaraj noticing. On one occasion I looked him up nervously, after months away, and was momentarily alarmed when he said “Ah yes, Mr. Wilson, I haven’t seen you for a while.” “Oops,” I thought, “I’m for it.” But no – his only reason for commenting on the time lag was that it meant I wouldn’t have seen his latest published paper, no doubt on Krishna’s love life, a copy of which he promptly handed me with no further comment on, or questions about, my prolonged absence.

Ann also got organized

I enrolled in the School of Fine Arts which was conveniently close to our Multi-flat Building. I was keen to do more of the diploma I had started at Canterbury University. But the system was totally different from New Zealand and I didn't have with me proof of my one-year preliminary course back home. So they gave me a practical examination. To my amazement and joy, on the basis of my exam efforts they admitted me to the final year of their three-year Diploma course.

Not without some drama however. Tuition was nominally in English, but lectures in History of Fine Arts, and in Geometry, were normally given in Hindi, in which lecturer and students were more fluent. My entry threw a spanner in the works. The teacher felt obliged to deliver his first lecture in English. Not only did none of the other students understand, but I was two years behind in the subjects. So I suggested he carry on as before and give me a list of books to study on my own.

I loved the practical art work, especially the life classes. No naked bodies as in Western cultures, but models were brought in off the streets – sadhus and gurus turbaned and with orange robes, rickshaw wallas with colourful necklaces, and so on. My teacher was good but frustrating. We were unable to understand each other so he'd take my brush and demonstrate on my work. Then, getting carried away, he would forget to give the brush back.

The composition teacher got around the problem by setting me to copy a print of an old masterpiece in traditional Indian painting style, similar to the teaching technique in past centuries in Europe I imagine. However I was rather taken aback when I came to class one day to find one of the senior students had completely gone over my finished work, without a word to me before or after.

Sculpture was another subject I really loved. I spent most of the year doing a detailed head of the Buddha. Sadly this was ruined when the chowkidar, who was looking after the school during a holiday period, failed to keep the clay moist by daily covering it with a wet cloth. When I came back from Nepal I found it dry and cracked in half.

The sculpture teacher, whom I liked very much, was the only one fluent in English. He often commented on my paintings, talking about hanging them on my walls at home in New Zealand to remind me of India. With this in mind I was horrified to be told at the end of the year by the crabby old head of school (who was always telling me off for sneaking into life classes when I should have been doing design with him) that my works were the property of the University because done with University materials, and that I wasn't allowed to keep them. So after exams, when we were about to disappear into Nepal again, we hatched a plan to liberate them. Jim drove me on our scooter to the school entrance. I walked in, said a pleasant hullo to the lecturer taking an exam for another class, calmly uplifted my portfolio, and hopped back on the scooter. We rode off, hearts in mouths. We'd pulled it off.

A row spluttered and flared for most of the following year, the highlight for us being a letter from the Head of Department which accused me of "skulkingly, along with your husband, removing your work to the multi-purpose building" (actually multi-flat, but multi-purpose sounded more interesting.) We wrote back explaining we hadn't done it skulkingly but openly and boldly. For a while the Head threatened to withhold my diploma unless the work was returned, but he must finally have given in because eventually I received my Diploma in Fine Arts with first class honours in practical and theory.

Throughout my time at Art School I had a very close friend, Arati Roy. She was very talented, and later traveled the world giving exhibitions and workshops with her beautiful batik designs printed on silk, two of which we have on our walls. This friendship made my time at Art School much more enjoyable, and we have since kept in touch, and once stayed with her on a return trip to Varanasi.

9. Materialism, Proto-scientific Theories, and Dualism

So began Hinduism's profound influence on me. My thesis was titled "The Grounds of Religious Belief in Indian Philosophy". I was thus extending into the Indian tradition the question I had wrestled with in the Western tradition: can religious beliefs be justified, or at least argued for, rationally? So I was still examining religion primarily with my mind. Valuable though this is, it is only one among a number of important ways of approaching religion. In due course India swept me excitingly into these other ways as well.

The advantage the topic had for my journey was that it allowed me to read very widely in Indian religious philosophy. That I could get away with a topic so broad, and therefore in the eyes of many western academics so superficial, was another of the many boons India bestowed on me.

Materialism and consciousness

My starting point was Surendranath Dasgupta's 5-volume *A History of Indian Philosophy*,[1] together with *A Source Book in Indian Philosophy*,[2] a compendium of religious and philosophical writings in English translation. Immediately I was struck by a significant difference from the Christian tradition of the West. There were startlingly different viewpoints including, to my astonished delight, a materialistic one. The ancient school of Charvaka believed only in physical reality, and in human lives as one-off physical occurrences. Their religious opponents all believed in a spiritual aspect of reality, represented in humans by our consciousness. They raised forcibly for Charvaka the central question for materialists: how can consciousness arise from non-conscious elements? As only fragments of Charvaka teachings have survived, and those set down in religious writings with a view to refuting them, we have only hints about their answer. But essentially they pointed to instances in our ordinary experience in which, from a mixture of ingredients, characteristics emerge which are not at all in evidence prior to mixing. For instance grapes and water, neither of which are intoxicating on their own, can be mixed and fermented to produce intoxicating alcohol. So too, Charvaka insisted, inorganic elements combine in complex ways to give rise to living organisms, and in even more complex ways to produce varying levels of consciousness.[3]

Charvaka fascinated me for two reasons. Firstly, it seems to me that in broad outline modern science is neither better nor worse off than Charvaka. In detail we moderns are far better off, for example increasingly linking various aspects of consciousness to specific areas of the physical brain. But we still have to accept that complex combinations of molecules, none of which on their own are conscious, give rise to consciousness.

Secondly, this seems the fundamental puzzle at the heart of all religious and non-religious viewpoints – how to account for consciousness – and the fundamental source of difference not only between materialistic and religious viewpoints but also between differing religious viewpoints. Certainly it is for me at the centre of the mystery of our place in, and relationship to, the universe.

Child studies suggest that when we are very young we make little distinction between ourselves and the 'external' physical world around us. We simply are. I presume this is why, when our grand-children were very young, they could be so unselfconsciously absorbed in a leaf or a stream or a bird. They were not aware of themselves as separate conscious observers of what is there: they simply experienced it. This may be what Jesus meant when he said – if he said – "Unless you turn and become like children, you will never enter the kingdom of heaven."[4] Certainly many Tantric Hindu and Zen Buddhist hints about the state of moksha or nirvana point to something like children's natural ability to be absorbed in the present moment, unaware of themselves as separate self-conscious observers.

As we grow older we become increasingly aware of ourselves as distinct from our environment and from other humans. This is partly because we are taught to be so by already self-aware and usually very self-conscious adults. But it is perhaps also necessarily so if we are to function as semi-self-sufficient individuals in a world of apparently external people and objects. We become aware not only of leaves and streams and birds but also of ourselves experiencing them. And our consciousness can seem independent of external physical things, and quite unlike them. We are subjects observing objects, and this division is so deep-rooted it is enshrined in the grammar of most languages.

Once we have reached this stage it is possible, and in the case of philosophers and religious thinkers irresistible, to wonder about the relationship between ourselves as conscious beings and the physical world we are conscious of, including our own physical bodies. And, very broadly speaking, there are three options to consider. One – the Charvaka and modern materialist option – is to believe matter is the only reality, and consciousness is one of its manifestations. The second, known as dualism, is to believe matter and consciousness both really exist but are fundamentally different from each other. Dualistic systems usually give priority to consciousness, and regard the apparent link between consciousness and matter as an unfortunate accident. Their aim – in the west also from Socrates and Plato on – is to free consciousness, the spiritual self or soul, from entanglement in matter, so that it can enjoy its true blissful and undying state. The third option is to believe consciousness is the only reality, and matter is in some sense an illusory construct, or magical display, of consciousness, in something like the way objects in dreams seem real while dreaming, but on waking we realize they have no reality independent of the dreaming mind.

Proto-scientific theories

In Indian philosophy Charvaka represents the first option. Orthodox Hindu schools, and heterodox ones of Buddhism and Jainism, can all be grouped under the other two options. The second, dvaita/dualism, has had little impact on my personal spiritual journey. I've never felt dual, never felt my mind and body are separate from each other. But the Indian version of the third option is advaita/non-dualism, and some knowledge of dualism is necessary to understand it. Indian dualism is of interest also because, taking matter seriously, some dualistic schools developed fascinating physical theories.

In ancient India, as in ancient Greece, philosophers wondered whether all the bewildering variety of physical objects and processes can be seen as different combinations of a few fundamental elements or energies. And in Indian as in Greek philosophy an atomic theory was proposed. In both, earth, water, fire and air were basic atomic elements, and in India there was a fifth substance, akasa (ether, or space, it is difficult to suggest an exact translation). In India the Nyaya school (famed also for its development of logic) proposed the atomic theory. Each element is composed of tiny irreducible particles, and all physical objects, including our bodies, are combinations of different varieties and numbers of atoms. Gold, for example, was regarded as fire atoms surrounded by earth atoms. And everything is subtly pervaded by akasa, which, for Nyaya, is non-atomic.[5]

The Samkhya school, also dualistic, went sub-atomic to explain why types of atoms differ from each other.[6] They postulated only one sort of original undifferentiated matter which combined with various particles of energy in various ways to produce the five types of atom. The akasa atom, the lightest and least discernible, was composed of a small amount of the original matter excited by a particle imbued with vibratory energy. The air atom had more matter, excited by vibratory and by pressure energy particles. The fire atom had more matter again which was excited by vibratory, pressure and light and heat energy. The water atom, with yet more matter, was excited by the three previous energies plus the energy of viscous attraction. And finally the earth atom, the heaviest and densest, added the energy of cohesive attraction to even more matter.

These physical theories mirrored their religious theories. Nyaya and Samkhya both believed in an infinite number of conscious selves (atman or purusha). These were permanently enduring individual and indivisible entities, as were Nyaya atoms and Samkhya fundamental particles. And, to round off this inadequate sketch of Indian proto-scientific theories, we can then see why the Buddhists took things a step further. Fundamental to Buddhism is the doctrine of no-self (anatman).[7] The Buddhist way of releasing us from believing we are enduring selves trapped by matter is to insist there are no selves. We are simply whirlpools of momentary feelings and thoughts, each moment causing another, but with no enduring centre or self (atman) involved at all. When they turned their minds to physics they proposed that matter likewise contained no enduring entities but consisted of momentary flashes of causal energy, each flash giving rise to another. The human mind – itself a flux of flashes – constructs enduring entities from other flashes, in similar fashion to how our eyes see a whirling firebrand as a continuous circle of light, or a whirlpool in a river appears stable but is only a pattern of continuously changing molecules of water. Or, as a modern Buddhist might suggest, in the way rapidly changing still images projected onto a screen are seen by the viewer as enduring people and objects moving through space and time.

This progression in ancient Indian physics is, in broad outline, amazingly similar to that in modern physics during the last few centuries. Atoms as basic particles have given way to subatomic but still enduring particles, and they in turn to quarks and bosons and mesons, etc., some of which are believed to endure only for nano-seconds, and to be difficult to describe adequately as particles at all.

Dvaita/dualism

Religiously, of the dualistic systems of India, Yoga is the best known even within India, and the only one widely known outside. Yoga developed a marvellous system of physical and mental exercises aimed ultimately at achieving enlightenment (moksha). Its disciplines were adopted by other Indian schools, and now by many in the west, for a variety of physical and mental and religious goals. Indeed nowadays many Yogic gurus and practitioners, in and outside India, are non-dualist, aiming at the realization that our apparent individual self is identical with Brahman, the Supreme Self. But originally the Yogic aim was dualistic, that is to free one's real individual self from entanglement with real matter. Individuality endures in dualistic enlightenment, but the self is free from rebirth.

In this Yoga was so similar to Samkhya that in most treatments of early Indian philosophy the two schools are linked together as Samkhya-Yoga. And yet – and at first astonishingly to me – Samkhya is atheistic, Yoga theistic.[8] How could the most fundamental division in western religious thought, between atheism and theism, be considered in India so unimportant that Samkhya and Yoga could be grouped together? The answer is that originally the God of Yoga was simply a Supreme Isolated Self who had never been trapped in the round of rebirth. His use in Yogic discipline was as an inspiring example to meditate on, not, as in Christianity, as an active Creator God able to assist us to salvation. In Yoga, as in Samkhya, it was up to each individual self to achieve release from rebirth; and, once released, it enjoyed bliss in isolation from other selves, including, in Yoga, the Supreme Self. So it was indeed a matter of small moment whether or not one added belief in a Supreme Self to the system.

10. Advaita/non-dualism

The aim of the dualistic schools of Hinduism is to release one's individual conscious self from the round of rebirth. This self was most commonly referred to as atman. It is probable that this dualistic strain in Indian religion stems from beliefs and practices of people who inhabited India when Aryan invasions began about 1500 BC. To understand advaita/non-dualism – or spiritual monism, as advaita/non-dualism is often called in the west – we need to see what happened to the conquering Aryans after they settled in, and began to be influenced by, India.

The religion of the invading Aryans[1] has striking similarities to the religion of the New Zealand Māori prior to European influence.[2] It is preserved in the *Rg Veda* which is often called a collection of hymns to gods and goddesses but is better viewed as collections of ritual chants called mantras, or, to use the Māori term, karakia. They are addressed to what could be called environmental deities, mainly male though some, e.g. Dawn, are female. The major ones are Indra, god of thunder and lightning and rain (cf. Tāwhirimatea, Māori god of wind), Varuna, sky god (Rangi), Agni, god of fire (Mahuika), and Soma, the hallucinogenic drink used to lift priests to ecstatic heights (no Māori equivalent).

Indra is especially dramatic. Drunk on Soma he careers his chariot across the sky with earth as wheel on one end of the axle and sun on the other. If he crashes, as drugged drivers are wont to do, we're done for! With his lightning bolts he bursts asunder the demon drought, Rta, and releases rain to replenish parched land. This is dramatic mythological depiction of dramatic seasonal events on which life in India depends. After the long dry summer vast monsoon clouds at last mass in the sky. But for days or weeks – and sometimes, disastrously, months – the clouds seem to be imprisoning rain, holding back its life-giving water. Then, abruptly, lightning flashes, thunder booms, clouds seem rent asunder, and rain pours down on thirsty land and desperate people.

Indra has to be praised, placated, even forced to do this deed by rituals performed by the priestly class, the brahmins[3]. And increasingly in the second stratum of sacred Hindu scriptures, the *Brahmana*, the belief grows that, if the brahmins correctly perform the rituals and chant the mantras, Indra has no choice but to oblige. This is because rituals and mantras tap into an unseen energy pervading the whole universe, and can channel it in ways beneficial to humans. This energy is Brahman, which at this stage is very similar to mana, the energy pervading the Māori world-view. And the gods are demoted; they are no longer supremely powerful but are subservient to this all pervasive force.

At about the same time Aryans were coming into contact with the dualism of indigenous Indian cultures, and with the associated meditative practices, including extremes of self-denial and self-infliction of pain, aimed at freeing atman from repeated rebirths into physical bodies. Some brahmins, it seems, were intrigued by these meditative practices, for the third stratum of Hindu scriptures is the *Aranyaka*, usually translated forest treatises.

I like to imagine that, impressed by the serenity of indigenous hermits meditating in forest retreats, they decided to try it themselves. Some must have accepted the dualistic viewpoints undergirding the practices, for these survive strongly into later Hinduism. But some meditated not on isolated selves distinct from matter but on the mysterious ritual energy activating the whole universe, matter and selves alike. For in the fourth strata, the *Upanishads*, also known as Vedanta (Veda's end, that is climax or fulfillment), we find the first powerful statements of non-dualism, which in my possibly biased opinion becomes the dominant underlying viewpoint of Hinduism. And the way it was expressed brilliantly united the meditative tradition aimed at freeing atman from rebirth with the ritual tradition aimed at channelling Brahman, the universal energy. The great Upanishadic vision is that atman and Brahman are one and the same.

Among many moving assertions of this, the simplest is that in which a father is explaining to his son the nature of the universal energy and of his own self. I paraphrase. "Take this seed, Svetaketu." "I take it, father." "Now split this seed in two, Svetaketu." "I split it, father." "What do you see?" "Nothing, father." "Yet, Svetaketu, though you cannot see it, in this tiny seed is the power to grow into a mighty Banyan tree." "This I know, father." "In the same way, Svetaketu, though you cannot see it, in all things there is the invisible power of Brahman. And that art thou, Svetaketu."[4]

These teachings, and the more systematic exposition of them in the 8th century AD by Sankara[5], the greatest of the advaitan philosophers, had a profound effect on me. They spoke to some deep-felt but not till then identified need. I have never felt dual, split into consciousness and body. I have always felt at one in myself and at one with my environment, the latter probably inspiring and then being reinforced by my mountaineering and other outdoor loves. I had also chafed at the duality in Christianity between God and the universe, and God and human selves. Part of my gut reaction against Augustine's "Justification by Faith Alone" stemmed from my dislike of being at the mercy of, and having to grovel to, a separate, powerful, personal God (whom David Hume described as having "a restless appetite for praise"). Perhaps also I still resented God trying to make me give up mountaineering! Now Hinduism presented me with a whole new way of viewing and feeling my relationship with the universe and with the spiritual energy infusing it and me.

I explored it eagerly, emotionally as well as mentally. And it felt great. This strange fascinating consciousness, which seems the unifying and to a considerable extent the motivating and controlling centre of my individual existence, is no different from the energy in everything. This isn't grandiose megalomania. I, as an individual self, am not the universe. But neither am I separate from it. I am as integral a part of it as are stars and earth and rocks and trees and fish and birds and other humans. My consciousness, and the body it infuses and informs, are together but a magical momentary manifestation of the Universal Consciousness, Brahman. And my religious destiny is not at the mercy of the arbitrary whim of another, and all-powerful, Person; it is up to me. Through meditation I can realize that atman and Brahman are one, that I am one with the universal energy, thereby achieving release from narrow selfishness; and that is moksha (enlightenment, liberation).

During this initial time in India, and later back in New Zealand, I had powerful experiences of this state of blissful oneness. On occasions these were enhanced by drugs. In India, especially in the Tantric tradition, this is an acceptable way of opening myself to such experiences. The blissfulness of oneness is partly due to contrast with much of my normal experience. While feeling and acting as if I am a separate individual negotiating a tricky external world (a dual situation) I am worried about the impression I'm creating on others, worried about what I should do with my life, worried about how I can come to settled peaceful terms with the changing objects and circumstances around me. Also I am often annoyingly self-conscious, aware of myself observing things rather than being totally absorbed in them as small children are. During my oneness experiences all this drops away and I become whatever it is that is happening around me.

The first time I got really stoned illustrates this. I'd taken rather too much of good Kashi hashish and was listening to a beat-up old record of Beethoven's Fifth Symphony. Too often when I listen to music I am in a dual situation, aware of myself listening to the music, distracted by other things, even imagining other people looking at me. On this occasion, though we had others in our flat and I was helping Ann by handing round drinks and nibbles, the music totally took me over. It was as if the music was being played through me, as if I was the music. Bjorn Borg vividly made the same point in relation to tennis when he said: "Usually it is me playing tennis, but sometimes, wonderfully, it is the game of tennis playing itself through me" (my paraphrase).

I intensely felt the music as a battle between good and evil, and when Beethoven suddenly changed from gentle melodies to a crashing intrusion of fearsome force I uttered a loud cry and clasped my heart. Most thought I was having a heart attack and rushed to help me, but a gentle Nepalese friend urged me to "take lemon Mr. Wilson, take lemon", knowing this would bring me down a little.

Not that I wanted to come down. I was enthralled by the experience, and craved more. And got more, enjoying similar experiences later, often with Indian flavours. I can vividly recall standing on the deck at our New Zealand home, high on acid, the clouds pulsating across a star-studded sky, and experiencing the whole universe, myself included, as powered by sexual energy, as in Shiva and Parvati mythology. Again I was enraptured, lifted clean out of my narrow individual life, so that it was not as if the individual 'I' was experiencing oneness but as if there was just oneness.

Knowledgeable Christians could remind me that ecstatic expressions of similar experiences can be found in Christianity. And they would be right. But even liberal theological colleges, such as the one I had studied at, didn't pay Christian mysticism much attention. In Christianity, and in Islam, mystics are mostly regarded with considerable reserve, if not outright suspicion.

For Christian expressions of the mystical experience suggest that the mystic becomes one with God, almost becomes God. And this runs counter to the main thrust of Christian theology and practice, namely that God is immensely above and beyond us humans – "For as the heavens are higher than the earth, so are my ways higher than your ways and my thoughts than your thoughts"[6] says Yahweh in the Old Testament. The aim is, by God's grace, to come into an obedient relationship with God. To try to, or claim to, become God, or even one with God, is to blur the distinction between us and God in a way certainly verging on heretical. In Christianity only Jesus is divine, and in Islam to claim this even of Jesus is blasphemy. In Hinduism, by contrast, spiritual monism (advaita/non-dualism), as expressed in "All is Brahman", is fundamental. So Hinduism is far more fertile ground for experiences of oneness than the Hebraic tradition.

Be that as it may, it was through Hinduism that I had my first real introduction to mystical unity with spiritual reality, and I'm glad this was so. Had I encountered it in Christianity I would have shared the suspicion that mysticism was not compatible with fundamental Christian belief. More importantly, any attempt by me to feel oneness with the Christian God would have been fatally hampered by my difficulty in believing there is such a god. In Hinduism I was free of both these difficulties. Coming to it anew I had no prior beliefs or disbeliefs to worry about, no orthodoxy I felt I had to justify myself to. And, in Hinduism, the aim is direct experience of spiritual reality, not correctness of belief. Beliefs are assessed in terms of their ability to help or hinder such experience, rather than in terms of truth or falsehood. Moreover, against the vast backdrop of samsara (beginningless and potentially endless rebirths in a cyclic universe of unimaginable size) it is taken for granted that different selves, human and other, will be at different stages or levels of spiritual progression. One set of beliefs, therefore, cannot be expected to suit all, so a variety of beliefs is to be welcomed.

Shankara, excitingly for me, takes this one step further. He is commenting on a passage which says of Brahman "whence words together with the mind turn away, unable to reach It."[7] He points out that human language has developed to deal with the apparent world of everyday events, in which we humans act and think as if we are conscious individuals interacting with other conscious individuals and with separate physical objects. It is therefore necessarily the case that words are not adequate to describe Brahman, or the experience of oneness with Brahman. Devised in, and therefore fatally infected by, a dualistic world, they are incapable of expressing non-dualism adequately. Even the classic attempt to express it – "That art thou" – posits identity between apparently distinguishable entities, thereby falsifying itself in its own utterance.[8]

This was a new twist to the 'Theology and Falsification' debate I discussed in chapter 5. I was so excited I eventually wrote an article about it: "Shankara, Ramanuja, and the function of religious language".[9] Ramanuja is the most important of Indian theistic philosophers, his system being known as vishistadvaita (distinctions within non-dualism).

Writing about 1100 AD he ridiculed Shankara in a way that uncannily anticipated Anthony Flew's attack on Christian belief.

Ramanuja argued that Shankara's attempts to express and defend pure advaita (non-dualism) were not false but meaningless, a misuse of language.[10] In my article I establish, to my own satisfaction at least, that Shankara had anticipated and rebutted such criticism. He not only admits, but insists, that words are inadequate to express non-dualism or to describe Brahman. He is equally explicit about what, then, is the function of religious discourse. It is to hint at and facilitate direct experience of religious reality.[11] Once directly experienced, of course, words are unnecessary. I inadequately attempt to describe to you the glory of a sunset only if you are not also looking at it. If we are looking together words are not necessary, though an "Ooh" or two, or a "Wow, look at that", often pops out.

So it seems Shankara is giving me the go-ahead to try for this blissful experience without having first to believe stuff about what really does or does not exist. I may assess his and all other competing or complementary religious utterances not in terms of whether they are true or false but in terms of whether they facilitate or hinder progress towards the ultimate inexpressible experience of reality. And indeed he goes far along this path.

Since I found temporary immersions in the experience of oneness so fabulous why didn't I devote the rest of my life to seeking to experience it permanently? Ah – alas? – because even in Shankara, and in my experience inevitably so, there is a limit to this 'belief doesn't matter' approach.

To devote the rest of my life to pursuit of this experience, rather than valuing it as one of many varied experiences I enjoy, I would have to be convinced it is the most desirable of all, and that it is permanently possible. But despite my delight in it I do not regard it as pre-eminent, preferring it as an equal amongst many. It infuses and enlightens the rest in a fundamental way, but is not, for me, an end itself. Nor am I convinced it is permanently possible. And this is because of what I believe, or deeply feel, is real. For I believe that the fundamental reality or energy is physical, with consciousness only one aspect of it, and a comparatively recent and rare one. I have on occasions tried to believe otherwise. But, unlike some, I am unable to believe whatever I want.

Or perhaps I don't want to enough? Which comes first, the belief or the desire? On balance I am very content with my present physically-based way of coming to terms with the universe. Is this why I find I don't believe in a primary spiritual dimension? Or, finding that I don't believe in one, am I simply making the best of a bad job by convincing myself that a physical universe only is what I prefer?

Be that as it may, belief surely has a fundamental part to play in whether one commits wholeheartedly to a spiritual quest, or wholeheartedly to coming to terms with a purely physical universe. (I suppose there is a third option, to vacillate between the two, but I don't fancy that: I prefer whole hearts.) And even Shankara, eventually, admits belief is vital. Despite the brilliant effort he puts into persuading us that his religious utterances are not to be assessed as statements true or false, but simply as pointers, he is in no doubt that fundamentally reality is non-dual, and that the least misleading hint as to its nature lies in our own experience of consciousness. "For," he writes, "it [moksha, enlightenment] does not depend on the will of man, but merely on what really and unalterably exists."[12]

There is another, vaguer, reason why I have never committed myself wholly to dissolving my self in a Higher Self. There is something paradoxical, verging even on the contradictory, in the idea. I am urged to lose myself, become selfless. Why? To experience the seemingly selfish reward of eternal bliss. This paradox is present in many religions. In the New Testament, for example, Jesus urges us to do good secretly. Why? Because then "your Father who sees in secret will reward you."[13] But it is most acute in Hindu non-dualism and in core Buddhism. However motivationally suspect may be the appeal in Christianity to act selflessly for others so that you can selfishly get your reward in heaven, at least it is believed that there is an individual soul to go to heaven and enjoy its reward. But in Hindu non-dualism, and even more in Buddhism, the aim is to realize there is no individual self. Hinduism doesn't worry too much about this seeming contradiction, though Ramanuja, with his usual perceptiveness, points it out to Shankara in no uncertain terms. But Gautama the Buddha, and much Buddhism, is deeply concerned about it, and tries a variety of interesting and sophisticated ways to overcome it.

I'll delay describing the main impact of Buddhism on me till a later chapter, because it wasn't till I had to teach about it that I delved deeply into it. But at this point it is relevant to mention a very interesting passage about Gautama the Buddha. He is consistently portrayed as being against metaphysical speculation, against trying positively to describe ultimate reality. He teaches only suffering, the cause of suffering, and the cessation of suffering. The cause of suffering, he tells us, is tanha, the flame of self-centred desire. To end suffering, therefore, all (!!!) that is necessary is to blow out this flame. And the way to do this is to realize there is no enduring self, and, in addition, no enduring physical objects for such a self to desire. Anatta (no self). This is at the heart of Gautama's dharma (teaching).[14]

The cessation of dukkha (suffering) is a purely negative hint about nirvana, about what happens when, by realizing there is no self, we blow out the flame of selfish desire. And Gautama's disciples, and many later Buddhists, wanted a more positive hook to hang their hopes on. They wanted Gautama to assure them that the experience of being blown out is blissful. But he was a wily old cove. To give them this would be to rekindle the flame of self-centred desire, albeit desire for a lofty goal, and one that would cause no suffering to others (except to his wife and small child whom he abandoned when he set out on his spiritual quest – cf. Jesus rejecting his mother and siblings, and Gandhi being extra hard on his family – this seems a common career hazard for spiritual pioneers). So Gautama refused to give his disciples anything positive to desire. "I teach only suffering, the cause of suffering, the cessation of suffering." Even more than Shankara, certainly more consistently, he remained true to the view that ultimate reality, and the experience of nibbana, being blown out or cooled, is inexpressible. So he refused to try to express it.

His disciples pressed him. "Lord, what happens to the self when it is blown out – does it exist, or not exist, or both exist and not exist?" This formulaic version, in texts written well after Gautama's time, is almost certainly the wording of later monks or scribes, but the question may very well come from the first disciples, and the answer from the Buddha himself. He draws his disciples' attention to the fire burning before them. "If this fire goes out," he asks them, "in which direction has it gone? Has it gone north?" "No, Lord." "Has it gone south?" "No, Lord." "East? West?" "No, lord. No, Lord." "Where then has it gone?" he asks them. "The question does not fit the case, oh Lord," they reply. "So too," says Gautama, "the question whether the self that has blown out the flame of desire exists or does not exist does not fit the case."[15] Not that even this completely avoids the problem. Even to want one's suffering to cease is a self-centred desire. But it mutes the stridency of the problem.

Subsequent Buddhism tries tirelessly to remain true to this austere stance, fails gloriously, then gamely tries again, and again. But of this more anon.

Meanwhile, back to my flirtation with Shankara's non-dualism, or spiritual monism as it can be called. It has had far-reaching effects on me, as I will make clear in chapter 23. But even at this time it had a very deep emotional impact on me, and one aspect of this was unexpected. My memory now is that it was during my initial time in India that I finally felt emotionally free of the Christian God. I may be mistaken in my timing here. For several years after our return to Christchurch we attended, and were communicant members of, Mt. Pleasant Presbyterian Church, which is curious if I really was free of God. So maybe it was during a later time in India that I felt free. What is clear, and still very vivid to me, is that my emotions finally caught up with my mind. I had intellectually abandoned belief in a Christian God; then, in a distinct and dramatic moment, I realized I was also emotionally an atheist.

Ever after I have likened the experience to that of taking off a 90lb pack after a long day carrying it up a Canterbury riverbed. It was the same intense sensation of lightness, of a heavy burden removed, almost of levitation. Of course I'm not saying there is such a God whom I suddenly removed from my shoulders. Either there is, in which case she or he is still on my shoulders, just riding lightly for a while, which I'm sure such a being could do; or there is not, in which case it was simply my mistaken notion I was rid of. But the relief was intense, and marvellous. And I give spiritual monism (advaita/non-dualism) much of the credit. It gave me at that time an exciting view of spirituality free of all the intellectual and emotional baggage with which I had burdened Christianity. In ways I've tried to indicate I responded to it enthusiastically without having to agonise over whether I believed in it or not. So I could shuck the Christian God off my shoulders without abandoning spirituality entirely. Given my intense involvement in religion till then this may well have been a necessary staging point for me, as well a very exciting one and, transformed into physical monism, an enduring one.

11. Hindu Theism

At the same time as I was flirting with spiritual monism, and getting the sober Christian god off my back, I was having a ball with whacky Hindu goddesses and gods, and taking a peek at the Hindu Supreme Deity. Even with God, capital G, the differences from Christianity struck me forcibly. In Christianity God is portrayed either as loving and creative or as judgemental and destructive, and these two aspects were never satisfactorily reconciled for me. In the Hindu God creation and destruction are presented as two complementary aspects of the one being. For in the Hindu cyclic universe destruction, terrible at the time, is necessary to clear the way for new creation, be it the next life of an individual or the next cycle of the universe. It was then easier for me to see God as creative and destructive and yet on balance good. This also felt more realistic to me, more in tune with what we humans experience. As was the case with spiritual monism I had no past baggage of belief, so was free to explore how this deity 'felt' without worrying about whether it was a real being or a picturesque personification of universal processes.

The Hindu Supreme Deity is symbolized by more than one persona or mask, the three most important being Vishnu and Shiva (male) and Kali (female).

Vishnu is the most sober and serious, but he, like the other two, is both creator and destroyer, and through his many avatars (descents or incarnations), especially Krishna, he has a very playful and a very sexual side too.

Shiva is decidedly wilder and fiercer, and central to his character is the endless alternation between creation and destruction, life and death. In the portrayal of Shiva dearest to my heart he is Nataraj, King of Dance; the many beautiful murti (images) of him in this role have him perfectly poised at the centre of a ring of flaming energy. It is his dance which creates and sustains the universe during its manifest stages, and awesomely destroys it at the end of each cycle. In another dramatic portrayal it is the sexual energy of Shiva and his consort Parvati, with whom he once made continuous love for 1,000 years, that keeps the universe in existence.

Then there is Kali, the Supreme Mother Goddess known also by many other names, especially Durga. Kali is often portrayed as primarily destroyer, with a blood-dripping human head in one of her many hands, a bloody sword in another, and a necklace of human skulls. Yet she is approached by her devotees with touching tenderness, and with confidence that her mother's love will protect and assist them, and that even her destructive side is ultimately for their benefit.

In addition to this triumvirate of deities Hinduism has hosts of other goddesses and gods, depicted in lurid posters and by a wild profusion of images and shrines and stories. They include an elephant-headed god, a monkey god and a snake god, as well as many human-like ones, some relatively sober and serious but many very zany indeed.

To one brought up on the thin gruel of an unimaged and soberly moral Presbyterian God this was sumptuous fare, and I devoured it enthusiastically. Had I grown up a Hindu I might have anguished over apparent contradictions within and between deities. But perhaps not. Hindus are not required to take all this as literally true. They are aware these are flawed human attempts to symbolize an ultimately inexpressible reality, aids to religious development which we can use if we find them useful, ignore or discard if not. So there was no pressure on me to worry about whether these fabulous deities were real; I could respond to them emotionally and aesthetically and religiously in whatever way I pleased. And so I did.

The more sober intellectual expositions of Hindu theism affected me less than Shankara's Advaita. I was very impressed, however, by the acute mind and clear discourse of Ramanuja. He argued persuasively that language is adequate to express the theistic viewpoint, which regards moksha as a close loving relationship between atman (selves) and Ishvara (the Supreme Self). He also claims that we need, and can have, the assistance of Ishvara as we struggle to free ourselves from rebirth.

At this point I was delighted to find, in Ramanuja's writings, the Hindu equivalent of my old friend the Augustinian/Pelagian controversy. Typically, it was expressed in colourful images. The debate was between the rival theories of cat salvation (cf. Paul and Augustine) and monkey salvation (cf. Pelagius). When a mother cat removes her babies from danger she simply picks them up by the scruffs of their necks and carries them – they are passive, doing nothing for themselves. So the cat salvation school comes close to the extreme Christian view that on our own we are helpless, and wholly dependent on God's grace. But when a mother monkey rescues her offspring they have to clasp their arms round her neck and hang on. They would not be saved without her strength and mobility, but they have their own vital part to play. So the monkey salvation school, though believing we cannot be saved without God's grace, believes also that we cannot be saved without exerting some effort on our own behalf. The dualistic and non-dualistic viewpoints, on the other hand, though they believe we could not save ourselves unless reality is as it is, call on no other external person, placing the ball firmly in our court. I certainly prefer it that way.

But my immersion in Hindu theism was not only at the intellectual level. It was also, most powerfully, at the ritual and emotional level. I went to many pujas (ritual worship) in mandirs (temples) and on Ganga's ghats (steps leading down to the river's edge). I didn't believe the goddesses and gods we were approaching literally existed, but I forcefully felt their presence, or, I suppose more accurately, felt I was in the presence of something immeasurably greater and more powerful than my puny individual self.

To me this is the archetypal religious feeling, and I experience it strongly when awed by nature – for example, mountains, or mountainous seas, or flooded rivers, or wild winds. Presbyterian services, on the other hand, with their emphasis on preaching the word, and their austere lack of ritual, had exercised my mind, but seldom my emotions to any great extent. To my dismay at the time, my attempts to 'feel' the the presence of Jesus especially strongly at communion services almost always failed. In a conventionally religious sense, prior to my encounter with Hinduism and Sherpa Buddhism, my most intense religious experiences had been my 'call' by God during the Christian retreat, and my night of torment in the Edwards valley, significantly in a natural setting.

Now, especially during attendance at puja in the university mandir, I was frequently and intensely getting this feeling of awe before something immeasurably greater. I would enter the inner shrine reverently and sit on the floor with my fellow Hindu worshippers. They seemed completely untroubled by my presence, not needing to check my beliefs or motives before welcoming me. I doubt it entered their heads that the presence of an unbeliever, if such I was, could in any way affect the efficacy of the puja; and if the puja affected me adversely that was my business. In all my times in India I have been declined entry to only two Hindu temples. At all others I have been warmly welcomed.

The inner shrine of the Banaras Hindu University mandir is a small square room. A large Shiva Lingam (penis) and Parvati Yoni (vagina), festooned with bright marigolds and their green leaves, takes up much of the central space. The ceiling is low, and it and the walls are concrete, acoustically very powerful. There are doorless entry arches on two opposite sides. For a while we would sit quietly, with only murmured mantras from some of the not-quite-crush of people. Then, clanging gongs and symbols, swinging incense and chanting mantras, one or more pujari (priests) would enter. The ritual would begin, then gradually work up to a climax of simply awesome volume and intensity of sound and sight and smell.

The mind didn't have a chance – it was simply overwhelmed by the senses. I suspect it would have been even if it could understand the Sanskrit mantras, which mine couldn't. The ritual never failed to lift me out of myself and into a blissful quiet centre in the midst of a maelstrom. And, significantly, I felt afterwards no need to think about it, to analyse what was going on and why it was affecting me so powerfully. Maybe, for mind-bound me, this was the greatest of the many wonderful gifts Hinduism gave me.

Small wonder that Hinduism became my favourite religion and remained singly so until joined by pre-European Māori religion. Small wonder that when I tried to describe Hinduism later it was largely a favourable description, skating lightly over the darker aspects of which, like all religions, it has plenty.

12. Ganga and Hinduism

During Ed Hillary's Ocean to Sky expedition, in 1977, we drove jet boats up India's sacred river Ganga. Subsequently, Ed asked me to contribute an appendix on Ganga and Hinduism to the book he was writing about the adventure.[1] I have so far given a very partial and piecemeal picture of Hinduism, because I have been concentrating on its influence on me. So herewith is my attempt at an overview as presented in an edited version of that appendix.

Brahman

Running through most of the diverse beliefs and practices of Hinduism is belief in Brahman, the underlying energy of the universe. This energy manifests in an immense variety of ways: in the cycling of stars and galaxies and in the microscopic vibrating urgency of an atom; in the germination and growth of a grain of rice or a mighty banyan tree; in the complexities and bewilderments and excitements of conscious human activity or the intricacies of an anthill; in the fiery death of a star or the dreadful dissolution of the universe at the end of each cycle; in death by drought of a tender rice shoot or by hunger of a tiny child.

In Hindu mythology living beings on this earth are but a tiny part, and normally understand only a tiny part, of this great flow of energy and life. The flow also ceaselessly cycles through countless other world systems, each, like ours, with its earth and its heavens and its hells, with its earthly life-forms and its deities and its demons. And while our final goal is to understand and get in tune with as much of this diverse manifestation as possible, yet our small human minds can be boggled by its immensity.

Ganga as symbol

So we need symbols – smaller and more familiar things within our experience that can stand for Brahman the immense, and can teach us gently a little more about it, preparing us for greater knowledge in future days or future lives.

Ganga is one such symbol, and a superb one. Like Brahman through the universe she runs her silver thread through northern India, from a human standpoint seemingly infinite in form and mood, yet one river, ever the same. There are many beautiful tales of people learning wisdom by watching and thinking about the river. For Ganga, like Brahman, is life as well as death. With her monsoon flow she brings water, and thus life, to earth dried to dust by summer heat. Almost overnight northern India turns green; almost you can hear new life thrusting up from the soil. With her monsoon floods, over untold centuries, she formed the fertile plains in which she annually renews life. And in the hottest driest summer she remains, though in diminished flow, then more than ever quite literally the essential support of life, water for irrigation and for drinking, and a pathway for the transport of people and goods. But what Ganga gives she also takes away. The same monsoon floods that built the land often eat it away, undermining houses and washing away fields; or they overflow banks and inundate crops and drown croppers.

As we moved up the monsoon flow and saw both the life it gave and the destruction it wreaked we became convinced that the villagers whom it affected understood this: that if they accepted and lived on the blessings of the river they must also accept the river's blows. Most strikingly this seemed so in two villages where half the houses had been washed away. To learn this from the river, then to apply the lesson to life as a whole – this is one way of expressing the key aim of Hinduism. Like the river, Brahman gives and takes in a way indifferent to human desires. Wisdom consists in realising that it cannot be otherwise, and enjoying when it gives and enduring when it takes. Beside this wisdom our restless Western attempts to force life always to give and never to take seem a brave but ultimately doomed alternative.

But the river in all her variety is still not easy to comprehend fully. Though we travelled her length, and were deeply moved by her diversity, we acquired only a piecemeal picture. So Hinduism goes further in breaking down the great into smaller images, easier to relate to. Ganga is personifed, thought of and modelled as a very beautiful woman, a goddess. We did puja before one such lovely image in the Ganga mandir (temple) at Dasashwamedh Ghat in Varanasi, before turning to continue the puja to the actual river herself.

It is at this point, often, that the mind of the outsider begins to get confused. For the beautiful Ganga is just one amongst a number of striking images or manifestations of Shakti, the active feminine aspect of Brahman. There are also Kali and Durga, often depicted as fierce and horrific as well as warm mother figures, to emphasise the destructive as well as the creative side of life. There is the exquisitely formed Parvati, daughter of

Himalaya and wife of Lord Shiva. There is Sita, chaste wife of Ram; Radha, Krishna's favourite gopi (cow-girl); Lakshmi, the goddess of wealth and good fortune; and Saraswati, goddess of wisdom and learning. Images and colourful pictures of these goddesses abound in most Hindu temples and homes. On this trip I also came across some more local goddesses, new to me – Banadevi, to whom the Sunderbans villagers pray for protection from tigers; Vindhyachal-Devi, whose temple near Mirzapur we visited; and Vaishno Devi, whose cave-shrine our liaison officer visited when he was anxious about a crucial stage in his career.

And these are just the feminine personifications or manifestations of Brahman. Amongst the male manifestations, Shiva, who catches Ganga in his hair and lowers her gently to earth, and Vishnu, from whose toe the celestial river first flows, are pre-eminent, each having a wealth of images and myths of his own. Shiva, especially as Nataraj (Lord of Dance), strikingly portrays the ideal of poise and balance in the midst of the wild unrestrained energy of the universe. Vishnu is above all the preserver and re-creator, and is often depicted lying on the coiled serpent, Shesha, the last traces of form in the ocean into which the universe dissolves between each cycle. In his dreams on this sinuous bed he gathers up and pieces together again the scattered elements of the formed universe. And there are many other male forms. Ganesh, elephant-headed son of Shiva and Parvati, is prayed to for success in hard tasks (we needed his help especially when trying to heave our heavy boats off sandbanks). Ram is the ideal of righteousness and fidelity; Hanuman, his monkey helper, of loyalty and courage. Krishna, like Ram, is one of the most important avatars (descents to earth) of Vishnu, and from his mischievous childhood through his loving youth to his lofty teaching in the Bhagavadgita he presents a fascinating and complex figure.

To these divine figures, through images, some crude and some exquisite, along the length of Ganga and throughout the breadth of India, Hindu devotees bring their offerings of flowers and fruits and milk and rice, and their chanted Sanskrit mantras or their simple prayers. They come with requests as basic and varied as their lives: for health when they or their children are sick; for rain when their crops wither in drought; for success in business deals or examinations; for a higher rebirth next time round; for a happy marriage; for strength in living a morally good life. With so many goddesses and gods, and such a profusion of requests, confusion seems at times to reign supreme, and Hinduism is thought by outsiders to be endlessly polytheistic and crudely superstitious.

Ek bhagavan

And yet, on this journey as on many others, I found complete unanimity amongst Hindus, whether villager or sophisticated city professional, whether ordinary devotee or learned priest or earnest sadhu. There is but one god – ek bhagavan.

At a reception in New Delhi, for example, I was talking to two very sophisticated women. One of them had been in a small plane to Namche Bazaar, a Nepalese village near the foot of Mt. Everest – a wild flight over wild country. "The light plane was tossing in turbulent air pockets," she recalled with a shudder, "and I remembered every temple in India and prayed earnestly. I was praying for the pilot – 'Oh God help him fly us safely out of this!'" "Praying to whom?" I asked, "Shiva, Ram, Kali?" "Our family has a family deity, Durga," she replied. "But", the other woman added, "our Hindu religion has so many gods we just call on God, not by any specific name."

In the Sunderbans, in a very different social setting, I spent a lot of time in the back of the largest launch where the boatmen prepared their meals on a small coke fire (and were happy to share them with me!). In a mangled mixture of broken Hindi and English we discussed India and New Zealand and the world, and politics and agriculture – and of course, above all, religion. They said prayers twice a day, they told me, "in the evening and again when we get up in the morning". "To Shiva?" I asked. "Yes," replied one of them; but another said, "No, my goddess is Kali." "Kali and Durga?" I asked, probing to see if this devotee made a distinction between these two forms or names of the great mother goddess. "Yes, yes, but they are the same," came the reply without hesitation. "What about Parvati and Saraswati?" I queried. "Yes, the same, all forms of Shakti." "And Shiva, is he also a form of Brahman?" "Yes, yes, ek bhagavan, bas" (there is only one God). I was so delighted at this impromptu piece of research into Hindu monotheism that, with the dark silence of the Sundarbans all around us, I sang to my friends the only Hindi bhajan (hymn) that I knew, a song of devotion to Ram. Despite excruciating mispronunciations of lovely Hindi syllables, and some wailingly off-beat notes and rhythm, this set the seal on our religious togetherness.

I confess my researches into how many gods Hinduism really has have been the butt of much hilarity and derision from many of our mob since a Nepalese jet-boat expedition of 1968. In that vintage year I managed to solicit the answer "ek bhagavan" from a fine range of Hindus – from a

Bengali truck-driver's assistant in crowded Calcutta to a remote Nepali pujari (priest) on the banks of the Sun Kosi. There was some suspicion – base and unfounded – that I made it clear in my questions that "ek bhagavan" was the answer I desired, and that my always polite Hindu respondents kindly gave me what I wanted.

So I was relieved that in the Sundarbans, on this trip, I had Graeme Dingle as witness to a completely unsolicited "ek bhagavan" response. We were ashore in one of the beautiful green villages which hide behind high protective banks, and in a wee temple beside a lotus pond we were shown a murti (image) of Gauranga. "Who?" I asked, for I had not come across this name before. After much discussion we gathered that Gauranga was a manifestation of Krishna. But the discussion ranged wider than that. Gauranga, Krishna, Jesu Christu, – and again, Allah, Bhagavan? – "ekais, ekais" (the same, the same) the villagers said over and again. "Aha!" Ding pipes up with the magic phrase, "Ek Bhagavan". "Haan! haan!" (yes, yes) they said, heads wagging in agreement. "And Shiva, Vishnu, Ram, Shakti – ekais?" I asked. "Haan haan," they replied enthusiastically.

Sophisticated Delhi dwellers, remote Sundarbans villagers, and an ebullient down-to-earth army officer too – all give the same answer. Throughout the trip our liaison officer, whom we called B.B. because his full name was unpronounceable by us, was superb in relating to us stories about Ganga and other goddesses and gods, and on occasions about his own religious activities and beliefs. He and Neelam, his wife, were both "sort of religious," he said; and he told us a moving story about how he felt he was helped at a crucial stage of his career by making a pilgrimage to the remote cave-shrine of Vaishno Devi. But the thing he didn't like about religion was the way people tried to push one god over another. He told of a Sikh friend who wouldn't go to puja with his Hindu wife but would sit outside waiting for her, for hours if necessary, rather than go inside the mandir; and of a Christian who likewise wouldn't go into a Hindu mandir. "I'll go to any ceremony, any time," B.B. said, "for under any form I just pray to the one God – whether one form or three forms or whatever, there is just one God."

This ability to make offerings and requests to different deities as if they are separate beings, and then turn and insist so decisively that there is only one God, is readily understandable once Hindu belief in Brahman is understood. It is of the nature of this One Holy Power to manifest itself in a great variety of ways. Amongst these manifestations are those we call goddesses and gods; and in one sense they are as separate from each other and from us as we are from each other and from mountains and rivers and trees. But they are, nonetheless, just manifestations of the one power; so from the point of view of deepest religious belief they are not separate beings.

Hindu theism, which regards Brahman as a personal supreme god, sees this varied manifestation in the form of many divine beings as part of the grace of God to limited human minds. We all have different tastes. One form may appeal to me and another to you. No symbol our minds can grasp can contain the whole truth about the energy of the universe; but gradually we may be moved by this one and then by that, building up from a simple to a more complex understanding.

Ramakrishna, a great Bengali saint whose temple near Calcutta we visited, put it this way: "…if God is formless, how then can He have form? Further, if He has a form, why does He have so many forms? These things do not become clear until one has realised God. He assumes different forms and reveals Himself in different ways for the sake of his devotees." Ramakrishna uses the image of a mass of water, uniform throughout and formless in its liquid state but in cold temperatures taking on separate forms as blocks of ice. So too God, who is everywhere and is everything, under the cooling influence of His devotees takes on separate forms.[2]

But even the personal imagery of one supreme god is just one way of viewing Brahman. It may be thought of as impersonal, not a being from whom we are separate but the power of consciousness, which is our own innermost nature.

The ultimate goal in Hinduism is fully to understand this power and thus enter fully into relationship with it or realise we are one with it, not separate particles battling forlornly against the flow. And those further along the path can dispense with partial forms and images. Mahatma Gandhi expresses this point in a typically tolerant way: "I do not forbid the use of images in prayer. I only prefer the worship of the Formless. This preference is perhaps improper. One thing suits one man; another thing will suit another man, and no comparison can fairly be made between the two."[3] A hymn by a South Indian devotee of Shiva makes the point more forcibly – a hymn I had to keep carefully hidden from my fellow travellers as it pulls the carpet out from under much of what we were doing on our pilgrimage:

Why fast and starve, why suffer pains austere?
Why climb the mountains doing penance harsh?
Why go to bathe in waters far and near?

Release is theirs, and theirs alone, who call
At every time upon the Lord of all.[4]

Dependent on Indian Oil barrels and Hamilton jets for our pilgrimage up Mother Ganga we were a long way from such lofty freedom from props of partial symbols and ritual acts. So too were a great many Hindus we met along the way, whether villagers at a simple shrine or sadhus making a thirty-five-year pilgrimage up the length of Ganga. What hope, for them or us, of attaining the goal of direct experience of the Holy Power in the brief years of limited groping left to us?

Samsara and karma

It is here that Hindu beliefs about time and rebirth are crucial: the doctrines of samsara and karma. According to these beliefs we have all the time in the world, literally, to work our way through to full understanding. For we have as many lives as we need in which to do this. Brahman manifests itself in cyclic, not linear, time. The universe itself repeats a cyclic pattern over and again, evolving from Brahman into its concrete diversity of form, then dissolving in fire and flood back into formless Brahman at the end of each age. The time scale of the universal cycle is enough on its own to boggle the mind – 311,040,000,000,000 human years for one cycle according to one computation.[5] Then Hindu mythology adds infinite space. "But the universes side by side at any given moment, each harbouring a Brahma and an Indra: who will estimate the number of these? Beyond the farthest vision, crowding outer space, the universes come and go, an innumerable host. Like delicate boats they float on the fathomless, pure waters that form the body of Vishnu. Out of every hair-pore of that body a universe bubbles and breaks. Will you presume to count them? Will you number the gods in all those worlds – the worlds present and the worlds past?"[6]

Not just the universe as a whole but all things within it, animate and inanimate, revolve through their own cycles within cycles, according to their diverse natures and to diverse laws. Many of these cycles are simple repetitions. But for living creatures purposeful spirals are possible, up or down a scale of spiritual ability. And the law which determines patterns of rebirths for us living beings is the law of karma. As we go through any one life we think and act in certain ways, consciously or unconsciously, and thus form habits of thought and behaviour. These habits create and express our basic character, and they have an influence long after their initial formation and far beyond their original sphere.

One writer gives the example of a businessman who, through long immersion in his job, builds up habits of seeing and dealing with every situation in economic terms. Such habits are beneficial, perhaps even essential, to the success of his business. But though he formed them they take control of him and go with him out of office hours and into his relations with family and friends. There of course, where less tangible and more complex techniques and measures of success are needed, these narrow habits are a disaster. And even when the sorry state of his relationships finally convinces him this is so, the force of habit is such that it will take him a long time and much effort to break these habits and form a new character and a new life.[7]

Hindus believe such habits and character traits have an influence over the barrier of death, causing, and determining the status of, our next life. It follows that our present status and nature are the result of our past deeds over a beginningless series of causally connected previous lives. This can give us peace of mind and a calm acceptance of the limitations of our present lot. It should not make us resigned to whatever the future may bring, however; for it follows also that our future is, within the limits of our past habits, very much in our own hands. As we act now, so we will be in our next life. Belief in karma encourages optimism, though outsiders often accuse it of engendering fatalism.

It can still seem a very daunting prospect: our future in our own hands, but with limited room for manoeuvre in any one life; countless lives to come; and an infinite cycling universe surrounding us. But again Hinduism gently breaks down the immense and incomprehensible into smaller more manageable chunks. It provides three frameworks to help us cope with and plan our slow progress towards full understanding.

Class and caste

For society there is the framework of the four classes, made incredibly complex through the centuries by the development within it of a great number of castes. The class and caste structure of Hindu society, with its associated ideas of the superiority and purity of some groups and inferiority and impurity of others, has undoubtedly given rise to, or been used to justify, some terrible aspects of Hindu history. The 'higher' classes have used religion to bolster their privileged position, the 'lower' classes have been confirmed in poverty and social inferiority. Many Hindus in many ages have protested about this aspect of the social framework, culminating in our time with Gandhi's outraged protest against the treatment of so-called untouchables.

But the framework of classes and castes has also a beneficial side. In a large and complex society an individual can feel lost and lonely. The caste groups, based originally on a variety of cultural or linguistic or occupational differences, give each individual a more intimate and comfortable slice of society within which they belong: something of a mutual aid society, indeed. A caste member, so long as he or she has not conspicuously transgressed against the rules of the caste, can be sure of support from other members, either by way of provision of the necessities of life or, if necessary, against a threat from other individuals or groups in society. It is the social application of this central Hindu theme: break down the big and incomprehensible into smaller more manageable bits. In our bit, our caste, we are 'at home' because from birth onwards we have imbibed the customs and obligations of our group. And in Hindu belief we are also at home at and by birth. In our previous lives we have built up habits and personality characteristics (karma) which fit us for this particular occupation and status in society, and indeed cause our conception in the womb of a member of this particular caste.

This same theme applies even more to the four great classes of traditional Hindu society, into which the castes are slotted, not always neatly. The servant class (shudra), the trading and agricultural class (vaishya), the ruling and military class (kshatriya), and the priestly and scholarly class (brahmin), it is believed, divide society into groups of ascending order of spiritual merit and ability. Each has its own dharma (duty, role) to perform in society, all essential to society and consonant with the characteristics of each group built up over previous lives. And so, surrounded by the vastness of the universe and the infinite duration of its cycles and possibly of our own, we are each provided by Hinduism with a finite and manageable span of space and time, in accordance with our abilities and merit built up in previous lives. In this present life we live out our allotted role in this group of society in this period of this age, in the confident belief that if we do so the law of karma will ensure we get the due benefit of a higher birth and more spiritual capacity in our next life. In this way progress towards the remote ideal of full understanding of Brahman is divided into small steps which we are, in theory at least, well fitted to take.

Four aims of life

The second framework is the four aims of life which perform a similar service in relation to the cacophany of desires competing for our attention in every one of our lives. First there are the two lower aims of material success (artha – wealth and/or social or political position) and sensual pleasure (kama – aesthetic and physical, including sexual, enjoyment). Far from condemning these aims and urging us to forgo them, Hinduism recognizes them as legitimate, indeed essential at certain stages in our spiritual development, and urges us to express and fulfill our desire for them. But Hinduism insists we should do so in accordance with the moral law, an over-arching dharma for all, central to which is the precept not to injure any other living thing. And it believes that in due course, maybe in this life, maybe many lives hence, we will learn by experience that these aims give no lasting satisfaction. Material possessions fade and decay, and relationships flow and ebb and end.

Then we will willingly move on to the third aim of social and moral and religious virtue (dharma in the highest sense). We will start to move away from the self-interest which underlies the lower aims and causes our rebirths as selfish individuals, and will begin to put others before ourselves. As we do so we will find, again by our own experience rather than by orders from above, that this brings far greater happiness to ourselves, as well as to others, than does the pursuit of possessions or pleasure. And we will build up habits and characteristics which fit us more and more for the fourth and highest aim – moksha, full understanding of Brahman by direct experience, and hence freedom from rebirth.

Four stages of life

Fine in theory! But when immersed in a busy life what hope of learning about these four aims and working carefully through them? Plenty of hope if we follow the third framework, the four stages of life. Here, for each life of an individual, Hinduism again breaks down the large into smaller portions.

First comes the student stage, during which we do indeed learn of the four aims of life and as much more of the beliefs and frameworks of Hinduism as we can comprehend with our current spiritual ability. If we are brought up in a traditional Hindu home we will learn from our grandparents and parents, and also from Hindu scriptures read at family or caste ceremonies. If we are very orthodox we might be attached to a priest or sadhu as disciple, helping care for the guru's material needs in return for his spiritual guidance.

Then comes the householder stage: we would be expected to marry and raise children, earning our living in the occupations appropriate to our caste, and contributing in this way to the well-being of society. This is the busy worldly period. We will be trying to keep to the rules of dharma, both in our moral conduct and in our offerings and devotions to deities. But we will be heavily involved in material matters (artha), and in at least some sensual pursuits (kama) in order to conceive a family, though for family and caste rather than for purely selfish motives.

We can be comforted throughout this stage, however, by anticipation of the third and fourth stages. When we see our children's children, that is when our family has grown to independence and our responsibility to them and to society is fulfilled, we have the right to turn more fully to spiritual matters. We may stay with our families and continue to help them, but have more time to devote to puja to deities and/or to meditation. Or we may, if we wish, leave home and family and wander off in search of enlightenment, first in a moderate way with still a modicum of possessions and a family home to retreat to, but in the fourth stage, if we are determined and serious enough, with no possessions and no ties at all.

Pilgrimage

There are many ways in which we can use these later stages of life to advance our spiritual capacities and enhance our prospects for our next rebirth. Some are very austere, repudiating all props and fiercely demanding of the mind direct understanding of the secret of self and the universe. But a more popular way is to go on a pilgrimage. And by far the most popular pilgrimages are those associated with Mother Ganga.

Small wonder, then, that we saw so much evidence of the way in which these latter stages of life are still taken seriously by many Hindus. On a 1975 reconnaissance trip prior to the expedition itself, Murray Jones and I chatted with a group of retired businessmen who were living in a small sacking tent on Ganga's banks at Hardwar. No ulcers and dying in harness, nor any retirement problems, for them. They had handed over their businesses to their sons and were discussing life's meaning and prospects in a companionable group. And on the main expedition, in 1977, as we made our way to and from Hem Kund, we passed many really elderly people, some being carried, some painfully but with moving determination struggling along on foot, to reach this high mountain lake sacred to Sikhs. Ed was moved to comment on how fortunate they were by comparison with many of our old people in New Zealand. There many are almost rejects from society, eking out their last days as a burden on resentful relatives. Here their religious beliefs and frameworks were giving their last days a purpose and a joy which was shining through exhaustion and pain.

For a pilgrimage of any sort is believed to bring great merit and hence lead to a better rebirth next time. And the more arduous the pilgrimage the more the merit. At Hardwar we spoke briefly to a sadhu who, like us, was making the full pilgrimage from Ganga Sagar to the source. Unlike us he was doing it on foot, with full attention to ritual detail at every stage of the way, and he had already been thirty-five years on the way! I felt he must either have hustled or omitted the student and householder stages of life – as Hinduism gave him every right to do if he felt that previous lives had fitted him for this. Even his efforts pale, however, beside stories that are told of performing the double pilgrimage, Ganga Sagar to Gomukh and /or Badrinath and back again, while 'measuring your length' – lying full length on the ground, making a mark with outstretched fingers, standing up again at that mark, then again stretching out full length ...! I lazily prefer the gentler method of quietly contemplating the flow of the river, but I have always been impressed by the fierce determination shown in such feats. And the belief underlying them – that the greater the pain and suffering endured the greater the merit acquired – was a great comfort to us on the few occasions when we imagined we were suffering on our pilgrimage.

The place Ganga pilgrimage has in Hindu culture accounts, at least in part, for the incredible reception Ed got as we progressed up the river. For Hinduism is endlessly tolerant of individual variations of method in pursuit of enlightenment. And though we were by no means in an orthodox fourth stage of life – even if some of our families thought we had been permanently on expedition, if not pilgrimage, for as far back as could be remembered; though we would return to households and possessions and all sorts of lowly desires and pursuits; and though we were travelling by the least arduous means imaginable; yet we were making the pilgrimage so many Hindus would dearly love to make.

Many people, particularly in villages, believed that by associating with us some of our merit would be transferred to them. And if this were so for us, the ordinary members of the expedition, it was a thousand times more so for Ed. Ed was a text book figure stepping out of the pages into their lives, for a commonly used school history book had a whole chapter on Tenzing's and Hillary's 1953 ascent of Everest. So he was already for many a symbol of the spirit of adventure. Now, with all the religious associations of a Ganga pilgrimage surrounding him, he was being toasted in speeches more generally as a symbol of the greatness of humanity, and, in the all-embracing Hindu sense, of the potential divinity of humanity.

This reached a climax in the puja at the Ganga mandir at Varanasi. Ed was welcomed by a Hindu priest at a Hindu shrine, or so it seemed to me, as the latest in a long line of great humans elevated to divine status in the capacious mansions of the Hindu pantheon. If this was what was in his mind he was echoing the thoughts of thousands of those who flocked to have darshan – to see and be in the presence of Ed – along the length of the river.

It was both profoundly moving and a considerable emotional strain for Ed, but as usual his sense of humour kept it all in perspective."You know," said an Indian Oil man at one of our enthusiastic receptions at a refuelling spot, "You know they think you're a sort of a god." "But you know I'm not a god," Ed replied confidently, for the Indian Oil man knew well by now our many failings and moods. "Oh yes, I know you're not," he said with a grin. Not so a devotee of Bhagavan Hillary further up the river at Karnaprayag. He mistook Graeme Dingle for Ed, and after a long earnest conversation with him asked "Sir, you are very great man – what is difference between you and God?" An awesome Hindu responsibility for a humble Kiwi to live up to, and Ed much preferred the kindly cynicism of the Indian Oil man.

The four classes, the four aims, the four stages of an individual's life – with these frameworks, as with the idea of many manifestations of the One Power, Hinduism breaks down the immensity of life and the universe into portions more easily digestible by ordinary humans. At the same time, and by the same means, it holds ever before us a higher goal: the heroic aim, indeed, of attempting to digest the universe itself, entire, to experience the holy Power as it really is, not as it is partially represented for us in image and in myth.

Ordinary Hindus live in tension between the two ends of this scale. Their pressing immediate problems are those of a limited life here and now: problems of physical well-being for self and family, of personal and community relations, and of emotional adjustment to an often harsh life. As students and as householders, concerned with the lower aims, they approach partial manifestations of Brahman through concrete physical images, seeking help and comfort. But always there are reminders that these lesser symbols and lower aims are not the final answer to life's problems. On the one hand the results of their petitions to deities can only be of limited duration. The sick family member may be healed but will sicken again and eventually die, as will we all; the crop may be saved by timely rain but the next crop will be at risk in its turn. On the other hand there are always abroad in Hindu society symbols of a loftier search for more enduring ends

– wild sadhus and gentle retired businessmen in the fourth stage of life, gladly supported by the community because they remind us of this higher goal. And around the images of deities to which ordinary Hindus bring their petitions there is always a sense of something greater, some One Power of which these many deities are but partial manifestations.

Above all this is so of the goddess Ganga. Small partial manifestation of the universal energy she may be, against the backdrop of our huge universe, but she gives in rich measure an image of the whole – nearly endless variety within enduring form, source of life and death, of fertility and destruction. I cannot help thinking that those who come with specific requests to this symbol are likely to stay and meditate more deeply, and to gain from Ganga something of the wisdom we felt in the people of the destroyed villages. And then they would indeed be moving from the lower to the higher aims of Hinduism: moving from specific requests to partial manifestations to the attempt to understand and accept life and death, pleasure and pain, as a whole, realising that we should try to alter not life's outer circumstances but our inner selves.

Moksha – attitude or control?

Of course Hinduism is not as simple as this – no religion is. I have painted far too unified a picture, simplifying what I see as main themes. And here at the heart of Hinduism there is a fundamental ambiguity. What does this acceptance of life amount to? Is it really just an adjustment to our attitudes, leaving life outside us unchanged and uncaring? Or are we then in a position to control life from its centre?

There is an old and pervasive human belief that knowledge is power, that understanding gives control. It was as evident in the magical rites of our ancient forbears as it is in modern scientific theories and technology, though with a great deal more justification and success in the latter than the former. This belief has always been strong in Hinduism. Yogic powers are believed to be evidence of it. Full understanding of Brahman is thought to give powers beyond the ordinary because one is in tune with the fundamental energy that activates all things. And yet side by side with descriptions of such powers in Hindu texts there are warnings against being beguiled by them, for they are not the final goal.

Indeed, Ramakrishna suggests such powers are little more than gimmicks. He tells of "a sadhu who acquired great occult powers" but was vain about them. God visited him disguised as a holy man, and asked if he could use his powers to kill a passing elephant. The sadhu did so. God then asked if the sadhu could bring the elephant back to life, and so the sadhu did. "Wonderful is your power," said God. "You have killed the elephant and you have revived it. But … do you feel uplifted by it? Has it enabled you to realize God?"[8]

Ramakrishna also tells a story about a great Siddha (a sage with yogic powers) who, disturbed by a storm while sitting by the sea, used his power to still the storm. But a ship passing with all sails set capsized as a result, and "the sin of causing the death of so many people accrued to the Siddha, and for this reason he lost all his occult powers …".[9]

Hinduism does dabble with, and delight in, the thought that full understanding of universal energy might give spectacular control over physical events. But she is too deeply imbued with belief in the orderliness and inevitability of the universal processes to do more than dabble. I think that fundamentally she inculcates, as does that part of her we call Ganga, the feeling that this energy is incomprehensibly greater than any individual manifestation of it. True understanding does not bring control of it by any individual – and in any case so interconnected are all its manifestations that any such control would be at the expense of other individuals. What true understanding can bring instead, more marvellously, is an ability to accept and delight in life: no longer are we isolated individuals fighting against the current, we are flowing harmoniously with it, an integral part of the whole.

We didn't learn this properly on our pilgrimage I'm afraid, let alone experience it fully. Many of us are rather unbelieving materialistic beings, immersed in possessions and pleasures (artha and kama). We were not really on pilgrimage to enhance our spiritual capacity in a future life. We just wanted to travel up Ganga from ocean to sky, against the current, in response to strong but not fully analysed desires for excitement and variety.

And yet even on our restless minds Ganga-mata worked her magic. As her flow and the life of her people mingled with our lives, albeit briefly, she imparted to us some of the gentle wisdom of Hinduism, leaving us a memory of a moving alternative to our excited search for adventure, should we ever need one.

PART III

Religious Studies

13. Early Years

Ann and I say of our lovely sons that they always fall on their feet. Indeed we believe that if Steev was dropped head first from the top of a tall building he would twist upright as he fell and, just as he approached the hard pavement, a cart full of hay would pass by and he would land in it unhurt and unperturbed.

But perhaps we should have been saying it about ourselves. For as our time in India was drawing to a close, and we were about to be dropped head first into the rest of our lives, a letter arrived from Michael Shorter, Professor of the University of Canterbury Philosophy Department from which I had graduated five years before. Michael had asked me then to stay and join his staff, rather than go to Dunedin to study theology. God-driven still at that time I had regretfully declined. Now he wrote: "A new subject has been started at Canterbury, Religious Studies, and has been placed in the care of our department. It has created a new position, lecturer in Philosophy and Religious Studies. If you are willing to read about, and work up courses on, comparative religion, you would have a good chance of being appointed. Are you interested?"

I'm not sure whether Michael didn't know what I'd been studying in India for the last two years or whether, vague as ever, he'd forgotten. But with my degree in western philosophy, my degree in Christian theology, and my admittedly not yet completed degree in Indian philosophy and religion I was tailor-made for the job. And was I interested?!!! This was the career equivalent of Steev's cart full of hay: a job studying and teaching about philosophy and religion, that is being paid for what I wanted to do anyway, and in Ann's and my home town. I applied post haste.

A month or two later I was at Camp 2 on Mt. Thamserku, Nepal. Four of our party had reached the summit and returned safely. I was on the radio to Ed Hillary who, far below, was finishing the airstrip he was constructing at the village of Lukla. Mountain and expedition business over, Ed added "Oh, and there's a telegram offering you a job at Canterbury University. They want to know if you'll accept." I told him ecstatically that I would, and he presumably informed them, though how their message or his reply got to and from Lukla I have now no idea.

That was in November, 1964. So when Ann and I finished at Banaras Hindu University, in May 1965, we returned to Christchurch.

Here we started not just a new job but also a new family. This latter set in riotous motion a change in our lives more dramatic even than our meeting and marriage, and at times seemingly more perilous than being dropped head first from a tall building. Steev and Guy arrived in quick succession, only 16 months apart, on the appallingly misguided belief that being so close in age they would get on well together! Seemingly endless sleepless nights, coupled with me working long hours at the new job leaving Ann to bear the brunt alone, put a severe strain on our sanity. But the new arrivals brought to us also intense love and wonder, increased yet further when Mac arrived a more sensible three years after Guy.

The new job was also an intense combination of strain and exhaustion, on the one hand, and exhilaration on the other. Initially I had to teach about all the major religious traditions, while Jim Thornton continued to teach a Philosophy of Religion course. I had studied in depth only Christianity and Hinduism, so with the others I was barely one step ahead of the students, and was frequently up till two or three a.m. preparing lectures or marking essays. But I quickly discovered there is no better way to learn about something than having to teach about it. And as far as my personal journey was concerned, immersing myself intensely in so many different religions proved very stimulating. While I was unable to accept the metaphysical beliefs underlying any of them, some of their attitudes to life and the universe, and some of their techniques for overcoming anger and inculcating compassion, influenced me a great deal.

In this chapter I shall discuss the influence that Judaism and Islam, and ancient Chinese religion, had on me. It will be obvious that I am not attempting objective, let alone comprehensive, portrayals of these religions.

Judaism

Judaism had the least influence during this period, but only because it had already influenced me almost overwhelmingly through its offshoot Christianity. The belief that there is one supreme God who created and controls all, and who is compassionate but also just and stern, arose in the experiences and thoughts of the tribes of Israel who, under their leader Moses, invaded Palestine probably about 1200 B.C. This belief flowed on into what is now called Judaism, and gave rise first to Christianity then to Islam. From a Religious Studies perspective these three religions are therefore very similar. They are together referred to as the Hebraic religious tradition, because the language of the ancient Israelites was Hebrew, as it is now of modern Israel. This tradition, in its Christian version, was what I had grown up in, and it was the Hebrew God Yahweh, in Christian guise, whom I believed had 'called' me to his service.

The Hebrew scriptures, shared by Christians but called by them the Old Testament, are what I had been studying under Lloyd Geering. And even before this study I had been greatly influenced by the sayings of prophets preserved in these scriptures because Dad preached from them regularly, pressing home their proto-Pelagian view that it was what you did that God was concerned about: whether you helped or cheated those less fortunate than you, not whether you believed the right things and performed the prescribed rituals and ate the right food.

Now, as I read and taught about post-Christian developments of Judaism, I was delighted by some of the zany stories by or about rabbis that abound in later Jewish literature. I also found the development of Jewish mysticism fascinating, coming close, as it did, to the impersonal monism of Shankara. But even this, in terms of direct influence on me, had been anticipated, in this case by Hinduism. So the additional impact of Judaism on my personal development was minor. My hopeless horror at centuries of persecution of Jews by Christians, culminating in Hitler's holocaust, is another story again. This naturally deepened my disgust at the divisive and cruel aspects of religion, and my distaste for these aspects of Christianity, but was of more general origin, from history and books and films, not from studying and teaching about Judaism.

Islam

Secondly, Islam. In these days, when many in my culture are consumed with hatred against Islam and Muslims, I feel bad saying it had little personal influence on me. But the reason is the same as for Judaism, and should be a reason for Christians to feel more kindly disposed towards it.

As noted, Islam is the third, chronologically, in the Hebraic tradition. Some 500 years after the followers of a Jewish prophet called Jesus invented Christianity, another prophet, Muhammad, rose to prominence. He drew inspiration from the same earlier figures Jesus looked back to, Abraham, Moses, and the Old Testament prophets, and believed he was inspired by the same God, the Muslim name for whom is Allah. But Muhammad was an Arab, not a Jew, and the religion he started came to be called Islam (submission). In Islamic belief the Qu'ran[1] records the words Allah 'spoke' to Muhammad.

Unlike Christianity which, bizarrely, came to blame all Jews for the death of Jesus, the Qu'ran regards Jews and Christians as the other "people of the book".[2] And unlike Christianity, which for a long time vilifed Muhammad, the Qu'ran thinks highly of Jesus, as do Muslims following its lead. But – and here I agree with them and disagree with Christians – they do not believe he was/is, nor that he himself claimed to be, the Son of God. They believe that Jesus was a prophet[3], preaching what all the prophets, including Muhammad, preached: submission to the commands of Yahweh, whom they call Allah. Jesus' followers distorted this message and committed the cardinal sin of deifying him, putting him up alongside God, beside whom there is no other. So, to pure monotheistic Muslims who have never made this mistake about Muhammad, Christians are not pure monotheists, but tritheists[4] (three Gods: Jehovah, Jesus and the Holy Spirit), or even quadtheists (add Mary). Given my difficulties with the Christian doctrine of the Trinity it is hardly surprising that my sympathies are with Muslims on this point.

As a delicious aside to this question that divides Christians and Muslims as to who is and who isn't God, and how many there are or aren't, and also as a revealing reflection on war-like intolerant tendencies in both these religions, I can't resist repeating a bit from the whacky and wonderful novel *Life of Pi*. Pi is a young Hindu boy who at one stage becomes interested in the other two main religions in India, Christianity and Islam. So he goes to a local Christian church and is eagerly befriended by the priest. Until then, Pi says, he knew little about Christianity except that it "had a reputation for few gods and great violence." He likes what the priest tells him about Christianity, and decides, to the priest's delight, to become a Christian.

But why stop there? About Islam he knew equally little except that "it had a reputation worse than Christianity's – fewer gods, greater violence" But he found the Islam of the local mullah to be gentle and compassionate and appealing and decides, to the delight of the mullah, to become a Muslim. As a Hindu it didn't occur to him that anyone would consider these religions were mutually exclusive. One day the Christian priest, the Muslim mullah and the Hindu pandit happened to meet, all together, Pi and his parents. Each, to the annoyed astonishment of the others, was loud in praise of Hindu/Christian/Muslim Pi. Pi, who was perfectly happy being all three, was embarrassed and bewildered when they nearly came to blows over which he really was.[5]

But I digress. Studying and then teaching about Islam was influential on me in exposing the distortions and slanders about this religion perpetrated by Christians over the many centuries of their bitter and bloody battles. For example, I had uncritically imbibed the prevailing western notion that Muslim men were beastly to their women, and that Muhammad himself, or Allah through him, had commanded women to be subservient to their husbands, and allowed men to have many wives. How convenient for Christians to forget that their own Paul had ordered women to be subservient to their husbands, and that till very recently Christian marriage services commanded the brides to obey their husbands, but laid no reciprocal command on the bridegroom. And to forget also that the emancipation of women in Christian cultures is of very recent occurrence, and is still far from complete.

Equally seriously, there had been in my experience of Christian portrayals of Muhammad and Islam no attempt whatever to set Muhammad in his historical context. Now I discovered that, against the background of Arabia of Muhammad's day, the Qur'an goes far to ameliorate the lot of women, requiring husbands to treat their wives well, and limiting the grounds on which they can divorce them.[6] As for polygamy, an accepted Arabian custom in Muhammad's day, the Qu'ran again limits the practice, requiring men to take no more wives than they can support and treat equally.[7] A cynic might well say this last requirement – equal treatment – effectively limits a man to one wife.

I also found in the Qu'ran the same puzzling mixture of loving compassion and fierce judgement as is present in the Old and New Testaments. All suras begin with the invocation: "In the name of Allah, the Merciful, the Compassionate."[8] And the same stern demands to care for orphans and widows and the poor as are found in the great Old Testament prophets and in Jesus are movingly there in the Qu'ran.[9] But, again as in the Old and the New Testaments, there are also stern warnings of the fiery fate of unbelievers.[10] How infinitely sad, then, that the three faiths stemming from the ancient Hebrews are so vehemently opposed to each other, when from a Religious Studies standpoint they are so similar.

And it is this similarity which accounts for the small influence studying and teaching about Islam had on me. I had already, when a Christian, been hugely influenced by this monotheistic tradition. I would have been similarly influenced had I grown up a Muslim or a Jew. To say that Islam had now little influence on me is not to denigrate this religion as less powerful or appealing than Christianity, but simply to note that its potential influence on me had been anticipated by Christianity. As I had moved away from belief in a personal all-powerful god my study of Islam enlightened me about Islam but had little effect on my personal journey.

Confucius

Chinese religions had more of an impact on me at this time because they were new to me. How I had the cheek to teach about them a few days after I'd started reading about them I prefer not to recall. I covered only the teachings of Kung Fu Tzu (Confucius) and the early developments of Confucianism; and the seminal texts of Taoism, *Tao Te Ching* and *Chuang Tzu*.

I immediately warmed to Confucius, and greatly admired his teachings. These were preserved by his disciples in a series of short sayings and stories, *The Analects.*[11]

Confucius' aim and teaching was political and moral rather than religious. Indeed, he was humanist rather than religious, and though he didn't deny the existence of spirits and deities he was for all practical purposes an atheist. What he wanted, intensely, was to get an effective post with the ruler of one of China's then many states so that he could influence that ruler's policies. The reason he didn't get one seemed obvious to me. His idea was that the ruler should govern for the welfare of his people not for his own aggrandizement. Even in his lifetime some of Confucius' disciples were employed by rulers for they were valued for their education and, even more, the scrupulous honesty and integrity which their teacher had inculcated in them. But Confucius himself, never. He was far too strong a personality, and far too determined that the welfare of common people should be put first.

He rarely complained, and kept trying to the end. But he found it hard, especially when his followers got posts and he didn't. Even harder was that he was once offered a post, but under a particularly unscrupulous ruler. His disciples were horrified that he should even consider it, and I'm sure he also knew he would be used by, rather then influencing, this tyrant. He declined, but the incident did wring a rare complaint out of him: "Am I to be a bitter gourd, left dangling on a string and never eaten?"[12]

Despite this, his essential good humour and lightness of spirit shine through the clipped phrases of *The Analects*. He evidently stressed to his followers that they should think carefully before acting. One day it was reported to him that Ji Wenzi, a warlord some generations before, always thought three times before he acted. Confucius replied, no doubt with a smile, "Twice might be enough."[13] He always wanted the spirit of his advice creatively followed rather than the letter of it literally applied. And though he seems to have enjoyed traditional rituals as a socially cohesive force, he did not rigidly prescribe them. The greater pity, then, that after his death Confucianism became hidebound in tradition and ritual, and was turned by rulers into a tool for keeping subjects in order rather than a prod to them to rule for their subjects' welfare. It also became tied up with traditional Chinese beliefs about spirits, and the need to honour and placate the spirits of departed ancestors. To this extent Confucianism became more of a religion in the supernatural sense. Hopefully something of Confucius' original intention shone through, and helped keep subjects' well-being alive in rulers' minds.

Confucius was dealing with heavy matters of how to run a state. But he never lost sight of what a well-run state should be for, namely making it possible for its citizens to enjoy the simple pleasures of life in peace. My favourite story about him illustrates this. Sitting in an idle moment with his disciples, he asks them "What would you most like to do?" Mindful of his teaching about running a state well, one after another the disciples declare that they would like to be prime minister of a state of this or that size, and organize this and that and the other with impeccable efficiency. Confucius listened without comment to these probably blatant attempts to give the answer they thought he wanted. Meanwhile one disciple, Tseng Hsi, was strumming away on his lute, saying nothing. "And you?" Confucius asked him at length. Striking a final chord, Hsi stood and said, bashfully, "My aims are quite different". "What harm is there in that?" asked Confucius, "We each have our own ambitions." Hsi replied: "In late spring, when the spring clothes are made, I'd like to go wandering with a few friends and servant boys, bathe in the Yi River, enjoy the wind at Rain-Dance Altar, and then wander back home in song." Confucius sighed deeply, and said: "I'm with Hsi."[14]

So above all Confucius he say to me "Be light even in heavy matters". Me, I say to Confucius "I try".

Taoism

Taoism also appealed to me greatly. I know little about its origins or its later developments, concentrating as I did solely on the two seminal texts, *Tao Te Ching* (attributed to the sage Lao Tzu)[15], and the sayings and stories of the whacky Chuang Tzu.[16] These both seem to me to stem from the period when the fluid and sensitive teachings of Confucius had hardened into a rigid system of dos and don'ts, bolstering a rigid family and ritual and social and political hierarchy. Lao Tzu and Chuang Tzu both portray this, in striking and amusing ways, as human attempts to force the natural flow of the universe into confined and orderly channels, attempts not just ineffective but positively harmful.

Lao Tzu often follows Confucius' pattern of giving advice to or about rulers, and declares "the best ruler is but a shadowy presence to his subjects",[17] i.e. lets them get on with their lives without interference. And this is because, according to Taoists, natural ways are best, and if rulers and subjects alike cease trying to master or channel nature, and instead go with its flow, all will turn out beneficially. The natural flow is the Tao, usually translated as the Way. It is often likened to water, which left to itself seeks the easiest way down a slope;[18] or to a flexible reed, which bends before the force of flood or gale, and is unharmed and ready to sway upright again once the storm has passed, whereas a dead and rigid stick tries to resist and is snapped off.[19]

As with the Upanishadic Brahman, Tao is inexpressible[20] and can only be hinted at and felt. There are suggestions in Lao Tzu, and to some extent in Chuang Tzu, that if you let go and surrender to the Tao then you will feel at one with it, no longer an individual fighting against it. In these early texts this is never elaborated into a fully-fledged system of mysticism, at least partly because Taoists delight in deriding any attempts at systematic anything – such human attempts in all their desperate variety are indeed the main problem. But certainly the desired state is to be so in tune with the Tao that one not only goes with its flow but also feels peace and harmony within it.

Chuang Tzu is even less systematic than Lao Tzu, and gets across his message mainly by telling zany stories of people not just accepting, but welcoming, whatever happens to them. Two in particular remain in my memory.

In one, a man is walking along the bank of a fast-flowing river as it tumults into a series of whirlpools and rapids through a narrow rocky gorge. Suddenly a Taoist sage appears from a cave and leaps into the river at the upper end of the gorge. "Alas poor fellow, he's a goner," concludes the startled observer. But no, after five minutes or so the sage emerges at the lower end of the gorge, shakes the water off himself, and strolls back up the bank. "Amazing," stutters the onlooker, "How on earth did you do that?" "Easy," responds the sage, "there are gaps and ways through the whirlpools and rapids; I just let my body go with the flow through these gaps, and with no effort at all emerge at the other end unharmed."[21] So too with life is the unstated conclusion.

In the other, Chuang Tzu's dearly loved wife has died. Instead of going into the prescribed mourning state, and conducting the prescribed funeral rites, Chuang Tzu sits down at his drums and thrums and sings the day away. A friend is shocked. "She raised your children, and lived with you for many years," he says accusingly. "It is one thing not to observe the prescribed forms, but drumming and singing – isn't this going too far?" Chuang Tzu looks up at him. "Do you think I'm not grieving?" he asks. "Of course I am sad. But sitting around with a long face would show I know nothing at all about the Tao. Sixty years ago there was a movement in the Tao and my wife was born. For sixty years she flowed with every movement of the Tao. Now there's been another movement and she is gone."[22] Being fully in tune with the Tao, it appears, enables one to accept even the death of a loved one.

I was and am deeply moved by this Taoist way. But, as usual, my critical mind, perhaps infuriatingly to some, declines to allow me to leap wholeheartedly into this exciting river. I think natural forces are indifferent to human needs, and require careful assessment before deciding whether to leap in and go with the flow, or to try to avoid or deflect it. Chuang Tzu's river advice would be excellent in most situations if one were already in the river, on purpose or by accident. I have used his technique to get safely across mountain torrents. But to accept it uncritically and, trusting to it, to leap into a river just above a savage rapid or waterfall, would be unwise to say the least. And if I accidentally fell into such a place, while I could do no other than go with the flow, this would be unlikely to save me from this flow dashing me savagely, repeatedly, and finally fatally against numerous rocks.

So Taoism influenced me and continues to do so in very enjoyable and beneficial ways. I do think we humans try far too strenuously and humourlessly to order and restrict and direct the flow of life, and, as a very healthy counter to this, Taoism is marvellous. I am very much in tune with this way, having all my life been irked by, and tried to refuse to be limited by, social norms and common expectations. But I do not accept the Tao as the sole or whole way to live my life. And again belief plays a crucial role in this. If I believed with the Taoist that natural ways are always beneficial to us if we flow with rather than fight against them, then I would eagerly follow only their way. Since I do not so believe, I very happily accept their way as part of my way, but not as the whole.

14. Buddhism

I have already said a bit about Buddhism in the chapters on my time in Nepal and India. During that period my contact with Buddhism was curiously disjointed. On the one hand I loved my immersion in Sherpa/Tibetan Buddhism at the level of everyday living and social interactions and ritual, without making any serious attempt to understand the history and philosophy behind it all. On the other hand, at Banaras Hindu University, during study for my thesis, I delved into some of the early and basic texts of Buddhism, and was awed by visits to Sarnath where Gautama first started teaching, without any involvement at all in day-to-day Buddhist life and ritual since Buddhism in India had largely been absorbed back into Hinduism.

Now, having to teach about Buddhism to western students, I had to be more systematic in my study of it, though solely from books. The author who best opened up Buddhism for me was a westerner who had become a Buddhist, Edward Conze. He wrote a very good book titled *Buddhism, its Essence and Development*, and also edited two books titled *Buddhist Texts Through the Ages* and *Buddhist Meditation*.[1]

Buddhism remains always for me the religion of actual experience, of 'try it and see', an approach that fitted very comfortably with my increasing inability to believe any religious doctrines. And the three aspects of Buddhism which most influenced me during this period are: some of their meditation techniques; the beautiful ideal of the Bodhisattva; and their heroic attempts, culminating in Chan/Zen Buddhism, to prevent Buddhists from becoming dependent on any Buddhist figures or practices or texts.

Buddhist meditations

Firstly, then, I was struck by some of the early Buddhist meditations. They pulled no punches. Like male hierarchies in most religions, Buddhist monks had a dim view of women as seductive temptressess away from the religious life and into the morass of worldly pleasures – a certain route to many miserable rebirths. In an interchange attributed to the Buddha and some disciples, which would be amusing in its panic-stricken terror were it not for its deleterious effects on women, a disciple asks, "How should we behave to women?" "Not see them," comes the stern reply. "And if we have to see them?" "Not speak to them." "And if we have to have to speak to them?" "Keep your thoughts tightly controlled!"[2]

How, in advance of such a fearsome fate as the close proximity of a desirable woman, can we men gain some measure of control over our thoughts? By meditation. What sort of meditation? In my experience only the Buddhists have come up with so radical a suggestion as this. You see in a woman the outer attractive skin and curves and eyes. But think for a moment. What is under that skin? Why, blood and bone and mucus and pus and piss and shit. How can you possibly desire, let alone bear close contact with, so foul an assemblage of putrid rubbish? So meditate mindfully on what a woman really is, and your desire will turn to disgust and your arousal wither away.[3]

To be fair to these early Buddhist males they equally strongly recommend that I meditate on my own body in a similar way, and on its inevitable death. How can I then regard my bodily life as desirable, or desire things to pleasure so foul and fleeting a thing?[4] In these, and other zany and earthy ways, Buddhist meditations seek to turn our desires away from physical things and towards higher goals of spiritual advancement and, eventually, nirvana, the blowing out of self-centred desire and consequent cessation of suffering.

Although these meditations intrigued and amused me with their strength and directness, they didn't really influence me. I was and am too fond of my body, and don't believe there is a higher goal beyond physical life. Other meditations, however, which aim at curbing hatred and inculcating compassion, became part of my repertoire for dealing with life. In their Buddhist setting they may be seen partly as a means of achieving the ultimate goal of nirvana. But even in this setting they can stand on their own; much of Buddhism seems to me to be recommending compassion as an end in itself and not just as a means to the goal of nirvana. And certainly I could and did take them as independent tools for increasing compassion. Not only did I feel justified in doing so, but I doubt any Buddhist would be unhappy that I am so using some of their techniques.

For example, suppose I'm consumed with hatred for someone, perhaps because they have wronged me, or, even fiercer, because they have injured or killed one of my family or friends. I should stop a moment and consider this person in the context of countless rebirths. I would then realize that in past lives this person whom I am now hating has been my father, carrying me over stony ground and swollen streams; and my mother, wiping away my tears and snot and cleaning shit from my bum; and my sister and my brother, playing with me, loving me. What? – should I be hating my own father and mother and siblings? "It is therefore not suitable that my mind should feel hate for him" concludes the meditation.[5]

This had, and continues to have, a profound effect on me. I haven't consciously naturalised it, i.e. reinterpreted it without rebirth; but probably unconsciously I have, along the lines of "We are all sisters and brothers, we are all humans sharing the same problems and delights. It is therefore not suitable to hate anyone". Not that I have achieved anything near perfection in this. I vividly remember burning garden prunings in a 44 gallon drum when our son Steev had just been born. Suddenly the bizarre fear popped into my mind "What if someone rushed up and threw Steev into these ferocious flames?" I knew with chilling certainty that I would kill that person if I could. Not much compassion there. Nor did I ever attempt, as our son Guy once did, to love Hitler; and having just read Vikram Seth's harrowing account, in *Two Lives*, of what the Nazis did to his Jewish relatives, I would find that even more difficult now. But at a lower level of difficulty I have no doubt this Buddhist technique has helped me curb hatred and inculcate love.

Even more effective for me, and requiring no belief in rebirth, is a stage-by-stage meditation aimed at inculcating unlimited friendliness towards all beings. It is so sensible and realistic, rather like trying to bike up a steep hill, starting some distance away on the flat to get up speed, and, if the first attempt grinds to a halt before the top, returning to the flat to get up even more speed for the next attempt.

For I am urged to start on an easy task – feeling unlimited friendliness towards myself. Easy – I am very fond of myself and wish only the very best for me. Okay, next step? Holding closely in my attention how I feel towards myself I am asked to try to extend that feeling to, for example, some respected teacher. If I succeed in this – and that is not too difficult – I am then to extend my feeling of unlimited friendliness to a very dear person, then to a person I am indifferent to, then to an enemy. If when I get to the indifferent person I find myself in difficulty, I should go back to the dear person, then back to the indifferent person, and so on till I succeed. Similarly, when I then move on to trying to feel unlimited friendliness towards an enemy, if I fail at first I go back to the indifferent person, or even further back to the very dear person, then try again.[6]

For me, however, there is a sting in the tail of this. I find myself resisting the final Buddhist aim of this progression. This is not only to feel something like the same unlimited friendliness and compassion to all beings that I feel towards my dearest, but to feel exactly the same to all beings.[7] Thus eventually, if I follow the meditation religiously, as it were, I would feel no more special love towards Ann and my family than I feel towards anyone else. No partisan special individual love at all, just even-mindedness towards all beings.

Interestingly, Mohandas Karamchand Gandhi, whom I admire enormously and will say more about later, also had this ideal as his aim. It is believed by some that he succeeded so well in it that he fouled his family up. That one son had a hard time of it is certainly true. I'm sure there were factors in this other than his father's heroic but arguably misguided attempts not to treat his family any better than anyone else. But I did come to feel that in these attempts Gandhi expected more of his family than of anyone else, and as a result was actually harder on them.

And this strengthened my natural feeling that, with him and with the Buddhist ideal, this is taking things too far. We are individuals and families, as well as wider social beings. I think each of us needs special love from mother and father and siblings and husband and wife, almost different in kind from general loving kindness. If this be considered a weakness in us then so be it. I'd rather acknowledge the weakness, and hope the need is fulfilled for all, than aim at an ideal I think impossible of full realization and potentially harmful to those closest to us. So once again I find myself admiring a religious ideal but not adopting it fully. Rather I see this Buddhist meditation as a very helpful counter to a natural human tendency to love only those dearest to us, to the exclusion and/or detriment of others; but not as a goal it is possible or desirable to attain fully.

Buddhist attempts to be even-minded towards all beings are but one aspect of wide-ranging Buddhist attempts to be even-minded in all things, so that one is at peace always, on an even keel and not heeling wildly first to one side then the other. As I understand it, Buddhism recommends that I iron out highs as well as lows, avoid intense excitement or happiness as well as intense boredom or misery, in order to blow out the flame of self-centred desire and end rebirth and suffering.

But, since I believe I have only one brief life, I am aiming not at release from suffering and rebirth but at as exciting and fulfilling a life as I can manage without hurting, or neglecting the needs of, others. For this – and here I think I speak as a mountaineer, or perhaps it is because of this that I became a mountaineer – I have found contrast, alternation between pain and cessation of pain, between boredom and excitement, between fear and the intense euphoria of surviving that which was feared, absolutely crucial. Buddhism has provided me with very useful tools for pursuing some of my aims in life, but not the goal for which these tools were originally intended.

A meditation technique to cope with pain also intrigued me, and I have tried to use it at times, with limited success. It involves the basic Buddhist notion of annatta, no self. When there is pain in the whirl of physical and emotional and mental moments which I mistakenly take to be an enduring self, i.e. 'me', my unenlightened mind thinks it is 'my' pain, and doesn't like it. But if there is no 'me' it cannot be 'my' pain. So I am urged to view the pain objectively and dispassionately, not thinking "Bloody hell, this pain of mine is unbearable," but "Oh, there is a pain there", in much the same way as I might think "Oh, there is a bird flying by".

It probably sounds whacky to some, but I have found this helpful in dealing with pain, though not so successfully that I have been able to be completely dispassionate and unworried about it, especially if the pain is intense like that following my knee surgery. I have probably been able to use this technique with some success because to a considerable extent I agree with the Buddhist analysis of 'self', namely that it is a whirlpool of moments succeeding each other in quick succession, with no underlying permanent entity at their centre. Modern physiology apparently confirms that this is so even on the physical level, with every atom/molecule/cell in our body changing constantly.

Bodhisattva

Secondly, the Bodhisattva ideal[8] moved me greatly. It is both attractive in its own right, and a very interesting attempt to deal with a problem shared by many religions. On the one hand we are urged to put aside self-interest and care for others. On the other hand the reason given for doing this is that it will give us eternal life, salvation, nirvana – surely a blatant appeal to self-interest albeit of a rarified religious variety. More than any other religion I know this seeming contradiction – be unselfish for selfish reasons – troubled Buddhists from the beginning. I think this was in part behind the Buddha's refusal to say what happens to the individual self when self-centred desire is extinguished.

The Bodhisattva ideal can be seen in this light. Surely it is selfish to want simply to follow the Buddha into nirvana so long as any beings remain enmeshed in samsara, and in need of our compassion and help. If we wish to be truly selfless and compassionate we should take the Bodhisattva vow to achieve enlightenment not for our own sake but so as to help others. So in Mahayana literature Bodhisattvas, unlike Buddhas who have gone beyond our reach, are still hanging round, hanging onto vestiges of individuality, so as to help us. The best known is Avalokitesvara (= something like Lord of all creatures), who, in a remarkable sex-change, evolves in China into Kuan Lin, Goddess of Mercy. It is believed that these Bodhisattvas, rather like Christian and Muslim saints, can be appealed to for assistance in a wide variety of needs. But the influence on me was as an inspirational model of true selflessness, along with a great admiration for Buddhism for tackling in so splendid a fashion this selfless/selfish conundrum that had so troubled me in Christianity and Hinduism.

Ch'an Buddhism

The third aspect of Buddhism that especially appealed to me was also Mahayana – the iconoclastic teaching and behaviour of Chinese Ch'an Buddhist monks. (When exported to Japan Ch'an became the more widely known Zen Buddhism.) I always think of Ch'an as an interaction between Buddhism and Taoism. But I'm not sure how historically correct this is, and the aspects I'll refer to could have grown out of elements already prominent in Buddhism, though muted in the more conservative and rule-conscious Hinayana/Theravada schools.

It has often been a problem for developed religions to prevent their adherents from becoming so devoted to their doctrines and symbols and scriptures that these start to hinder rather than help, obscuring rather than revealing ultimate reality. This in part explains the vehement Muslim prohibition against images of Allah. Only my beloved Hinduism, imbued as it is with the belief that "God is not in a hurry", has been relatively immune from this worry.

Buddhists take the problem very seriously. And, typically thorough, they devised many stratagems for dealing with it. The basic and baffling doctrine of sunya (emptiness) is central here – the emptiness of all human concepts, including not just the concept of enduring selves but also Buddhist teachings and concepts and figures. Ch'an Buddhists observed that their fellows had reified, i.e. taken as real, and virtually deified, i.e. taken as divine, the Buddha and Boddhisattvas, images of them, and Buddhist scriptures. So they took drastic action. Before the horrified gaze of less radical Buddhists they lit bonfires and heaped on them sacred images and scriptures. In my favourite Ch'an drawing a Buddhist monk has made a fire of wooden images of the Buddha and, lifting up his robes, is warming his bare bum by the flames.

This is just the most dramatic and humorous of repeated attempts by Buddhists through the ages to prevent fellow Buddhists turning the Dharma (the Buddha's teachings) into a hidebound sacrosanct thing, rather than piecemeal and imperfect hints about how to blow out self-centred desire. As the Buddha himself is reputed to have said: "You yourselves must strive. The blessed ones are only teachers." Only our own efforts, and, hopefully, our own direct experience of decreasing self-centred desire and increasing loving-kindness and even-mindedness, should have real authority.

I came from a Christian background in which people had been burned at the stake for differing from the church in small points of doctrine, where sensible humane Pelagius was declared a heretic, where theologians argued over how many angels could dance on the point of a pin, and where for centuries controversy raged over a single letter in a Christian creed. I also had acquired, presumably from Mum and Dad (no hat in church for Mum) a very healthy disregard for pompous pontificating authority. Small wonder that I read of these spectacular Ch'an displays of contempt for suffocating sacred images and creeds with undiluted delight.

Ch'an also struck a chord with me in its insistence that enlightenment did not mean withdrawal from the world but a changed attitude to it. I'll deal more with why this appeals to me when I come to Tantric Hinduism in the next chapter. Here I'll just mention the Ch'an saying, brief and cryptic as most are, which best encapsulates for me this reversal of the world-denying aspects of many religions. "Before enlightenment hewing wood and drawing water. After enlightenment hewing wood and drawing water." What has changed in enlightenment is one's attitude to these everyday worldly activities, not one's withdrawal from them.

15. Hinduism Again

Of the main religious traditions, however, it was Hinduism still that influenced me most during my religious studies period. Partly this was because it was the religion I was primarily responsible for. Over the first five to ten years of my job student numbers in Religious Studies grew rapidly, from about 20 in Stage I at first, if I remember correctly, to a near unmanageable 200 or so. This allowed us to increase staff numbers and my responsibilities mercifully dwindled from the whole lot to just (just!!!) Hinduism, and my Indian Philosophy course. My teaching about other religions declined, and my teaching about Hinduism increased as Stages II and III and M.A. courses were progressively added to our offerings.

But partly also Hinduism appealed to me even more than Buddhism. One has to bear in mind here that I always think what I've got is the best possible. Ed Hillary was wont to say of me, wryly, that no matter if it be Ann, or our beat-up Toyota station wagon, or our sons, or our cats, or our yacht Karoro, it is always, according to me (and I should know!), the best there is. And no doubt there is something of this in my love of Hinduism. But as with Ann and our boys and daughters-in-law and grandchildren, so too with Hinduism, it is true for me that it is the best. It is so colourful and varied, so whacky and wonderful, has produced so many amazing people, and has influenced so many other cultures, that I have come to love it dearly despite the horrific dark side that seems inseparable from all religions. And, of course, what you love most influences you most.

Hinduism's initial impact on me is covered in Part II. Here I'll discuss four of the ways this impact widened and deepened during my Religious Studies career.

Tantra

Firstly, Tantra, which appealed to me as soon as I started reading about it. It is one of the zaniest branches of zany Hinduism. It also seems to me the logical conclusion to Advaita (non-dualism/spiritual monism), so is important as well as zany. I used to devote a whole lecture to it in my Stage I course.

One reason Tantra tickled my fancy brings in yet again the fascinating topic of sex.[1] Most religions have very negative attitudes to sex, and, as a result, wrack many people with guilt about urges deep-rooted in us all, and essential to the survival of our species. I think this negativity comes about because so intense and ecstatic an experience of intimacy with another person is seen as rival to, and distraction from, the religious ecstasy of intimacy with the divine. Tantra turns this on its head. Once they have attained a high spiritual level, a Tantric practitioner of a certain class may use sexual ecstasy as a springboard to spiritual ecstasy – that is, use it as one of his techniques for directly experiencing oneness with Brahman. I say "his" advisedly. In common with much religion this is, alas, mainly presented from a male perspective. But at least one piece of instruction in one text, insisting that the male and the female involved in the ritual must be of the same spiritual level, seems to imply that the female will also benefit from the rite.[2]

So Tantra offers a refreshing counter to negative religious attitudes, and I can see how sex could be an effective way of experiencing oneness. At its best, sexual intercourse comes as close as is possible to bridging the gulf between self and other. One melts into the other, physically and emotionally, feels at one with her or him, at the same moment as physical sensation explodes in ecstasy. This union is intense indeed. So experienced while focused on Brahman, by people who have long been practicing disciplined meditation on Brahman, it could well catapult one into an even more ecstatic and intense experience of union with everything, dismantling all boundaries between self and other.

To some this may sound like a license for licentiousness, and it may have been used as such by some yogis. There are rogues in all systems. But the Tantric texts stress that this sexual technique is to be used only by the Vira (Heroic) class of Tantric practitioners,[3] and even they must be already at a very high level of spiritual insight and discipline, and be judged competent by their guru.[4] To untrained people it will do more harm than good. This is, of course, why I have never tried it!

The sexual aspects of Tantra, however, are just a minor delight in its overall influence on me. For Tantra reverses not only the negative attitude to sex but, more expansively and importantly, the negative attitude to the whole physical world inculcated by many religions. The classical advaita of Shankara regards the world as appearance only, as maya, the magical display of Brahman, almost an illusion. The aim is to see through this illusion to the underlying reality, Brahman. Worldly beauty and pleasure trap us in the illusion, and we are encouraged to withdraw from the world, and meditate on the spiritual reality behind it. Much the same is often true of theistic systems like Christianity. The world is a vale of tears from which we long for deliverance, and its few pleasures distract from devotion to God, the only worthwhile aim.

And yet the logic of non-dualism, and to a lesser extent also theism, surely points in the opposite direction. The world is Brahman; everything is Brahman. Or, in theism, the world is made by God, and in the Genesis account God sees it is good. To me, the Tantric conclusion is the obvious one. If all is Brahman all is real and all is holy and wonderful: trees, birds, mountains, stars, sex …[5] So, far from viewing the world as illusory, and a fatal distraction from spiritual advance, Tantra glories and delights in the world. Moksha is a state of mind within the world, not a withdrawal from it. What one sees through is the injurious notion that I am separate from trees and birds and other people. Once I have truly experienced that all is Brahman, including me, I can delight in anything and everything, seeing diversity not as illusion but as the real and wonderful display of Brahman.

Tantra influences Buddhism as well as Hinduism. It is important in Tibetan Buddhism, the religion of my Sherpa friends. And I suspect it played a part in the development of Ch'an and Zen Buddhism which, as already mentioned, insist that enlightenment occurs within everyday life, not in withdrawal from it.

Like all Hinduism, Tantra is far more complex than this brief picture given here. For example, it proved a welcoming home for all sorts of magical and ritual practices, some intending benefit and some harm to fellow humans. Given its fundamental belief that everything is Brahman, the One Holy Power, it makes sense to believe that therefore one can channel this power in ways which influence physical events, for example healing people by mantra and rite or, alas, harming them in the same way.

I once had an interesting experience which I think was a Tantric attempt at the latter, that is to harm me. I had followed camels across the Jamuna river at Agra in order to view the Taj Mahal from that side – the river proving indeed low enough for me to wade across, though coming rather higher up my legs than up those of the camels. As I sat entranced in the uninhabited grass and scrub of the riverbank a wild looking sadhu began circling me, muttering mantras. He continued this for some time and I became convinced he was trying to lay a spell on me so as to render me helpless and rob me. It was one of many times I was glad I didn't believe in the supernatural; I might otherwise have been very frightened for there was no one else in sight. As it was, my increasing conviction about his intention delighted me. I eagerly joined in the game, circling round him in an opposite direction muttering what I hoped he would think were counter spells. He looked very disconcerted, and after a short while ceased circling and departed, leaving me half amused and half ashamed of myself.

My only other direct contact with a Tantric sadhu was an altogether more convivial affair. While Murray Jones and I were on a reconnaissance in preparation for Ed Hillary's jet boat expedition up the river Ganga, I spent several hours, in a rural area by the Hooghly River near Calcutta, sitting under a palm tree with a shaggy and generous sadhu. His generosity consisted in his insistence that I share his hookah of hashish. Tantric sadhus regard hash as an acceptable aid to mystical experience. We got very comprehensively stoned together. His English was even more limited than my Hindi, and my Bengali, his language, was non-existent. So I cannot claim to have learned anything about Tantra from this encounter other than that at least one of its sadhus is a friendly fellow. But I greatly enjoyed non-lingual close communion with a fellow human, one of life's dearest treasures.

Ramakrishna

When I sat down to dream up a Stage II course on Hinduism, I decided we would look at recent developments, and concentrate on just four influential figures so we could study them and their sayings and writings in depth. Amongst the four I chose was a Bengali saint called Ramakrishna (1836–1886). In his intense relationship with the goddess Kali, and his strange relationship with his wife, he highlighted in extreme form the experiential side of Hinduism; and in addition he had very colourful and effective ways of sharing his views, often by relating stories from past and present Hinduism. His was a sort of theistic monism, common in Hinduism, and sitting comfortably with basic Hindu beliefs about Brahman being manifested in a rich variety of ways. I've touched on this in chapter 12, and mentioned there his stories about sages using their yogic powers unwisely.

It was from Ramakrishna that I first got the wonderful tale of Ganesh and Kartikeya, sons of Shiva and Parvati, in a race around the circumference of the universe. Ganesh is rather portly, and lean and fit Kartikeya thought he had it made as the race was started and he sped off like a spacecraft. But Ganesh uses his head as well as his body. Getting up off the ground in a leisurely fashion, and glancing at his brother's cloud of dust in the distance, he slowly walked round his mother who was sitting nearby. Then he sat down again. He knew that the whole universe is contained in Mother Kali, and so easily won the race.[6]

It is this ability to warm up the otherwise austere Advaita of Shankara that is the mark of what I call theistic monism. It takes the personal manifestations of Brahman seriously enough to relate to them, and tell stories about them, but not so seriously as to lose sight of the ultimately seamless whole of Brahman. This influenced me considerably by giving me a basis for my enthusiastic participation in Hindu – and, later, Māori – rituals, even though I don't believe the beings appealed to are objectively real. True, I didn't believe either, as did Ramakrishna, that they are real as manifestations of Brahman. But in the broad permissive atmosphere that I so love in Hinduism, and which had freed me from Christian doctrinal hangovers, this didn't seem to matter.

Ramakrishna is important not just for himself but also for the Ramakrishna Movement which flowed from him. This movement, which spread beyond Bengal, provides places for meditation retreats, and also sharpens the social focus of Hinduism, providing food and refuges for the poor and homeless.

Rabindranath Tagore

Even more important to me was another Bengali, Rabindranath Tagore (1861–1941). He was a wonderfully multifaceted person: poet, playwright, story-writer, song-writer, artist, philosopher, educationalist, peaceful patriot. The rote learning and harsh discipline of many Indian educational institutions of his day had, he wrote, led him to "fear not so much evil itself as tyrannical attempts to create goodness".[7] So he set up a very radical school, for girls and boys, on his family estate at Shantiniketan, encouraging loving interchange between teachers and pupils.

His songs, for which he wrote the music as well as the words, have become part of the fabric of Bengali life, constantly sung in fields and villages as well as on city stages. Some have religious themes, but many are simple but powerful evocations of Indian life, with the theme of our common humanity undergirding all. I read many of his short stories, often heartbreakingly sad, and many of his plays. But the work we studied at Stage II was a more systematic exposition of his religious views. He titled it, at a time before feminism alerted us to the bias, *The Religion of Man*.[8] Starting from common human experience and an awareness of modern scientific theories, he sought to find a base for understanding, and a space for preserving, a religious aspect of life.

In *The Religion of Man* Tagore seems often to be responding to the wonder and mystery of the purely physical universe, highlighting human consciousness as the key to this response. At other times, however, he seems sure there is a Supreme Self to whom we are responding in religion. So on the one hand he writes of "a popular sect of Bengal, called Bauls, who have no images, temples, scriptures, or ceremonials, who declare in their songs the divinity of Man, and express for him an intense feeling of love. …[this] gives us a clue to the inner meaning of all religions. For it suggests that these religions are never about a God of cosmic force, but rather about the God of human personality."[9] This can be interpreted as saying religions are not about metaphysics but about human responses to physical nature. But he also writes: "The vision of the Supreme Man is realized by our imagination, but not created by our mind. More real than individual men, he surpasses each of us in his permeating personality which is transcendental."[10] Theists would have no difficulty with this. So he occupies a half-way house, as it were, between a spiritual/metaphysical view of reality and a purely physical one. Because of this – and I realize this more clearly now than I did when first reading him – he eased for me the transition between spiritual and physical monism, and I owe him a great debt for this.

Gandhi

But of those we studied at Stage II it was Gandhi who had the greatest influence on me, and continues to do so. It would be impossible to summarize all that Gandhi means to me, so I will have to be content with a series of not well-ordered glimpses. Overriding all is the way he remained humble about his own fallibility and failures, and compellingly honest about them, even after he was widely believed by Indians to be an enlightened Mahatma (great soul). Ever after I have used him as a measuring rod to assess the many gurus and claimants to enlightenment which India produces in full measure. If they demand unquestioning acceptance of whatever they utter, and prove prickly when questioned, let alone challenged, I reject their claims out of hand. If, on the other hand, they discourage unquestioning acceptance, preferring listeners to think about what they say, and question or challenge as they see fit; and even better if they can poke fun at themselves and/or at their followers' tendency to take them too seriously; then I am happy to read or listen to them.

I am talking here not just about those whom I have read, but also about many who visited Christchurch to drum up or encourage disciples, for in my job I was a sitting duck to be invited to attend their often excruciatingly egocentric rantings. I would sit thinking of Gandhi writing about some of his interesting but sometimes bizarre experiments with diet for curing various ills. On occasions he would disarmingly point out that even when his 'patients' recovered after changing their diets he could not be sure that it was because of this change, but that "I added somewhat to my reputation as a quack".[11]

Even the subtitle of his autobiography, 'The Story of my Experiments with Truth' , shows this lack of dogmatism that so endeared him to me. In virtually all he wrote, and it was an enormous amount, his approach was "Here is what I have tried, and for me this worked and this didn't. What do you think?" I think this is the first of two main reasons why people take seriously what he tried, and his conclusions about it.

The other main reason is that he displayed such wonderful energy and courage in trying to alleviate the lot of the oppressed, with remarkable successes as well as heart-breaking failures. After nervousness overcame him in his first case as a lawyer in India, Gandhi went to work for a law firm in South Africa to start afresh. Very quickly he became involved in the struggle for rights for non-whites there, initially only for Indians, but soon realizing it had to include also the even more oppressed Africans. When he returned to India he joined the fight for independence from Britain, for which he is now justly famous. Probably less widely known is that he was equally indefatigable in fighting against inequalities and oppression within Hinduism, especially what he called the blot of untouchability (to orthodox high caste Hindus the persons of the lowest castes were viewed as so impure that even their touch would pollute).

Gandhi's methods, developed in South Africa then applied in India, are usually referred to as non-violent. And certainly they were inspired in part at least by the deep-rooted Hindu ideal of ahimsa, non-injury to any sentient being. But he himself called his method satyagraha, literally holding fast to truth. Increasingly this became a religious theme for him, and the truth to which he held could be referred to as God. But, as with Tagore, there was fascinating ambiguity here which greatly appealed to me.

One year, for an M.A, course, we went carefully through all the volumes of his *Collected Works*.[12] As we did so it became clear that in his early South African years it was the British Empire and British justice to which he appealed, and in which he put his faith. Only gradually, as these failed Indians again and again, do references to God begin to replace those to Britain. Moreover, as references to God take over, he repeatedly uses "God" and "Truth" interchangeably, as if "God" is just a convenient emotionally charged word for Truth. Indeed at one stage he wrote: "If it is possible for the human tongue to give the fullest description of God, I have come to the conclusion that God is Truth. Two years ago I went a step further and said that Truth is God."[13] However it is equally clear from other passages that he thought of Truth/God as something underlying and sustaining all human worldly affairs, and that he gained strength from it/him to continue his struggle. "[God] whispers constantly into our ears, 'Trust in Me alone'. If we do not listen to His sweet words, having ears we are deaf. If we do not see him sitting by our side, having eyes we are blind."[14]

Of his political struggle and legacy I will note only two things which especially appeal to me. The first is his wonderful feel for the right symbolic action with which to challenge British rule non-violently. Pre-eminent here is his protest against the iniquitous salt laws. Salt is a critical ingredient in Indian cooking, so every family from richest to poorest uses it. The manufacture of salt was the monopoly of the British Government of India, and the salt laws protected this by declaring it illegal to manufacture your own, whether for your own use or for sale. Gandhi organized a huge protest march which wound its way for many days and for two hundred miles from his ashram inland to the little village of Dandi, on the seashore. There they simply picked up salt lying on the beach.

Gandhi and his followers then urged Indians everywhere to break the salt law in similar fashion. "Every villager on India's long seacoast went to the beach or waded into the sea with a pan to make salt." The Government responded with mass arrests, including, about a month later, Gandhi himself. By so doing they made laughing stocks of themselves and the law they were upholding.[15] This simple and entirely non-violent protest reverberated around India and the world, and was a significant additional nail in the coffin of the British Raj.

The second, and even more radical and moving, is Gandhi's suggested method for taking the heat out of Muslim/Hindu rivalry for power as independence from Britain neared. This was part of his impassioned but tragically unsuccessful attempt to prevent the partition of India into (largely) Muslim Pakistan and (largely) Hindu India, with all its consequent horror and bloodshed. Muslims were, understandably in my view, deeply fearful of entering independence as a minority in a Hindu-dominated state. Gandhi believed in general that, in any dispute between two parties of unequal strength, those in the stronger party should always give most say to those in the weaker, for the weaker have more reason to fear. So he pleaded with the Hindu-dominated Congress party, virtually certain to become the first government of independent India, to accede to all Muslim demands, even to the extent of giving Jinnah's Muslim party the final say, and most power, in any government.

Sadly, even for Jahawarlal Nehru, let alone for the majority of politically active Hindus, this was too much. So India was partitioned, and millions of Muslims and Hindus fled from India to Pakistan and vice versa, to the accompaniment of appalling scenes of violence and murder. Gandhi was heart-broken. He refused any role in Nehru's Indian Government and threw himself into using his influence with Hindus to try and moderate some of the worst violence. In a move typical of his complete disregard for his own safety, on hearing of Muslim/Hindu violence in Bengal, itself due for division into West Bengal and East Pakistan, he and his friends went to the worst affected villages and tried to prevent further violence.[16] But overall even he was powerless against the tsunami of fear and hatred and cruelty that overwhelmed India for many tragic months, and led to the violent death of millions.

Vegetarian at last

From my first study of and contact with Hinduism I had been struck by the huge difference from Christianity and the west in beliefs about and attitudes to living beings other than humans. Christianity, indeed the whole Hebraic religious tradition, has always put humans in a privileged position far above other animals. In the Hebrew creation account in Genesis in the Old Testament, which Christianity took over, God creates humans last and says to them "Be fruitful and multiply, and fill the earth and subdue it; and have dominion over the fish of the sea and over the birds of the air and over every living thing that moves upon the earth." I have only now noticed that he continues: "Behold, I have given you every plant yielding seed which is upon the face of all the earth, and every tree with seed in its fruit; you shall have them for food."[17] A clear command to be vegetarian I would have thought.

Jewish and Christian practice and thought did not follow this command, however. Both religions were greatly influenced by the Socratic/Platonic belief in a soul which survives the death of the physical body, and insisted that such souls are confined to humans. Thus an unbridgeable gulf was created in the western intellectual and popular mind between humans and all other living things.

Religiously this is expressed by believing humans have souls, and hence potential for life after death, while other beings do not. Intellectually and emotionally it comes out in refusal to believe other animals have feelings and thoughts and social networks in any way comparable to ours. Despite Greek influence via Aesop's fables, and countless western children's stories, and despite many westerners' close contact with other animals through farming and through keeping pets, the dominant intellectual view was that to attribute feelings and thoughts to other animals is anthropomorphism, by which was meant wrongly attributing human-like characteristics to other animals. I think it is these beliefs underlying Western attitudes to other animals that make it possible for us not only to use them to assist in agricultural work, but also to farm them for slaughter and consumption, and to perform often excruciatingly cruel experiments on them.

Indian beliefs and feelings are quite different, due partly at least to belief in rebirth. I may be reborn next time not as a human but as a member of any one of the myriad other life forms we share this planet with. And in previous lives I would almost certainly have been a member of most of these other species. This includes insects, and gives rise to an amusing and enlightening cartoon. At a desk sits a spiritual official with a queue of souls before him waiting their turn to be told what they will be reborn as. To the one at the head of the queue the official is saying: "Ah yes, Mr. McGillicuddy, you're to be reborn as a mayfly. Have a nice day." (Mayflies live for one day only.)

So in the Indian tradition we are not radically distinct from other animals but are with them part of a continuum, admittedly at the more complex end. All living beings have, or are part of, a spiritual essence, including, in Jainism especially, plants. And the Hindu concept of ahimsa, non-injury, applies to all living beings, not just to humans. This surely makes it more difficult carelessly to misuse and ill-treat them, let alone eat them. If we push this too far and decline to eat even plants we would starve to death, and this is the preferred and admired end for extreme Jain sadhus.

From the beginning of Hinduism's influence on me I had been feeling increasingly uneasy about eating meat. And while Ann and I lived in India those first two years we were virtual vegetarians. But this was because in that hot climate meat dishes were suspect hygienically, rather than because we had imbibed the Hindu attitude to our fellow living beings. On occasions, in restaurants, we did eat meat; and on our return to New Zealand we reverted to our old carnivorous ways and brought the boys up likewise.

Indeed the influence of Hinduism in this respect took a long time to come to fruition with me and, as I'll relate shortly, I needed a nudge from our son Guy before I took the final step. But as I continued to teach about

Hinduism, and even more as I undertook research amongst Hindus many of whom became my friends, my uneasiness increased. Because I was so interested in Hinduism, and so obviously loved it, many of my friends assumed I was a Hindu. When they discovered that I ate meat, though they were too tolerant and polite to say anything, their disappointment showed in their eyes. This was particularly so in Fiji (see next chapter) and with the boatmen in the Sunderbans whom I mentioned in chapter 12. I'd discussed Hindu goddesses and gods with them, asked about their puja, sung them my bhajan (Hindu hymn); but when they asked me did I eat meat, clearly expecting me to say no, I had shamefacedly to admit I did. Why I didn't give the practice up there and then I cannot now understand. I must have been an avid carnivore indeed.

So thank goodness for Guy. In his early teens he became an equally avid animal rights advocate. To Ann's and my mingled admiration and alarm he set off one night to liberate the animals held in cages in a New Brighton zoo, unsuccessfully to our shamefaced relief. On another occasion he and his equally brave friends placed themselves between ducks and their shooters at Waihola (Lake Ellesmere) at the start of a duck-shooting season. But most amazing of all was his spontaneous action one evening when he and a group of others were working for the Department of Conservation on an island reserve off the coast of Fiordland. His companions had somehow acquired some live crayfish and had put a large pot of water on the fire. As it roiled to a boil Guy looked on in horror. "Are you going to drop them alive into that," he asked incredulously, for his sheltered upbringing had not included knowledge of this appalling New Zealand habit. "Yes," they answered, surprised that Guy didn't know this was what you did with live crays.

Guy leapt to his feet and, before any other could react, seized the bucket full of crays and bolted barefoot down a long bouldery slope to the shore. Howling with rage the others likewise leapt up and set off in hot pursuit. Guy easily outstripped them and tossed the crays into blessedly cool seawater. Calmly then he turned and walked back through the slavering mob who fell back before him like the Red Sea parting before Moses. I have ever since regarded this as proof of the saying "His strength is as the strength of ten because his heart is pure." But I confess that I do have a reputation for exaggeration! – the bones of the story are true, but in Guy's more sober version there is only one crayfish, and only one person chased him down to the sea.

Less dramatically, but with lasting results, he looked round our meat-laden table one evening and asked us "Do you have to eat meat?" "I could do without," said Mac. "So could I," said Steev. I happily followed, and that left only Ann who waited a week because she couldn't bear to waste the sausages she had in the freezer! For me this change has been fabulous. Ever after I have been able to look my Hindu friends in the eye. I have also felt much better physically as well as morally. Though I'm not sure "morally" is the right word here – "emotionally" might be a better term. For through Hinduism and through Guy I feel so much at one with other living beings that eating them would feel as awful to me as would eating humans. I have a long way to go, however, to reach the highest Hindu standards. I still try to squash sandflies and mosquitoes before they bite me!

Day-to-day Hinduism

As my teaching about Hinduism expanded I began to realize that my treatment of it was badly overweighted in favour of 'higher' Hinduism, that is the fundamental beliefs undergirding it, and the monistic and theistic paths to enlightenment. Of the day-to-day Hinduism of ordinary people – their rituals, their use of their religion to comfort and support them in family and survival affairs, the social implications of their religion – I knew too little and taught hardly at all. So in two ways I started to remedy this and, as usual, this affected not only my teaching but also my personal journey.

One way was to return to India frequently and take slides of as many rituals and ceremonies and shrines as I could to use in my teaching. This was made possible by another of those stunning coincidences of interests with which my life is studded. I was by this stage deeply involved with Ed Hillary's Himalayan Trust, and with the projects he undertook in Nepal. I had winkled myself into Ed's affection and trust in my usual cunning way, by being nice to everybody and working hard. So he frequently invited me to work with him on his aid projects in Nepal. He also included me in his adventures in Nepal and India, most notably his jet boat journeys up the Sun Kosi and Mother Ganga, and, with Ann and Mac as well, a film Mike Dillon made while Ed was New Zealand High Commissioner to India.

Now to go on all these wonderful trips I needed leave from the University Council. Lo and behold they were willing to grant me this since my teaching specialty was Hinduism. Though it always seemed to me one of those disgraceful rorts we University staff specialize in, hiving off to exciting places on full pay, it actually did make academic and teaching sense to allow me to return to India and Nepal, both largely Hindu countries, as often as possible.

It is true that even the long-suffering University Council eventually baulked. Bert Brownlie, the Vice Chancellor, came to me one day with a wry grin on his face. I had just lodged yet another application for special leave, this time to join Ed in Nepal primarily to assist in rebuilding the immense supporting rock wall of the Thami Gompa courtyard (so religiously orientated, and in fact I spent fascinating hours sitting with young trainee Buddhist monks in their classroom). But this was my umpteenth application for special leave, and, said Bert, Council felt there seemed now to be not two but three kinds of leave – sabbatical leave, special leave, and Wilson leave. I was overdue for sabbatical leave (most of a year off teaching duties every seven years to do further study and research). Could I see my way clear, asked Bert, to re-submit my application but this time for sabbatical rather than for special leave? Council would find it easier then to grant it. "A rose by any other name smells just as sweet," I replied, and promptly applied for and got the leave I sought, with just a change in nomenclature.

So on this occasion, and on many others on my way to or from Nepal, I wandered the streets and villages of northern India participating in countless rituals to goddesses and gods and, when permission was given, as it almost always was, taking slides of shrines and murti (images). One highlight was the Varanasi puja on the Ganga trip, mentioned in chapter 12. Another came when I stayed with a friend's brother and family in their ancestral village deep in rural Bengal, a village that had then no motor road linking it to the rest of India, and no electricity. Khris' brother Bata, like me, was personally not religious, but respected his late father's habit of having daily puja in the house. Often I was the only one present other than the village pujari conducting the ritual, and I got a real feel for the way in which these rituals are felt to have protective power for the house and family simply by being performed, without need for family members to be present.

Even more moving was when, with Bata's and Mira's then five-year-old daughter Tumpa, I got up at 2 a.m. one brilliant moonlit night to watch and listen while the pujari performed the harvest puja to Lakshmi, goddess of prosperity. In a way typical of Hinduism Lakshmi was represented not only by a small image of her but also by samples of the harvest she had provided, sheaves of rice with ears of grain still on, and samples of other crops and vegetables. For Hindus the goddesses and gods, the murti (images) of them, and the natural things they personify or bestow, merge seamlessly together in a way I found very powerful.

In these ways I deepened my understanding of, and feeling for, the ways religion comforted and sustained ordinary Hindus, not primarily as a means of achieving the ultimate goal of moksha, but as an aid to coping with the trials and crises, and the successes and joys, of everyday life. I have tried to convey this in a systematic way in chapter 12. Here, for completeness, I am just noting that it was during my Religious Studies career that I more fully immersed myself in this aspect of Hinduism. Once again there was a happy and very powerful interaction between my teaching needs and the expansion of my own experiences and understanding. And once again, as with experiences in the Banaras University temple, I was able to participate in and be uplifted by puja to goddesses and gods without worrying about whether I believed they existed outside of human imagination.

16. Fiji: Cultural Adventures

The other boost to my understanding of everyday Hinduism was Fiji. Here again was a stunning co-incidence of interests, and again an outrageous academic rort which was nonetheless justified. In how many jobs is it possible to go off for ten months on full pay to a tropical island inhabited by not one but two races of fabulous people, and surrounded by warm clear sea, coral reefs and fish?

How could this be justified? Well, consider what my job was – to teach about Hinduism in a New Zealand university. Hindus were a small proportion of the population in Aotearoa, and they tended to maintain a low profile to avoid anti-Indian and anti-any-religion-other-than-Christianity sentiment. India, Hinduism's home, was far away. How then to make Hinduism more relevant to our home in the South Pacific?

Easy. A few short hours away by plane, on islands visited by thousands of New Zealanders, was a large vibrant Hindu community – the Fijian Indians. It was obviously my duty to go to Fiji, study Fijian Hinduism, and return to teach about it. The University Council agreed, and granted me permission to spend my first study leave thus. So from August 1972 to June 1973 our New Zealand family transmogrified into a Fijian family. I later published articles about Fijian Hinduism, and became more or less the world's leading authority on the subject for the simple reason that no other Religious Studies person had studied it.

As with Nepal and India, my studies, and their effect on my journey, were not even half the story, so herewith some general information on our fantastic Fijian frolic. Socially we had the best of both Fijian worlds – the Indian and the Fijian. My lovely Indian friends I'll introduce later, for they came with my work. Our most wonderful Fijian immersion, on the other hand, happened by fortunate accident.

After a trying month sharing a house with another New Zealand family in a rainy hill suburb of Suva, we rented a house right by the sea in the little village of Lami, a few miles west of Suva on the King's road to Nadi. The family next door had a Fijian housegirl, i.e. servant, something we hadn't even considered as servants are a foreign concept to New Zealanders like us. But the housegirl next door had a close friend who badly wanted a job, and it took only a little urging for us to think “Why not? – we can afford it”.

Alumita

So burst Alumita into our lives. She was tall, muscular, beautiful, hilarious, outrageous – I could heap adjective on adjective for ever and still not do justice to her. And to our delight we were immediately friends with her, not employer and servant. No choice, mind you, even had we a mind to try to treat her as a servant, for anything less servile than Alumita is impossible to imagine. She and Ann used to do what little housework there was together, laughing uproariously the while, often at Alumita's wicked and usually suggestive teasing of me. She happened on me in the shower one day, and ever after referred to me as “sausage in his pants”, which appellation I accepted gratefully as a fine tribute to my manliness.

Alumita was married to Vili, whom we also immediately liked. They lived in a village further along the coast. To get there you took a bus for several miles then walked along a muddy track through guava forest to coastal mangrove swamp. If the tide was low you then walked along sand and mud and shells seaward of the mangroves for maybe two or three miles. If the tide was high a thin track led you over low grassed hills and through numberless creeks and mudholes. The village comprised 20 or 30 thatched bure (houses) and, typically, a sturdy concrete Christian church, Methodist I think. Church and bure scattered themselves picturesquely over a grassy promontory that sloped down to mudflats or sea depending on the tide.

Alumita adored our youngest son, Mac. Indeed her main assistance to Ann, as distinct from the pleasure her friendship gave us, was to play with Mac and make sure he didn't drown in the sea while Ann took Guy and Steev for their correspondence school lessons – all five minutes of them usually, before they tricked her into letting them have a quick swim from which they wouldn't return for several hours. Early on Alumita began taking Mac with her on Friday afternoons when she returned to her village for the weekend. We needed no persuading. Dearly as we loved Mac, he was only about 18 months old, and there were many things we could do easily with just Steev and Guy which would have been more of an effort with a toddler. So Alumita would grab a spare nappy, hoist Mac onto her hip, buy him an icecream, hop on a bus, and disappear.

We had not a moment's concern over Mac disappearing into a remote ‘native’ village. But Ray, Ann's mother, had when told of it by letter. “What if he wanders off and falls into the sea?" she asked. When we relayed this to Alumita she roared with laughter. "Fall in the sea," she spluttered, "he doesn't even touch the ground." Apparently this tiny beautiful blonde cherub was snatched from hand to hand by large Fijian mamas from the moment he and Alumita arrived till the moment they left. Unfortunately he was then too young to have now conscious memories of the fabulous experience of living in a remote village laved by love. But we think that in the remote subconscious level, which influences so much of what we do and are, this experience is one of the reasons why Mac is so calm and confident.

Then came Hurricane Bebe, in November 1972. In common with many Fijian villages Alumita's and Vili's was badly damaged, only God's house remaining unscathed as a refuge from God's wrath. It is unfortunate to benefit from others' misfortunes, but this had a wonderful effect on our lives. While their flattened bure was being resurrected Vili and Alumita came and lived with us, cementing our friendship with both, and in addition leading to wonderful Friday evenings with their friends descending on us after work, with beer and guitars and harmonious voices, to party under our big tree by the sea. Through them, in this way, through visits to their village, and in a host of other ways, Vili and Alumita ensured that we were not normal expatriates living lives in isolation from the locals, but became a warmly welcomed part of the Fijian way of life and love. We owe them an incalculable debt.

It gave also some dramatic and traumatic moments. How could it be otherwise once accepted into Fijian life? After their bure was rebuilt Vili and Alumita returned to the village, Alumita once more coming to us only by day. Then, inexplicably, she didn't turn up for some days. Ann eventually ran into her at the shops and was shocked to see her looking severely depressed and with a badly bruised face. Ann forced the story out of her. She had adopted a small baby from a mother too young to cope. About the same time Vili's sister from another island came to live with them. Alumita was soon enraged by the laziness of this sister who left the baby unfed and in her own mess while Alumita was away all day. She spoke her mind about it, no doubt forcibly, that being her style. But telling off a guest, and a husband's sister at that, was definitely tapu and Vili, enraged in turn, beat Alumita up.

Alumita was so miserable we told her she was welcome to bring her baby and come and live with us. Which she did. Unfortunately she also, unknown to us, spread word that we were displeased with Vili and wouldn't let him set foot in our compound. Fortunately I ran into Vili some time later in town. He told me how hurt he was by this, and I was able to assure him it was quite untrue and that he was most welcome any time.

After Alumita and the baby had been with us for a while a deputation of three village elders visited us and made it clear that the baby must go back to the village where she belonged. As Alumita was still persona non grata there it was decided that we should be the ones to return the baby. So, having naively and probably outrageously interfered in an affair when we were almost entirely ignorant of the cultural intricacies involved, we found ourselves, boys and all, squelching through the mud on the coastal route to the village carrying a small black baby girl.

For us who love intense experiences, good or bad, this was very exciting, especially when we were accosted by a huge Fijian with a tree trunk slung casually over one shoulder. "I know who you are", he said menacingly to me. "You're the one who crooked (=stole) Vili's woman and baby. You won't be welcome where you're going." Fortunately for me I was carrying the baby on my shoulders at the time, so he couldn't knock my head off with his tree trunk without also smashing the baby to bits. He let us carry on, his scowl piercing fiercely into our backs. Our trepidation at our temerity was not lessened by this encounter, but as we were friends with Vili again, Alumita-induced mis-understanding cleared away, and as we knew he also wanted the baby returned to the village, we pressed on.

A village meeting was called on our arrival. Lovely Niko, a young man of the village with whom we'd become friendly, and whose English was good, translated for and to us in the heavy drama which followed. We were determined to give Alumita's side of the story, and our feelings about it, even though we'd only heard Alumita's version. We were heard out in courteous Fijian fashion before their take on it was put to us very firmly and we had to agree to differ. I like to think that in this, as in many other cross-cultural exchanges we've had, the sincerity of our human feelings mitigated the affront of our impertinence. Despite seemingly great differences in superficial customs we are all human at heart, and this is intuitively recognized by all but a few, and makes meaningful meetings across cultural chasms relatively easy.

Encounter with a cannibal chief

My brother Hugh was involved with me in yet another intense encounter of the Fijian kind. I had long gazed in wonder at an amazing peak in the interior of Viti Levu. It was called Korobasabasanga because it looked like the jagged comb on a rooster's head and neck. When Hugh visited us he eagerly fell in with my suggestion we climb it. With a Fijian friend who came from a village near its base we set off up the Singatoka River. We travelled first by a local boat powered by an outboard motor which was cunningly raised not quite out of the water to get us up shallow rapids. We then proceeded on bare feet through deep mud and over stony river bed carrying fairly heavy packs. We were barefoot because we reasoned that if our friend and all other Fijians could do it so could we. This reasoning was unsound and our feet suffered as we deserved, but eventually we reached our friend's village.

As dusk deepened to darkness we found ourselves in a large bure with a very old chief and his fellow elders. After dinner we conversed through our interpreting friend. I was interested in old Fijian beliefs and customs, and in response to my queries our friend volunteered the information that the chief dated back to the good old days when Fijians were allowed to eat their enemies. "Oh, what do we taste like?" I asked, for I have no objection to humans eating each other, only to the hypocrisy of human horror at it when we blithely eat other animals. My question was translated to the chief.

His answer needed no words of either language. Hugh was sitting next to him and in those days of very short shorts was displaying a large expanse of tasty-looking thigh. With a perfectly straight face the old man reached across and pinched a portion of this thigh between thumb and forefinger, pretended to transfer same to his mouth, then lovingly licked his lips. We were sitting in a tiny space of wavering candlelight surrounded by the deep dark of the rest of the bure. Beyond the bure walls the even deeper darkness of the forest stretched for many miles before any assistance in not being eaten could even be imagined. Of course we knew – or we thought or at least hoped – the chief was joking. But for a timeless moment a frisson of terror curiously mingled with excitement ran up and down our spines. Then the rest of the bure exploded in laughter.

Next day, with our friend and another young villager, we set off along dwindling tracks through dense forest, then through dense forest previously trackless but with our guides cutting a track with cane knives almost as fast as Hugh and I could walk. The last stretch to the summit was as curious a bit of climbing as I've experienced. We hauled ourselves up vines and branches protruding from a vertical cliff, always several yards horizontally out from the cliff face. The dog who was our third companion had to settle for waiting at the bottom of the cliff since four legs, while faster on the flat, are less use than two legs and two arms for this sort of aerial gymnastics.

We knew we had reached the top when we could look down the vertical vegetated cliff on the other side, but other than that we could see nothing but trees and vines. Our friends wanted the villagers below to know we had summitted, and to botanist Hugh's horror began laying about them with their cane knives till what looked to Hugh like a tennis-court size clearing had been created. Still we couldn't see over the surviving trees, nor were our friends sure our shouts could be heard. Nothing daunted, but daunting Hugh still further, they heaped the murdered trees together and set fire to them. We briefly wondered if the plan was to roast us, and the smoke a signal to the chief to come up for lunch. But the surrounding surviving trees failed to ignite, the brief fire smouldered out, and we lived to descend the cliff to the waiting dog.

Back on the track we were brought to an abrupt halt by a raised hand and excited discussion as our friends examined marks on the forest floor too faint for us even to see. "A young pig passed over here less than half an hour ago," they explained to us. "Wait here a minute." Dog in the lead they plunged into the impenetrable vegetation, and within five minutes mingled barking and squealing proclaimed their diagnosis correct. Five minutes more and they reappeared with a young pig, legs tied together, squirming on the shoulders of one of them. With no abatement of pace because of the added burden we continued down to the village, where the previously wild pig was added to the semi-domesticated ones who kept the village clean and who were, presumably, destined to be replacements for the long pig (human) flesh our chiefly friend had once enjoyed.

Racial tensions

During our ten months in Fiji our three boys mingled with people of different skin colour and different culture in natural ways impossible to duplicate in then largely mono-racial and mono-cultural Christchurch. They have now little conscious memory of this, but the influence on them at a subconscious level is probably considerable. I think it accounts in part for what seems to me their complete lack of racial prejudice, more complete and unconscious than mine.

Our times in India as part of a tiny minority group had already given me deep sympathy for Māori in New Zealand, a minority group in their own land. Our time in Fiji gave this sympathy more depth and insight. For in Fiji, despite tensions with their Indian compatriots (later cynically exploited by coup leaders), native Fijians still lived their own culture in a way as natural as breathing, and surrounded by fellow Fijians. I could not help but contrast this with the heroic, and now thank goodness increasingly successful, Māori attempts to save their language and culture from extinction by the arrogant dominance and all pervasive influence of Pākehā (European) culture. There are regions in the North Island where Māori ways are still an everyday natural thing, and Māori people a sizeable proportion, and in some areas a majority, of the population. But until recently, for Maori elsewhere in New Zealand, experiencing their culture tended to be something separate from their everyday life, taking place on marae (Maori ceremonial and social sites) or in haka and other performance groups.

As for Fijian-Indian tension, my experience in 1972–3 persuaded me it was not so pervasive or negative as media and politicians would have us believe. When I stayed on the farm of a friend's brother I found relations between this Indian farmer and his Fijian farmer neighbour were warm and friendly. They lent equipment back and forth, and helped with each others' harvests and other tasks.

Even in Suva, where tensions were higher partly because most businesses were Indian owned and run, and because Indians formed a larger proportion of university students and of the educated and professional classes, on the personal level tension seemed to me minimal. Often I would be walking with Indian friends who on occasions had given me the typical Indian stereotype of a Fijian – lazy, uneducated, not able to manage money or run businesses or government departments; almost word for word, indeed, the same stereotype many New Zealanders have about Māori. But then down the street towards us would saunter a Fijian whom my Indian friends would hail with joy and greet as obviously a good friend. As we walked on I would quiz them: "Hey, you told me Fijians are a shiftless feckless lot. How come you have one as a friend?" "Oh so-and-so is different," they would assure me sheepishly. And often also I would be walking with Fijian friends who had frequently assured me that Indians are a sly tricky lot, interested only in money, etc. Then they would hail and greet an Indian friend warmly, and in response to my teasing would say "Ah, yes, but we were talking about Indians in general, so and so is different."

And when Rabuka and succeeding coup leaders whipped up anti-Indian feeling amongst disaffected Fijian youths, to further their own scurrilous aims, the only heartening thing to come out of the resulting chaos was that there were many instances of Fijians protecting or hiding Indian neighbours and friends from rioting mobs.

Equally impressive and heartening was the response of my Indian student friends to quotas set in an attempt to lessen the Fijian-Indian imbalance in government service, in universities, and in businesses. These quotas, requiring that a certain percentage of government jobs and university places, for example, be filled by Fijians, meant that on occasions my friends would find a job or scholarship given to a Fijian applicant far less qualified than them. They admitted this was hard to take, but understood and supported the system as a way of easing the imbalance and the resulting tension between the two communities.

17. Fiji: Religious Adventures

Now what was our excuse for being in Fiji for all this fun? Oh yes, I was there to study Hinduism in Fiji. As it turned out I also taught some Religious Studies at the University of the South Pacific, under the kindly auspices of Ron Crocombe of their School of Social and Economic Studies. Ron, a lovely man married to a lovely Cook Island woman, was adept at grabbing visiting academics to add variety to the then new and comparatively sparsely staffed university. I was more than happy to respond to his request.

Teaching and research

So, amongst other things, I taught about Hinduism to a group composed mainly of young Hindu students, an odd situation which nonetheless was mutually very beneficial. I had an over-all 'Religious Studies' perspective on Hinduism, and also knew more of its history and its ancient texts than they did; they, of course, had a much more intimate and everyday acquaintance with Hinduism than I did. We eagerly swapped perspectives with each other.

They also gave my research direction, indeed made it possible. They willingly agreed to fill in a questionnaire for me, and then to be exhaustively interviewed. A group of students on its own does not constitute a cross-section of Fijian Hindu society. But they gave me access to a wider sample, through their families and friends, and through taking me to shrines and puja and enabling me to talk to priests and participants there. Some of them also became close friends, in particular Shiu Prasad, and Babu, a strikingly handsome young man of whom Ann did a striking pastel portrait.

I found myself leading a most enjoyable double life. I would talk earnestly about religion with my Indian friends, attend puja with them, and join them in wonderful sessions singing bhajan and ghazal, Hindu and Muslim devotional songs. I imagine they thought me pious and religious, and so I was when with them. But then hey ho off I would go to wild and sexy Fijian nightclubs with Ann, or to Alumita's and Vili's village, or to yarning and drinking with Fijians on our sea wall on a Friday evening. No doubt some moral systems would expect me to be thoroughly ashamed of myself. I revelled in it. How wonderfully I had progressed from the naïve and devout young Presbyterian called by Yahweh to be his minister, and tormented by fears I was favouring mountaineering over Yahweh and crucifying Jesus.

At this stage in my Religious Studies career I was in full flight on my mission to find out more, and include more in my teaching, about everyday Hinduism as distinct from lofty levels of philosophy and enlightenment. In Fiji I concentrated on two aspects: firstly on what I termed the uses people put their Hinduism to, and secondly on ways in which they used their Hinduism as an overall framework for their lives. Running through both was my interest in finding out how much ordinary Hindus knew and/or cared about the basic scriptures of Hinduism on which I had largely based my understanding till then.

The titles of the two articles I published reflect this. Under the general heading of "Text and Context in Fijian Hinduism", the first was subtitled "Uses of Religion", and the second "Religion as a Framework for Living".[1] I discovered that the basics of Hinduism I later tried to outline in Ganga and Hinduism (see chapter 12) were indeed well known to all my informants, and were very influential on them. They had learned about these things, however, not by reading the Upanishads or the writings of Shankara but by listening to and retelling and reading the great Hindu epics. To Hindus in Fiji the *Ramayan* was best known, but parts of the vast *Mahabharat* were also familiar to them, especially the most loved portion, the *Bhagavad Gita*. On my return to Canterbury I hastened to include these in my courses. As one would expect, my informants' Hinduism was also imbibed from an early age from parents and grandparents and aunts and uncles, and by participation in puja, and by singing Hindu hymns. Nothing spectacular or new about these findings, but it was useful to elucidate them with reference to the beliefs and practices of Hindus in Fiji: useful for Religious Studies as this had not previously been done; and useful for my teaching since it gave me first hand material from the largest community of Hindus close to New Zealand.

Personal experiences

The effect on my personal journey was likewise not spectacular or new. But it further deepened my appreciation of how Hinduism operates on the thoughts and behaviour of its adherents, and perhaps added to my deep desire to work out a framework for living which suited me as well as Hinduism suited them. It also gave me more experience of the awesome impact of religious shrines and rituals. I will mention only two particularly intense incidents out of a host.

My friend Shiu Prasad took me to stay at his brother's farm on the second main island, Vanua Levu. Not far from the farm there was a shrine to Nag Baba, the snake god. This was not a shrine built by human hands but a large rock shaped – by natural or by divine forces? – uncannily like the hood of a giant cobra. Shiu and I talked with some of the devotees making their offerings and puja while we were there, and I was deeply impressed by the certainty and sincerity of their claims about, and experiences at, the shrine.

Nag Baba likes milk, and an oft repeated story told me there was that offerings of milk, poured into a depression in the flat area of rock below the over-arching hood, are always gone next morning, as are other prasad (offerings). A sceptic might snort and suggest hedgehogs or other nocturnal creatures are gratefully availing themselves of this bounty. If pressed to explain the situation this is what I would think. But at the time I felt no inclination so to explain it away to myself (I would never be so rude as to try to do so to the devotees.) I just felt profoundly moved by the faith of the devotees, and their joy that their offerings, and they believed also their requests, had been favourably received. And a thrill compounded of mystery and excitement ran up my spine.

So too with the other certainty of devotees of Nag Baba, related to me by Shiu, that the rock cobra hood is growing. I was told that since it had been recognized as a manifestation of the god, and offerings made, it had measurably risen in height. The whole atmosphere of the place and of the devotees gave me a vivid sense of what one writer calls the "numinous"[2] – a sense of being in the presence of a power mysterious, vastly greater than human, and potentially either beneficial or baneful to us.

This was the very sense which I had struggled to feel at quarterly communion services, when I was trying to feel the presence of Jesus as I ate the bread and drank the 'wine' in remembrance of his sacrifice for me. I am not sure why in Sherpaland, in India, and now here in Fiji, I had this sense so powerfully without straining for it, when in my native Christianity I strove for it in vain. But I suspect it was partly because my beliefs were not involved, my mind was quiescent; and partly because I wasn't striving, wasn't feeling I ought to feel it. This links these ritual experiences to the other times I am most movingly in awe before forces vastly greater then me, namely when I am involved with great objects and forces of nature, mountains, rivers, the sea, the wind. Here too awe overwhelms me without any effort on my part.

The other special incident was more personal. I have Shiu again to thank for it, and for so much else besides. He told me about a Kali mandir (temple) at Nausori, just east of Suva. Devotees brought problems and petitions to the priestess who, going into a trance-like state, would communicate their concerns to Kali. Kali would then reply through her, advising or comforting the petitioners. So to this mandir we went, Shiu and I. Again a thrill ran up and down my spine and my hairs stood on end. One by one people went forward and in a normal and not especially distinguished voice the priestess would ask each one to state her or his problem or request. Then she would close her eyes and begin to sway markedly. Suddenly a different and very impressive voice would come from her mouth in pure clear Hindi which even I could partially understand. "This is Kali speaking through her," Shiu whispered to me.

After a while there was a pause in the procession of petitioners. "Go up and take a turn," urged Shiu. "But I haven't any problems," I replied, both honestly and as an excuse, for I was feeling way out of my depth. "Doesn't matter," insisted Shiu, "Kali will read your thoughts". Nothing venture, nothing gain, so up I went. The priestess laid her hands on my head, went into a trance, and Kali spoke to me. I understood some of it and Shiu translated the rest for me afterwards. It was very complimentary – Kali either didn't know of my double life or, more likely, approved of it, for she is a wild thing herself. "You have a good heart and will do well in life" was the general gist, though Kali put it much more eloquently. Then, still I think in a trance, the priestess went over to the altar, took from it a simple plastic image of Ganesh, the elephant-headed god who helps in hard tasks, and gave it to me – a gift from Kali. It was stained with the offerings of countless devotees. I felt inordinately privileged.

Once again I had no inclination to seek naturalistic explanations of this spine-tingling experience. I simply accepted with great joy the intense exhilaration I felt. And as with all such incidents, it not only enhanced my ability to teach about Hinduism, it also affected me personally in a deep and beneficial way. These sorts of experiences form a very important part of my journey. Even though, if I cared to exercise my mind to seek an explanation of them, I would not accept the devotees' account, the experiences not only link me to the devotees, they also infuse my response to the universe.

I had only one religious disappointment in Fiji. I was keen to find out about pre-Christian Fijian religion, both for its own sake and to compare it with pre-Christian Māori religion. I failed almost entirely. There were no books about it in the university library, and Fijian friends I asked about it seemed to have no knowledge of, or interest in, their race's religious past, though most were enthusiastic and harmonious participants in their race's current immersion in various sorts of Christianity. Sadly, it seemed to me that Christian missionaries had, as usual, not only converted the 'natives' to Christianity, but had made them ashamed, and/or ignorant, of their previous religious beliefs and practices.

18. Māori Religion

Of religions that influenced me during my Religious Studies career there remains only pre-European Māori religion. I put it at the peak of the ascending order of influence during this period for it was new to me, whereas Hinduism had already influenced me enormously. Overall, the influence on me of Hinduism and Māori religion is about equal.

That Māori religion was new to me is a dreadful indictment of prevailing pākehā attitudes and educational system ("pākehā" is the Māori term for people of European descent.) Though I had grown up in Te Waka a Māui (The Canoe of Māui) I was almost completely ignorant of the rich culture of Māui's people, and equally unaware of how they had been cheated out of their own land and then marginalized in it.

My parents, on the other hand, were aware of, and deeply concerned about, the treatment of Māori by Pākehā. My brothers and my sister Margaret remember that Dad came home furious one day accompanied by some young men from the North Island who had come down for a Church conference. One of Dad's parishioners, who had agreed to billet them, had refused when she discovered they were Māori . They lived with us instead during the conference. This was an example of Mum's and Dad's admirable championing of people discriminated against. I imbibed this general attitude, and this later swung me fully on to the Māori side. But at this time I was largely unaware of their plight.

I became a little more aware of the situation during my university days, but don't recall doing anything about it. I made no effort to learn about Māori culture, despite being very concerned about Pākehā New Zealand's obsession with Britain and Europe to the exclusion of Asia. And when I started teaching Religious Studies I knew far more about Hindu belief and mythology than about those of my own country. I even knew more of ancient Greek religion and mythology than of Māori .

So there was no way I could teach about Māori Religion. Or was there? Here was the situation. We were the first university Religious Studies department in New Zealand. We taught about Christianity, the religion then dominant in the country even amongst Māori . We covered the other major religious traditions, with increasing expertise as new staff were added. But not a word about the original religion of our land. Unbelievable? Alas, true.

I became increasingly concerned about this. But here was the problem. At that time there wasn't even a Māori Department at Canterbury University, so we couldn't direct students to experts in the field. And none of us knew anything about Māori religion. For an ignorant Pākehā to teach about Māori religion, probably under the watchful eye of resurgent Māori pride, would be impertinent and stupid. Clearly out of the question?

Well, no. Life is seldom about choosing between good and bad alternatives. It is about choosing the best practicable alternative, with none ideal. So, gulping deeply, I chose to read about Māori religion and introduce it as part of a Stage I course, regarding this as preferable to our department not looking at Māori religion at all.

And was it ever under watchful Māori eyes! In the first or second year of my temerity a positive phalanx of Māori kaumātua and tohunga (elders and priests) filled the front row of the lecture theatre, including, if I remember rightly, Hui Vercoe, later to become Māori bishop of New Zealand, Peter Ruka, later to become a close friend through my involvement in his Greenstone Trails, and Maurice Gray, a Rāpaki kaumātua and Anglican minister. Some were doing the whole of the course, others sitting in on the Māori section to check out this impertinent Pākehā. As has been my unfailing experience when I have ventured into the Māori world it was neither a hostile nor a suspicious checking out. They listened politely and intently. It surely increased my trepidation at what I was doing. But Māori religion had captivated me immediately, and I comforted myself with the hope that my enthusiasm and love for the subject would shine through, and compensate for any inaccuracies or breaches of tapu.

Nonetheless my nervousness reached a climax when the time came to deal with the sacred heart of Māori religion: mana and tapu, and their counterpoint, noa. Once I got going I felt better, for I really enjoyed trying to convey to Pākehā students something of the power and excitement of this central topic. But at the end of the lecture, unusually, the Māori contingent rose as one and came up to me in formidable formation. "Oh dear, I'm for it," I thought. "I have ignorantly trampled on their most sacred taonga (treasure)." Nor did their opening remarks reassure me. With solemn faces they said: "Well, that was interesting Jim. None of us could have dealt with the topic in that way." Could have, or would have? I wondered; were they offended by my treatment? But then broad smiles broke out, and they explained what they meant: that, immersed in the tradition as they were, they couldn't have stepped back and discussed it objectively in a Religious Studies manner; and that they had found it not only interesting but helpful. I breathed again.

So much for why and how I came to teach about, and thus be influenced by, Māori religion. Why did it influence me so? Well, for two main reasons.

Firstly, a pattern in my long journey was emerging. I had been brought up in, and for a while intensely accepted, a metaphysical/supernatural framework for living, namely Christianity. My acceptance of this framework had weakened, and then faded right away, but my need for a framework remained as strong as ever. I needed, and still need, to have some understanding of the universe, and of my place in it, on which I can base my response to life – physical, mental, moral and emotional. I suspect this need is strong in many people, and is one reason for the continuing widespread acceptance of religious frameworks. Whether it is strong in everybody I don't know.

Hinduism and Buddhism, and to some extent the other religions I'd studied, assisted me in a staged withdrawal from a metaphysical framework. Hinduism especially helped me with its fundamental idea of an impersonal universal energy which activates all things, including me, and its stress on the need for me to alter my understanding of, and attitude to, this underlying energy, rather than throw myself on the mercy of a personal supernatural being. Brahman is metaphysical, but not as separate from the physical as is Yahweh. Moreover there is some similarity to the fundamental idea of modern physics that a single basic energy underlies all. I could leave aside the question of whether to interpret this energy metaphysically or physically, and explore and appropriate the rich and complex Hindu suggestions of how to relate to it.

Māori religion provided further assistance in this staged withdrawal. I have been wont to describe it as the least supernatural of all the religions I have studied, but it is more accurate to say that it does not make a distinction between natural and supernatural in the abrupt way the major religions do. To clarify this, and to explain why it had and has such an influence on me, I need to give a brief and inevitably inadequate sketch of Māori religion.

The origin of the world

In its account of the origin of the complex world we live in Māori religion doesn't have a supernatural person bringing form to the formless by creative command, as does the Hebraic account in Genesis. Nor does it give a metaphysical universal consciousness a primary role, as does non-dualist Hinduism. The Māori karakia (chants) of origin tell rather of immense periods of impersonal evolution of form from the formless, which seems more akin to the modern scientific account than the Hebraic or even the Hindu.

First there was Te Kore, the Nothingness, the Void. In a way I was to find typical of Māori karakia and mythology adjectives are added one by one to the bare name Te Kore – it was the nothingness in which nothing could be seen, nothing could be felt, nothing moved. Nothing was ever before or since as nothinglessly nothing as was Te Kore.

But over vast periods of time Te Kore became denser, ever so slightly more substantial, till at length Te Kore became Te Pō, the Night. Again adjectives powerfully elaborate on the nature and slow evolution of Te Pō – the intensely dark night, the night in which nothing could be seen, the night in which nothing moved – but, at long last, no longer the night in which nothing could be felt. For slowly Te Pō also became denser till it evolved into the night so intensely dark the darkness became almost tangible, almost could be felt.[1] Just so sometimes, moon and stars occluded by cloud, nothing visible or audible, intensely dark nights can seem to be tangibly pressing down on us with the weight of their impenetrable darkness. What I find so powerful in Māori mythology and song is the way imagery drawn from nature around us is used to build feelings and imagination to a deeply felt climax, like much of Hinduism bypassing my mind and infusing my whole being.

Now there is no longer nothing. There is something, albeit not yet easy to grasp, on which slow evolution can work. Here the karakia employ a variety of images to suggest the slow transformation of this almost formless something into distinct and recognizable forms: the power of plant growth – tentacles of roots and vines snaking through the darkness; the force of desire focusing darkness to a more intense point.[2] And over another immense period of time not only does the something become more substantial, it also begins to stratify into layers. Here I like to use the analogy of a pool of muddy water, with the earthy element under the influence of gravity settling to the bottom of the pool, and the water gradually clearing to translucence above it. Perhaps better, though, would be a swirl of dust in the air settling down as the air stills, becoming clear air above a denser layer of matter. For two distinct layers form: Papatūānuku, our mother the earth, lies below, while Ranginui, our father the sky, lies above.[3]

With Rangi and Papa we enter the realm of persons, to which realm other persons, their children, are added. But not only with Rangi and Papa, but with their children also, the natural forces or things behind the personifications are clear.

Rangi and Papa embrace in love and give birth to the great gods: Tāne, god of forests and birds; Tū, god of war and of humans; Tāwhiri, god of winds and storms; Tangaroa, god of the sea; Rongo, god of kūmara and other cultivated crops, and of peace; Haumia, god of fern root and other uncultivated crops; and, last born, Rūaumoko, god of volcanoes and earthquakes. These sons love their parents, but as another immense period of time passes Rangi and Papa lie still in close embrace, and the children endure a cramped existence between the breasts and in the armpits of Papa. At length they tire of having no room to tupu (unfold, expand) into full rich life. So they kōrero (discuss) how they might enlarge their space. Tū, abrupt and bloodthirsty, says "It is well, let us kill them." The others are horrified, and Tāne suggests a milder alternative. "No, let us separate but not kill them. Let Rangi be thrust far above and become a stranger to us, but let Papa remain close to us as a nursing mother."

Good idea, but how? Each brother tries in turn except for Tāwhiri, who is against the plan, and Rūaumoko, who is too young. Tū hacks at the sinews binding Rangi and Papa together, drawing blood which makes some of Papa's earth red, the sacred colour. But he fails to separate them. Rongo and Haumia try to push them apart, but their power of growth is too gentle for the formidable task. Tangaroa raises huge waves furiously but also fails. Then Tāne. First he stands erect between earth and sky and pushes with his mighty arms, but moves his parents only fractionally apart. Then he puts his massive shoulders on the ground and pushes with his great tree-trunks of legs. Slowly, slowly, with much rending of tissue and tendon, and to cries of distress from his parents, he pushes Rangi up and away till at length he is indeed far above, a stranger.

All this time Tāwhiri is holding his breath in rage. Now, the deed he feared done, he releases his breath in a storm of fury against his brothers. Rongo and Haumia are so frightened they hide underground, from whence their offspring, revealed by their tell-tale leaves, can still be harvested. Tāwhiri then turns on Tangaroa with such ferocity that half Tangaroa's children flee in fear to land; and then on Tāne, toppling his trees so they lie on the ground and become food for grubs or fall into the stormy seas and disappear. Finally he turns on Tū, god of war and of humans. This battle is long and fierce, but inconclusive. Neither can he vanquish Tū nor is he vanquished by him, a wonderful evocation of the interaction between us and the weather, an intense life and death struggle which we can never finally win but which, as a species, we have not yet conclusively lost. (Now, who knows, human-influenced climate change may at last give Tāwhiri victory.)

A wild start to the wild world we live in, and the story is not finished yet. Rangi's grief at his separation from Papa is so intense, and his tears so copious, that earth is in danger of being submerged completely. So Tāne turns Papa over so that her most desirable parts are no longer directly under Rangi's frustrated gaze. The rains that fall are still Rangi's tears, and rising mists are Papa's sighs of grief, but the torrents dwindle. Rūaumoko, still at Papa's breast when she is turned over, is carried underground, but is given fire to keep him warm. In volcanoes this fire bursts into the open, and earthquakes are Rūaumoko turning over in his subterranean home.

Tāne, who loves both his parents, is deeply grieved at what he has had to do. So now he clothes Papa's torn and naked body in trees and other plants, and propagates birds to fly and sing amongst them. And the sun by day and the moon and stars by night he places as jewels in Rangi's firmament.[4]

Mana, tapu and noa

Though it is not to my knowledge explicitly stated in the karakia, the rest of Māori religion makes me sure that it is mana that powers the evolution from Te Kore through Te Pō to Rangi and Papa and their children. As already mentioned mana has much in common with the original concept of Brahman. In early Indian scriptures Brahman is a mysterious universal energy which can be channelled by mantra and ritual in ways beneficial to humanity. So too with mana. It is all-pervasive and mysterious. It is not a person but an impersonal energy which powers all the world's myriad processes: the growth of plants, the rising and setting of the sun, the birth and unfolding (tupu) of human individuals and communities.

In itself mana is neither malevolent nor benevolent toward us humans. Because it is immensely more powerful than us it can be very dangerous, and needs to be approached with great caution – this caution being the key sense of the concept of tapu. But, if approached correctly, by karakia and ritual actions performed by trained tohunga for major activities, but by ordinary folk for minor ones, mana can be channelled beneficially into human activities. And not only can it be, it must be, for without mana nothing succeeds, indeed nothing whatsoever happens.

In teaching about mana I compared it with modern dependence on electricity, an equally mysterious force to me. We use electricity for many things nowadays – cooking, heating, lighting, powering tools, and so on. If we are careful, and if the insulation on wires and switches is adequate, ordinary people can channel electricity safely and beneficially into hot water jugs and electric drills. With low voltages, as on our yacht *Karoro*, I can even do the wiring and channelling myself, with no more than a sharp tingle if I make a mistake.

But fooling around with the voltage involved in houses, as I did once at our mountain hut, is a risky business that can result in serious injury or death. I assume this is because I myself, brain and nerves and muscles, am powered by electricity but of tiny voltage and current. High voltage and current is way beyond what my wires can handle and, lacking a fuse to blow, it will blow me apart instead. So normally it is wise to get an electrical tohunga – for the word basically means expert – to do wiring and switches for much higher voltage. And, of course, even more do we need high tohunga – highly trained and experienced electricians – to repair high voltage lines, let alone to design and build powerhouses and transmission lines carrying thousands of volts.

So too with mana. Ordinary Māori had a stock of karakia and ritual actions adequate to channel the mana needed for everyday activities. For example, before a fisherman set out to sea in his canoe he would use karakia and ritual to placate Tangaroa (god of the sea). But for larger more important activities – whether of Rongo (peace), like planting and tending and harvesting the kūmara crop, or of Tū (war), like a raid on another hapū (sub-tribe) or iwi (tribe), or of Te Whare Wānanga, the house of learning, where tohunga were taught – highly trained experts were needed. And while they were thus channelling high voltage mana, and in a residual way at other times also, these high tohunga, and also the ariki (chiefs) and rangatira (nobles) could be likened to live wires, charged with intense mana and therefore themselves dangerous to non-expert people or things which are noa.

These experts, their persons and their karakia and rituals, are tapu. Tapu is not a negative counterforce to mana. It is simply the condition of being infused with much mana, and a sign warning that this mana is dangerous to untrained people. Tapu is the mana equivalent of the electrical high voltage symbol placed on major transmission line pylons to warn of danger; and is also the equivalent of the insulation on wires, preventing wastage of energy. Noa is its opposite, often translated as "common", with an implication of inferiority, but more usefully viewed as meaning neutral, safe to approach, because involving only small amounts of mana. Were it not possible to neutralize oneself after involvement in high mana situations, such as war parties or kūmara rituals, ordinary life would be impossibly restrictive. So noa is not fundamentally a negative term but a descriptive one.

I have said enough now to explain why I say Māori religion is the most naturalistic and realistic of all the religions I have studied. It is almost pointless to speculate on whether mana is a supernatural or a natural energy. Because karakia and rituals are used to channel and protect mana it is possible to liken it to such supernatural powers as Yahweh or Brahman. But because it powers all natural things and processes it cannot be classed unambiguously as supernatural – that is, different from and superior to the natural world. And in the Māori context it is unhelpful even to introduce this distinction between natural and supernatural, an import by western scholars from our background supernatural religions. True, the Maori gods may to us seem supernatural – they are invisible for example – but on closer examination they are seen to be seamlessly a part of the whole of which we too are a part. They are the children of Rangi and Papa, sky and earth, 'natural' things if it were useful to use that term. And we are descended from them, for Tāne fashioned the first human, Hineahuone, from earth stained red with the blood of Rangi, and through her propagated us.

So perhaps I shouldn't have said that Māori religion is the most naturalistic, but that here the natural/supernatural dichotomy I had grown up with is so muted that it is almost non-existent. And I feel that this has much to do with my ability to absorb and appropriate its fundamental emotional attitude to life without getting hung up on supernatural elements.

Māori religion's fundamental attitude

What is this fundamental attitude? Well, it is in striking contrast to the fundamental Christian attitude. Christianity gives to humans a special and cosseted place in the universe but a very subordinate one. God has made us only "a little lower than the angels", he cares for and guides us, he sees everything we do, knows the secrets of our hearts etc. But this parental favouritism and protection comes at a heavy price in powerlessness. For we cannot question God's ways without grave risk of his disfavour and wrath. We must endlessly sing his praises and throw ourselves humbly on his mercy, for we are miserable sinners. We cannot save ourselves, but must be saved by God though Jesus Christ. Hume had a point when he spoke of God's "restless appetite for praise". And Nietzsche was even more scathing, despising the way Christianity forces humans to grovel before a despotic potentate. He compared this very unfavourably to what he regarded as the more manly Greek attitude to their gods, namely being wary of their power but outwitting or tricking them whenever possible. Had he known of it, Nietzsche would have loved Māori religion.

For what is the Maori attitude? Certainly that one must be careful, indeed meticulous, in channelling mana and dealing with the gods, for its power and their power could blast us. But if this care is taken we can channel mana to our benefit and can force gods to do our bidding. I particularly like it that some tohunga were reputed to be able to capture Tāwhiri's winds in a gourd then let them out when needed – an ability that would be of great assistance to sailors like Ann and me. We are highly admired if we do such things successfully, and are admired even if we fail, so long as we fail boldly. The fundamental attitude Māori religion inculcates in me is that of careful daring in a world not made for us but in which we can succeed, though equally may fail gloriously.

I'm not sure now how much I made the connection at the time, but Māori religion, I certainly see now, is the mountaineer's religion par excellence. *Nothing Venture, Nothing Win* is the title of one of Ed Hillary's autobiographies. To venture involves taking risks; and it is not despite the risks but because of them that one gains the great rewards, of fierce satisfaction and self-knowledge, in victory over one's fears and weaknesses.

In this fundamental Māori attitude to life there is no servile dependence and much bold self-reliance. This is not to the exclusion of interdependence with others. Far from it, the whānau (extended family) and the hapū (sub-tribe) are crucial, and to be cast out from one's community for some hara (offence or mistake) is devastating. But even this can be seen as challenge rather than catastrophe. The individual to whom this happens and who then creates a new whānau and hapū is highly regarded. The greater the challenge faced and overcome the greater the achievement.

I've never liked subservience. I was alternatively praised and reprimanded at school for standing up to and being angry with teachers who I thought were wrongly treating or accusing me. I enjoy interdependence between mountaineers together on a rope, and between friends on tasks impossible on one's own, if it is founded on mutual respect and trust. But I do not like being dependent on others, indeed am not good at accepting help from others, even when I need it, preferring to do things not only in my own way but on my own.

Māui

So to find a culture and a religion infused with such a daring and independent attitude was exciting and affirming for me. And it is in the stories about the culture hero Māui[5] that this attitude is most clearly displayed. Māui is born prematurely and his mother Taranga, thinking him dead and not wishing to bother with the lengthy rituals prescribed, cuts off the top-knot of her hair, wraps him in it, and places him sorrowfully in the sea. But he is not dead, is protected by Tangaroa, cast up on a beach, finds his mother and brothers, and demands his rightful place in the family. He tracks down his absent father and asserts his rights with him also, then, when he grows up, embarks on an amazing series of adventures.

The results of many of these adventures are beneficial to humanity. He slows down the sun's race across the sky, for example, giving longer daylight hours. And he tricks his grandmother Mahuika, goddess of fire, and escapes being burnt to death only by calling on Tāwhiri to send down a deluge. Ever after humans have been able to get fire by rubbing together two pieces of wood taken from trees into which fire fled. But in none of his exploits is his motive to benefit others. It is love of adventure pure and simple; love of a challenge, of danger, of the spice of risk of death. When he went to trick Mahuika, despite his mother's warnings of the danger, it was because he hadn't had an adventure for ages, and was bored. Afterwards, singed and lucky to be alive, was he abashed when his relatives said "We told you so"? Not at all. "Do you think I'm going to change because of this?" he asks them scornfully. "Never. I'm going to go on being the same forever."[6]

And here what I call the realistic note of Māori religion reaches its clearest expression. Māui did not go on being the same forever, because death puts an end to forever for all of us. We can believe something goes on after the death of the body – I'll come to that in a moment. Or we can whinge and cringe before the inevitable end. Or we can treat death as one more challenge to face up to with daring and excitement. Māui represents this last alternative, and gives for me the most satisfying of all treatments of death in human culture.

He announces to his brothers that he is off to kill Hine-nui-te-pō (Great maiden of the night), goddess of death. "You're mad", they tell him. "No way we're coming with you on this one." So Māui sets off to the west, where great Hine lies, accompanied only by small birds. Hine is asleep when he arrives, lying on her back with her legs apart. Māui's plan is to enter her body via her vagina – and we don't need Freud to point out the sexual allusions here: a vagina is where the sperm went in to make him and from whence he emerged into the mortal world as a baby born to die. Now he's out to reverse the process and become immortal by killing death. He will crawl through her innards, cut out her heart, and emerge triumphant through her mouth.

He decides to turn himself into a caterpillar – not a good choice as it turns out. Urging his feathered friends on no account to make a sound till he emerges with Hine's heart, he crawls and humps his way into Hine's vagina, which is set about with teeth of obsidian and greenstone. But in doing so he looks preposterously comical. The birds try their hardest to keep quiet, but it is too much for little pīwakawaka (fantail). His wee cheeks puff out in a vain attempt to suppress his mirth, then he splutters into laughter. Hine wakes, realizes what is happening, and snaps her legs shut. Māui is crushed to death.[7] The cycle is completed, though not in the way he intended.

But the tale does not bemoan the fact. "For Hine nui always knew what Māui had it in mind to do to her. But she knew that it was best that man should die, and return to the darkness from which he comes, down that path which she made to Rarohēnga."[8] The unspoken message is clear. Death is inevitable, but it is possible to pack into life an amazing treasure of excitement and achievement if one refuses to be cowed by fear of death, and lives life to the full despite its inevitable end.

Māui also highlights for me another aspect of Māori realism, and another stark contrast with Christianity. Māui is an inspiration to me, but most definitely not a moral example. He was cruel and capricious. He starved one grandmother so he could get her jawbone as a weapon, then beat the sun unmercifully with it. He repeatedly tricked another grandmother and his brothers. He was always playing tricks, often unkind ones. The moral message of the Māui tales is a harsh one: the strong and the powerful are not always gentle, and you tangle with them at your peril. I fear he would have snorted in disbelief or derision had he heard Jesus tell us to love our enemies. And he wasn't keen on forgiving a brother for even one offence, let alone 70 times 7. "What are ya, a wimp?" he would probably have said; though he would have been impressed by the way Jesus challenged the authorities of the day, at great risk to himself, and by his forceful cleansing of the temple.

It is interesting to contemplate a conversation between Māui and Jesus. Lacking such a conversation, for considerable historical and mythological reasons, I am happy that I can take what I want from each. "Live life to the full though death be the end." Thank you, Māui, I have tried to and will continue to try, and your example has helped me in this. "Love your neighbour as yourself – love your enemies – judge not that you be not judged." Thank you, Jesus, I haven't done so well here, but your teaching and example, and that of many of your followers, has certainly contributed to what little success I've achieved in this respect. How fortunate I am not to be confined to one tradition but to be free to call selectively on many.

Is death the end?

I've been suggesting that Māori religion accepts that death is the end. Those who know it well will be bursting to contradict me here. For it is true that the Māori view of humans is that we are not just tinana (body) and mauri (life force) but also wairua (spirit). And when death ends the unfolding of mauri, and tinana rots away, the wairua carries on. But – carries on to what?

Here Māori religion is, I think, ambiguous. On the one hand the tūpuna – the ancestors, the old ones – are an integral and moving part of present Māori communities. They are always greeted and honoured in the meeting house and at hui (gatherings). Their guiding and protecting presence is keenly felt. But there are also hints that their existence is a thin bloodless one compared to the full rich experience of those still living. Where they are now has definite similarities to the ancient Hebrew Sheol, a place of shadows, the abode of the dead. Most striking of these hints are the words of karakia recited at tangi (funerals). The wairua of the dead person is praised and honoured, but then very firmly and emphatically ordered to go to the abode of wairua.[9] Why? I think because wairua not properly honoured then sent away may lurk among us and cause mischief, because they are jealous of the full rich existence of the living.

So though beliefs about wairua certainly blur the sharp edges of the attitude to life I've been outlining, they do not completely annul it. And as usual I feel free to pick and choose, to sharpen my version of Māori attitudes to life by playing down or ignoring beliefs about wairua which I don't share.

Io

But ambiguity about the state of the wairua after the death of the body is slight compared with the uncertainty and controversy over Io, the Māori Supreme God.[10] Māori was not a written language till Europeans came to Aotearoa (New Zealand). Early written accounts of Māori religion are either European reports, often by missionaries anxious to convert Māori to Christianity, or material told or dictated to Europeans by Māori . And in these first written accounts, dating from the early 1800s, there is no mention of a Supreme Personal God. The Māori account of origins begins, as I have outlined, with Te Kore, and progresses by impersonal stages through to Rangi and Papa and their children.

But about 1860, a group of North Island tohunga announced through their leader, Te Matarohanga, that Māori belief had always included a Supreme Personal God, Io. It was by his mana and under his guidance that the slow evolution of form from the formless had taken place. Te Matarohanga's account, including very powerful and therefore highly tapu karakia, does not replace the Te Kore to Rangi and Papa account but leads seamlessly into it, and into the subsequent details of what was by then a widely known account. And the beautiful and powerful Io karakia heap adjective on adjective in typical Māori fashion – Io the parentless, Io before whom was nothing, Io the all-powerful, Io the all-knowing.

This disclosure was very influential and important to many Māori, and has been ever since. For the European religion, Christianity, loudly proclaimed that its monotheism was the pinnacle of religious development, and denigrated Māori rituals to many nature gods as polytheistic. This was a part only, but psychologically and religiously a very damaging part, of the general European put-down of Māori tanga (culture), and Māori self-esteem had been seriously eroded by it. Now here was a meeting of their most prestigious tohunga, through Te Matarohanga, assuring them Māori religion had always been fundamentally monotheistic. Though, as Te Rangi Hiroa puts it, "The discovery of a supreme god in New Zealand was a surprise to Māori and Pākehā alike,"[11] the boost to Māori self-esteem was very significant. And I think many Māori today believe Io was their Supreme Being from the beginning.

Many Europeans were not so sure and directed searching questions at Te Matarohanga, all of which, in my opinion, he answered convincingly in terms of fundamental Māori beliefs. Why did only a small group of very high tohunga know about Io, and not the rest of the Māori people? Because, replied Te Matarohanga, this was by far the most tapu of all knowledge and karakia, involving the most mana. For it to be known to, let alone used by, untrained people would put both them and the sacred knowledge at risk. It would blast the user and allow much mana to leak away.

Then why reveal this knowledge now, not just to untrained Māori but also to Pākehā? Because, responded Te Matarohanga, the Māori situation is now so desperate that the risk of going under because Io our protector is not widely known is greater than the risk of the knowledge and karakia being misused. Who could query that? Māori were in desperate straits, physically, militarily and religiously. Europeans were taking their land, European diseases were striking them down and leaving Europeans, who had built up immunity, untouched, European soldiers with guns were increasingly defeating the bravest resistance, killing warriors from a distance beyond the reach of spears and hand-held weapons. The popularly known Māori gods seemed powerless to protect, and when increasing numbers of Māori switched allegiance to the seemingly more powerful European god, they found Jehovah had a strong European bias and was deaf to Māori pleas for healing from illness or victory in war.

But – was Te Matarohanga really revealing a previously secret and higher stratum of Māori religion? Or did he and his fellow tohunga brilliantly Māorify Jehovah? The phrases used of Io do bear striking resemblance to Jewish and Christian descriptions of Jehovah: all-powerful, almighty, all-knowing. Even Io's use of powerful words to bring Te Kore into existence and to set it on its evolutionary course is similar to Yahweh's creation in Genesis. And the name, Io, is not too far removed from Je-ho-(vah). Of course none of this is conclusive. If there is a Supreme Creator who has revealed himself to Māori as well as to the Israelites one would expect name and attributes to be similar. And some have believed Māori are the lost tribe of Israel, in which case the Io doctrine is simply the Māori development of the same original revelation. Moreover, while Yahweh creates by simple command, Io does so in true Māori fashion by karakia.

My view of the matter is biased. I prefer Māori realism and nature gods to Christian monotheism. So I like to think the former is the authentic original tradition, and I regard Māori conversion to the latter with sorrow. And I do think Te Matarohanga's doctrine of Io is a brilliant attempt to Māorify the Christian god, akin to those of other great Māori prophets. If so, it is the most fully Māori of all those attempts, for it does not forsake old ways and old gods but adds a layer to the existing tradition. If Te Matarohanga created it then I agree with Eric Schwimmer who regards him as the most intelligent person in Aotearoa in the 19th century.[12]

I live here

I have digressed from explaining the two main reasons Māori religion so influences me. The first is its realism and closeness to nature, which I have taken so many pages to expound. The second is equally important but can be more briefly expressed. I had grown up in a religion whose land of origin was far away from me, and completely unfamiliar. As a child I had to have elements in stories about Jesus, and images in his teachings, explained to me. And even in the form in which it came to me, via Scotland, Christianity was set in a foreign landscape and climate and people, as was English literature which dominated the novels and poetry I read or studied. Māori religion, on the other hand, evolved in Pacific islands which are our close neighbours, then was naturalized in New Zealand by centuries of development here. The trees and plants which figure in its karakia and waiata (songs) are the trees and plants of the land I grew up in and love more dearly than any other place in the universe. The winds with which furious Tāwhiri battered his brothers are the winds which buffet me in my beloved mountains or terrify me on the great ocean of Kiwa, Tangaroa's realm. I know Haumia's bracken, I eat Rongo's kūmara, I walk in Tāne's forest and am entranced by his tall trees and beautiful birds. I feel Rūaumoko's subterranean rumbles and stand in awe before his volcanoes and geysers. As a well-written New Zealand novel has special appeal to me, so too Māori religion; for its allusions and imagery and landscapes need no explanatory notes, they are my own.

19. The Greenstone Trail

My lectures on Māori religion were based on written sources only, and dealt mainly with fundamental beliefs and attitudes. I had had no contact with everyday rituals and emotions of Māori religion such as I had so enjoyed with Hinduism and with Sherpa Buddhism. Indeed, in my ignorance, I thought none was possible, believing all the old ways had been swept away by the disastrous flood of European people and their Christian religion.

In 1990, to my delight, I discovered this is not the case. 1990 was the 150th anniversary of the signing of the Treaty of Waitangi, an agreement between Māori chiefs and the British government on which New Zealand governance is based to this day. Government funds were made available to people or groups who were keen to stage events to commemorate the occasion. Amongst the many who applied successfully for some of this money was my friend Peter Ruka, along with his friend Makere Schraeder, and his brother Mac.

Their plan was an ambitious and exciting one. In olden days South Island Māori had established routes through the Southern Alps along which trade, especially in pounamu (greenstone), flowed between west and east. One important greenstone trail came up the Arahura valley from the West Coast, crossed the Main Divide past what is known to Pākehā as Lake Browning, and over Browning Pass, then followed down the Wilberforce and Rakaia rivers to east coast settlements. Peter, Mac and Makere decided to link re-opening this trail and revitalization of associated lore and ritual with a sort of Outward Bound experience for disadvantaged youth, both Māori and Pākehā.

Mac and Peter had been steeped in the appropriate Māori lore and ritual by their grandfather, hence could ensure the ritual safety of the parties. But they lacked modern mountain expertise to keep the parties physically safe. So they cast about for mountain recruits to their cause, and Makere, who knew my sister Alison, asked me to join their venture.

For me the timing was perfect. I was a year into my retirement, living a family-oriented and very hedonistic life at home and on our yacht *Karoro*.

I was still very young (a mere 53) and vigorous. And my Presbyterian conscience and my parents' example were whispering in my ear "All very well for you, but you're not doing much for the needy." Ann was, as ever, supportive of me disappearing into the mountains yet again. And yet again there was a stunning coincidence of interests – being useful to others in the mountains and finally getting some real personal involvement in Tāngata Whenua (People of the Land), and at a critical time in the multi-racial development of New Zealand. My affirmative answer to Makere was pre-ordained.

Preparations

My greenstone trail experience started with a training camp based at a lodge on the shores of Kaniere Moana (Lake Kaniere), a little inland from Hokitika. I had something else on the day the camp started and, when I arrived a day late, I proved my incompetence for the job of teaching bush and mountain lore by getting temporarily lost as I tried to find my way from the lodge down to the lake shore, where the group was learning Māori lore.

It proved the perfect introduction. With a huge grin Peter announced to the group that this was their bushcraft instructor arriving by an unusual route. Their hoots of appreciative laughter, in which I joined heartily, completely broke any ice there may have been between me and the young participants. We could put aside any misconceptions about me being an expert who knew it all, and I could share my experiences and ideas with them as useful things to try, and accept, modify or discard, rather than as the only right way to do things.

That night, after the youngsters had in theory gone to bed, Mac and Peter told how they had come by their Māori lore and ritual. When they were about five or six years old their grandfather had chosen them to be the recipients of his sacred knowledge, after a series of memory tests posed to a number of children of the hapū (sub-tribe). He pulled them out of school, overriding the protests of educational authorities, and for several years schooled them in Māori matters. "He would recite a karakia or waiata (song) or tale," they told us, " and we would have to repeat it back to him word for word after only one hearing. It was as though he took the top off our skulls and simply poured his knowledge in."

The material was in very ordered form, rather like sections and chapters in written books, and for each portion a trigger word was given. Now they had only to repeat to themselves, or be reminded of, a trigger word and that whole portion would pour out of them without conscious effort on their part. I was enthralled. While studying Hinduism I had learnt of the way the Vedic scriptures, though eventually written down, had also been preserved orally by groups of brahmins in various parts of India over the millennia since Vedic times (about 1500 B.C.) I knew similar methods had been used in Whare Wananga (sacred schools) here in New Zealand, before European writing enabled written preservation. To hear first hand that this had happened between Mac and Peter and their grandfather was very exciting.

This was solemn sacred stuff, but to my delight it was delivered in anything but a solemn way. Mac and Peter found it impossible not to make a joke out of almost everything, and we who were listening were frequently hooting with laughter. And yet, in a way I found very reminiscent of my immersion in Sherpa Buddhism, this mirth accentuated rather than diluted the seriousness and sacredness of what we were discussing. I have since found this common amongst Maori , and very much to my taste. Again, as with Sherpa religion, part of the appeal was by contrast with dour Presbyterian Christianity, and the strained reverence I had felt in church.

Suddenly one of the older youths burst into the room and blurted out to Mac "Come quickly, so-and-so is about to have it off with such-and-such" – such-and-such being a very beautiful but very young niece of Peter and Mac. Big Mac rose formidably to his feet. "Oh oh", I thought, "here's where things do get serious." Not a bit of it. Very soon Mac came back, grinning broadly. "Wow, a close thing," he said as he sat down. "I was just in time. Young so-and-so had mounted the saddle and was about to ride off into the sunset when I grabbed him by the scruff of the neck and hauled him back." "And what did you do then?" I asked when our laughter died down, probably thinking of how such a thing would have been treated in a heavy judgemental way if it had occurred at one of my youthful Bible Class camps. "Sent them both back to their own beds," replied Mac, in a tone which implied "Why? What else needed to be done?".

Again I was very impressed, this time by comparison with how nearly all Pākehā adults in charge of youngsters would have handled the matter, given how strange are our attitudes to sex. All the Māori kaumātua (elders) present took it for granted that in a group of young people this sort of thing was natural and inevitable, to be prevented if age or relationship or pregnancy issues made that necessary, but certainly not to be treated as shameful or requiring punishment. And perfectly acceptable incidents to have a good laugh about. Laughter, almost no matter what: that is one of my most powerful impressions of my contacts with Māori , all the more impressive since in many cases my Māori friends were at the poverty end of the economic scale, and sometimes also on the wrong side of Pākehā law.

Already at this preparatory camp I began to see the powerful effect Outward Bound type experiences could have on young people. I had talked with friends involved in such ventures. And I had taken our boys, and on occasions others, into the mountains. But I had never had first-hand experience of encouraging urban young people to accept challenges in the wild, and it was wonderful to see how they responded as individuals and as groups.

I particularly remember when we introduced them to river crossing. After going across with them in a fairly mellow place, giving them an idea of the basics, we went to quite a deep swift place with a good run-out below it, and asked them to go across in their own groups, with us 'experts' loitering in the run-out area to hoick out any mishaps. It was very scary for many of them, and to see how the stronger and braver encouraged those frightened, with no attempt to appear superior themselves, was inspiring. One girl was in tears on the bank before her crossing, and a big tough-looking boy was very gentle in urging her to have a go, assuring her that he and the rest of the group would keep her safe. They didn't push her at all, just talked her quietly through her fear till she herself said, with a gulp, "O.K., let's go". They made a slightly shaky but eventually successful crossing and the girl, in tears of triumphant joy, flung her arms round the boy who had most encouraged her. I was left in no doubt that this successful rise to a concrete physical challenge, this overcoming of intense fear, was a major milestone in her development.

The main adventure

Then, in December 1990, the main adventure got underway. An Electricity Department premises near Lake Coleridge were converted into a temporary marae (Maori ceremonial and social site) and we were all carefully but humorously instructed in the correct ritual procedures to be observed. The plan was for three groups of 12 youngsters to tramp to Lake Browning from this marae in the east, while a further group of 12 were ready to set off from the West Coast side to meet us at the lake. As a concession to modern ritual the groups on both sides of the alps were equipped with radios so the timing of the meeting could take account of weather and speed of progress. Kete (baskets) of pounamu had already been placed in the lake from the West Coast side, and we were to retrieve them and bring them on to the east coast.

We were a wonderfully diverse group. Mac and Peter, and two or three of their brothers, along with other kaumātua from the Ruka whānau from Whangarei, made up the senior Māori contingent charged with ensuring everything was done with correct ritual and observance of tapu. Barry Law, from the Outdoor Education Department of Christchurch Teachers' College, was in charge of ensuring everything was done with due observance of mountain safety procedures. Barry was very good at getting the kids enthusiastic and in raising their self-esteem, and I enjoyed his company very much. He was assisted by Airini Caddick and me. Barry and I are Pākehā, but Airini was in an intriguing and at times awkward in-between space. She is of Samoan descent but was brought up in a Pākehā family. She described herself as a brown-skinned Pākehā. The awkwardness came from her often being taken by the youngsters as Māori when, because of her adoption and upbringing, she knew very little even of her Samoan culture, let alone of Māori. But she coped with this admirably, and was fantastic in everything she did.

On the West Coast side Barry Brailsford's son Peter, who was a mountain guide, was responsible for the physical safety of the party. Barry Brailsford himself was in a curious position. He is a Pākehā historian who wrote a good book on Māori Greenstone Trails[1] and, in the process, came to regard himself as expert in Māori ritual matters also, almost as a tohunga. He was therefore in charge of ritual correctness in his party, and this later gave rise to an embarrassing situation.

Of the 'youngsters' about half were Māori and half Pākehā. I have been referring to them as 'youngsters', and most of them were in their early to late teens, but some were in their twenties and thirties. Some, though not all, came from difficult backgrounds, and may have been sent on this trip by authorities and/or caregivers in the hope it might 'straighten them out'. But I think most were there because, in the case of the Māori, they wanted to get more in touch with their Māori roots, and, in the case of the Pākehā, because they wanted to find out more about Māori culture. One of the many wonderful things about the venture was the effect this mingling of Māori and Pākehā had on the young Māori, many of whom had previously had very low self-esteem. They had grown up in a culture dominated by Pākehā ways and had tended to think of Pākehā as cleverer, better copers, more knowledgeable.

Suddenly, now, they were in a situation where their Māori culture was the centre of attention, the guide to correct behaviour. And suddenly they were being looked to as authorities by their Pākehā companions. I felt I could literally see them standing straighter, looking more confident. There is a Māori saying from olden times comparing a man who had failed with a man who had succeeded: "Surely you lie curled and cramped, but I stand straight." And there is a dominant theme in Māori culture that a main aim in life is to be able to tupu, unfold or expand, like a koru, the unfurling frond of a tree fern. That's what I felt was happening to these young Māori. From being bent under the weight of negative Pākehā attitudes to them and their culture they were straightening up, unfolding, expanding.

Equally inspiring was seeing the joy of the Māori kaumātua as they walked in the footsteps of their tūpuna (ancestors). I became especially close to one of them, a man from Whangarei who, like me, was in his fifties. He was always simply known as Uncle Jim. No confusion with me as the kids had nicknamed me Uncle Pooh, after I had ridiculed their obsession with daily showers, and told them I bathed only once a year. One day as we walked up the valley together Uncle Jim pointed to a patch of summer snow high on a peak. "See how it is the shape of a woman," he said. Indeed it was. "That is Hine so-and-so" (alas I have forgotten her full name). "She was the one who first found this route," he told me, awe in his voice. (I think I remember that correctly – certainly she was one of the early ones to use the route.) I will never forget the joy on the face of this gentle man as the conviction that his ancestress was looking down on and after him suffused his whole being.

Ritual versus mountain lore

But not all was sweetness and light between the ritual tohunga and the mountain tohunga. This was very embarrassing, because the ritual tohunga were all Māori in our party, and the mountain ones Pākehā. On the second night out, after we had pitched camp on a high terrace above a tributary stream, Barry Brailsford called us by radio from the Arahura party on the other side of the Divide. His toko toko (carved ceremonial walking stick) had flown out of his hand as he crossed a creek, he said, had been swept over a waterfall, and had been retrieved only with difficulty by his son Peter. This could only have been, he insisted, because some hara (ritual error) had been committed. He had closely questioned all his party and was convinced the error was not on his side. Now I probably would have put up with this if it had been a Māori tohunga telling this tale, though reluctantly even then. But for Pākehā Barry Brailsford, who, I was convinced, had slipped and lost hold of his stick, to be trying to cover up his clumsiness in this way stuck in my gullet.

However our kaumātua took the matter seriously. They asked us all to think carefully whether we might inadvertently have done something wrong. After a while two girls came forward tearfully and announced they had by mistake brought some jewellery with them in their toilet bags (we had been warned to leave all jewellery behind, I think because it would have been in conflict with the pounamu). Our kaumātua consulted, then announced the two girls would have to be cleansed by a ritual performed naked in the stream below. Uncle Jim was appointed to conduct this ritual. Well, if I'd been skeptical and bolshie before it was now nothing to Airini's outrage. She felt very strongly that this would be a terrifying and humiliating ordeal for the girls, and she spoke out fiercely though unsuccessfully against it, supported by Barry and me.

It was intense stuff. On the one hand we thought Barry Brailsford was clumsily trying to cover up his clumsiness, and that our kaumātua should have told him to back off. On the other hand, aware of 150 years of Pākehā arrogance and put down of Māori ways, we felt terrible trying to interfere in the matter. And truth to tell it may have been a moving experience not a terrible ordeal for the two girls involved. Like the rest of the group they were very moved by immersion in things Māori. They probably felt bad that they had by mistake breached the tapu they had been instructed in, and may have felt much better when that breach was ritually removed. And, as we discovered later, our opposition didn't worry our kaumātua – they accepted that we differed from them, and were not offended by it.

A day or so later I had my own difficulties with ritual instructions conflicting with my party's safety. At least I think it was a day or so later – it may have been a year or two later when a party of us went back to undo a hara (ritual offence) we had committed at the lake. My memory now confuses together incidents from these two trips. In increasingly threatening weather we were pressing up the final stretch of the valley. The side of the river we were on, I knew well from past trips, became increasingly steep and bluffed, so I sought for and found a crossing to the other side.

One of the party looked very alarmed. "What's the matter?" I asked. "We were told that other side of the river is tapu, and that we must stick to this side," she replied. I was sure I had been told no such thing, and was even surer that if we tried to continue on this side we would have no hope of reaching the next campsite before rain and darkness put our inexperienced party in real physical danger. But the worried one was equally sure that if we crossed the river the party would be in real ritual danger. "Oh boy," I thought, "this is a good way to make a difficult journey even more challenging and exciting." In the end I simply had to override her concerns, assuring her that if she was right I would take full responsibility and bear all the consequences – easy for me since I believed there would be none. She reluctantly agreed, we made camp safely, and on checking with the kaumātua found, to my relief, that she had mistaken the instructions – indeed all the other parties had also crossed there.

To the lake

It took three days to nurse our charges through blisters and rivers and rituals to the junction of the Wilberforce and Cronin rivers, where we set up camp beside the Park Morpeth hut. From here Browning Pass looks more mountain than pass. A steepening slope of scrub and snowgrass leads up to an even steeper and ever narrower scree gully sneaking up between rock bluffs. Many the hearts that were daunted by the sight. Next day, drizzle turning to rain and cloud enclosing the tops, Airini and Barry and I left those daunted hearts in their tents and went up to improve the sort-of zig-zag track that Barry and I had scraped up the final gut on an earlier reconnaissance trip.

Down below Peter and Mac, in radio consultation with weather forecasts, with Barry Brailsford's party, and with kaumātua and helicopters back on the plains, decided the next day was on for the final push. It was a logistical nightmare, and we were glad we had only to help carry it out, not plan it. The day was forecast to start fine then deteriorate to afternoon cloud, then drizzle, then rain. We had to get 36 novices up to the pass and around the lake to its western end in time to rendezvous with the Brailsford party with its 12 novices coming up from the west. Meanwhile helicopters were to bring in from Christchurch a group of mainly elderly kaumātua, including Peter's and Mac's mother. Greenstone had to be retrieved from the lake and distributed to our parties to the accompaniment of lengthy rituals. Then we had to get everyone safely off the pass, especially the helicoptered elderly, before rain- and wind-induced hypothermia wiped us all out. Just the sort of challenge to remind us of the fragility of life and the need to live it fully – or foolhardily? – nonetheless!

Next morning, fine as forecast, we chivvied our charges to the foot of the pass then up the lower slopes. These were easy, for before the carriage road was formed over Arthur's Pass an attempt had been made to form one over Browning Pass. Remnants of it zig-zagged up snowgrass and scrub slopes before failing to angle up a rocky bluff. From this last zag the narrow shingle slide reared up alarmingly. In summer, with no snow on it, it was not really dangerous, but to those unused to mountains, and they were the majority of our party, the slope seemed frighteningly steep and exposed. As usual, some revelled in the challenge and were as surefooted as chamois. But others were very, very frightened.

I coaxed my crowd up to the final and steepest gut, and here we came to a halt. One girl in particular – I can't now remember whether it was the same one who overcame her fear so bravely in the river-crossing practice – was utterly terrified. Nine tenths of her was shrieking "I can't do it – I'll be killed – I must get down to flat ground." But the final tenth, more quietly but with equal insistence, was saying "Oh, but how very much I want to reach the lake where the old people traded pounamu, and take part in the ritual for which I've come so far and already braved such difficulties."

I am not good at trying to persuade people to do something they don't want to do, and fortunately I didn't need to. Once again the peers of the petrified one did the job perfectly, not forcing her against her fears, but talking her through them. Eventually I could see the part that wanted to go on gaining ascendancy, so I suggested to her that I could lead her up on a tight rope, no more than three feet between us, and that she could not then fall. With an abruptness that scarcely left me time to tie the knots she said "Yes, but we must go NOW before I change my mind."

I led off at a brisk pace, but not brisk enough for her. "Faster, faster" she begged. Looking back at her I saw her eyes were tightly closed as she stumbled determinedly in my footprints. I have always believed that bravery is to be measured not by objective dangers tackled but by subjective fears overcome. As with my sister Alison on the Franz Josef Glacier years earlier – she was hysterically afraid before, then conquered her fears and leapt over, a wide deep crevasse – I was lost in admiration for this young lass – or would have been had she given me time.

We shot over the top of the pass like two pocket rockets. She opened her eyes. There below us lay the lake, a green gem nestled in tawny tussock. With tears in her eyes she turned and hugged me her thanks.

Some of the rest of my twelve had followed us up. I left her in their care and went back down to rope and bring up the nervous remainder, fortunately none so nervous as to need to climb with their eyes closed. With the sun still shining, though clouds were thickening in the west, we walked around the lake towards the group gathered by the outlet at the western end. When we were halfway there helicopters whirled up behind and then over us in a crescendo of clatter, to land in a flurry on the foreshore.

We gazed aghast as the choppers disgorged their passengers. Most seemed incredibly old to our eyes. Moreover they had evidently boarded in the nor'west heat of Christchurch, for most were very inadequately dressed. Peter's and Mac's mother, Mrs. Ruka, took first prize in this respect, having on only a thin cotton summer frock. But I doubt any of them felt the cold. Their eyes glowed with rapture as they looked around them, and continued to glow as a long and very impressive ritual unfolded.

I can't remember the details now, nor did I understand the karakia then. But I was intrigued, as always, by the seamless weaving together of invocations to my old god, Yahweh/Jehovah, and to their old gods, especially Tāne. Hopefully there were also karakia to Tāwhiri, for as the ritual drama passed the one and then the two-hour mark the meteorological drama was proceeding apace. First the sun disappeared as cloud rolled in above us. Then the wind strengthened and grew colder, seeking out gaps in our clothing and racing razor-like round our bare legs. Then drizzle set in. The ritual was already sending shivers down our spines, and now the weather was doing the same.

Early on I decided I was responsible only for my twelve, and was reasonably confident of getting them down safely in any weather. But Barry Law could not be so cavalier. Not only had he over-all responsibility for the safety of the party, but also his professional integrity and reputation was at stake. He told me afterwards that as the storm drew nearer, while the end of the ritual seemed not to, he began to imagine what might happen if the cloud closed right down and the helicopters couldn't whisk the scantily-clad kaumātua to safety. If we had to herd a frail and failing party across to and down from the pass it was highly likely that some would pass away, especially Mrs. Ruka. So he sidled up to her and asked her to put on his jacket. She emerged briefly from her absorption in the ritual. "Why would I want to do that?" she asked, surprised. "Because otherwise you might die of hypothermia," replied Barry. She considered this for no more than a moment. "No problem," she informed him cheerfully. "If the tūpuna want me to join them now I'll be very happy. I can think of no better time."

Barry's imaginings then went a step further. He was being cross-examined at the coroner's inquest into the death of Mrs. Ruka on Browning Pass. "Now tell me Mr. Law, the deceased was wearing only a thin cotton dress in deteriorating weather at 4,000ft. in the mountains?" "Yes, your honour." "And you were the person responsible for the physical safety of the party?" "Yes, your honour." "Why then did you not get Mrs. Ruka to put on more clothing?" "I tried to, your honour." "And what was her response?" "She said she was happy to die there and join her ancestors." "I see Mr. Law. And what is your occupation? – let me see – you are a lecturer in outdoor education and mountain safety at Teachers' College?" "Yes, your honour." "I see, Mr. Law!"

We actually made several attempts to hurry the ritual along, Barry most assiduously of all. But as that was akin to trying to turn aside a typhoon by waving our arms we were not successful. Undoubtedly, in the minds of the Māori tohunga and kaumātua, the consequences of incomplete ritual were far worse than anything the weather could inflict, and in any case complete and correct ritual would protect us from weather as well. And maybe they were right. As drizzle morphed into sleeting rain, and the cloud level lowered to a few hundred feet above us, the ritual was finally completed, and at the last possible minute the helicopters took off with their underclad clients.

There remained only 48 mountain novices to be conducted back to and down the pass by five mountaineers, and in the relief at seeing the choppers disappear this seemed an easy task. And so it proved. Though sleet turned to snow as we trudged back round the lake, the wind was at our backs, and our troops were now battle-hardened and, of course, ritually inspired and protected. In reasonably short order, and in remarkably good order, our flocks were back in their folds, or, as we would call them, tents, and we were back in the smoky hut cooking meals and distributing them to hungry mouths. It had been quite a day.

Kōrero

We retreated down valley on subsequent days and arrived safely back at our temporary marae at Lake Coleridge. Here we acted out a final drama. It seems Māori culture anticipated long ago the modern custom of debriefing after important activities. So, after the hygienic youngsters had raced each other to the showers and poured amused scorn on unhygienic Uncle Pooh for not joining them, we gathered for korero (discussion). What ensued was mingled anguish and delight.

The anguish was due to a request to us physical safety 'experts' to give our opinion of the adventure, a request which included a warm invitation to criticize anything we had been unhappy about. In my experience there is something about a Māori gathering which encourages frankness, and we were frank. While stressing our admiration for all the positives of the experience, we also poured out all our frustration about ways in which ritual requirements had at times conflicted with mountain safety requirements. And we vented our anger at the way in which the young girls who had inadvertently breached tapu had been, we felt, humiliated. No problem, you might think – except the line of us venting this frustration and anger were all essentially Pākehā, even brown-skinned Airini, while those on whom we were venting it were all Māori .

It felt absolutely terrible – here we go again, Pākehā pouring scorn on Māori ways, and we were in tears not only of rage but also of shame and embarrassment. But wonderful are the ways of Tāngata Whenua (people of the land). If you did think, three sentences ago, "No problem," you were right. As soon as the korero was over I rushed over to Peter and Makere and said, again in tears, how sorry I was that we had felt impelled to be so critical. They looked at me in amazement, then gave me a big hug. "Brother," they said, "that is the purpose of this kōrero – to bring all such feelings into the open so we can honour them and deal with them as necessary. We would be upset if we had discovered later that you had these feelings and did not tell us; that would be terrible. That you have expressed them is wonderful." They re-hugged me warmly, and I felt warm and happy again.

The delight was hearing the views of the youthful participants, though this delight was tempered by sorrow that their past had so often been so devoid of self-esteem and love. One after another they came forward and told us how much the experience had meant to them, how they felt stronger, more confident, more able to relate lovingly and supportively to others. We felt humbled at how warmly they expressed their gratitude to us for giving them this experience, and a glow, not of pride but of pleasure, that we had done so. Again tears flowed freely, but this time mainly happy tears. However, when one small lad said simply "This is the first time I have felt loved", the happiness that he now had was mingled with horror that he never had before.

Equally moving was the foster mother of another youngster, Ricky. Ricky had been the most helpful of all of them, always eager to do all he could to assist us. One of our campsites was on a terrace which was beautifully sheltered by stands of mānuka from wind and rain, but high above the nearest water. It was Ricky who, despite the rain, eagerly volunteered to descend to a stream and carry full buckets back up the long steep slope. To our amazement when we met his foster mother at the kōrero we discovered she had been at her wits' end in trying to cope with a surly and uncooperative Ricky. When we told her how helpful and delightful he had been she was amazed and delighted, and after he had said his piece she asked if she could say something. "I don't know what you people have got," she said, close to tears, "but I want some of it." I enquired about him a few years later and he was still the new Ricky. I can't claim to know for certain, but I feel certain that he will remain so, and that the change in most if not all the others will likewise have proved enduring.

Controversy

Because of this, and because my field is religious studies not history, I am unconcerned about the controversy that swirls about Peter Ruka. Before the North Island invaders, Ngāi Tahu, took over Te Waka a Māui (South Island) there were two earlier iwi (tribes) here, Waitaha and Ngāti Māmoe. Peter says that he and his brother Mac were the recipients, via their grandfather, of ancient Waitaha lore. Subsequent to the greenstone trail adventures Peter committed this lore to writing, publishing a book entitled *Song of Waitaha; The histories of a nation.*[2] The book explains how Waitaha were peaceful people, not warriors like Ngāi Tahu and other North Island iwi; and that they were very environmentally responsible.

Quite a number of South Island Māori with whakapapa (genealogical) links to Waitaha now look to Peter as their tohunga, and became deeply involved in attempts to establish Waitaha as a separate iwi, with the right to be consulted on environmental and tapu issues in this island. Ngāi Tahu vigorously contested this, claiming Waitaha and Ngāti Māmoe have both been assimilated into Ngāi Tahu by intermarriage, and should not be considered separate from that iwi. I think they also question the authenticity of Peter's version of Waitaha history and lore.

I was aware of considerable tension between Peter's Waitaha and Ngāi Tahu during and after my involvement on the trail. But as I considered it none of my business, and because I had seen first hand what a beneficial effect the trails experiences had had on many, I never bothered to go into the matter myself. Undeterred by the controversy and opposition, Peter then published a second book, *Whispers of Waitaha*,[3] lore and ritual and environmental wisdom told him by a group of Waitaha kuia (women elders). I was involved in a minor way with both books, at Peter's request suggesting improvements to clarity and style of his English, and proof-reading.

The second book, especially, I found very interesting and moving – but also puzzling. To me it is a powerful appeal for greater care of Papatūānuku presented as the kaupapa of the ancient Waitaha matriarchy. The puzzling aspect is the extent to which modern scientific and ecological theories are woven into the grandmothers' story. Clearly there are two conclusions which could be drawn from this. One is that the Waitaha matriarchy anticipated, in broad outline but very strikingly, modern ecological wisdom. The other is that Peter's informants, or Peter, have woven this material into ancient material. If the latter is the case then the kuia, or Peter, or both, are to be congratulated on a brilliant interweaving of ancient and modern into a moving environmental plea which would, in my view, have a very beneficial effect on readers' attitudes to our planet, especially readers who identify themselves with Waitaha.

Here is where my religious studies approach comes to the fore. Religions are never static affairs, but are always adjusting to changes in beliefs and customs both in their own developing cultures and in cultures they conquer or are conquered by. The way Vedic religion was influenced by pre-Aryan beliefs and practices and developed into Hinduism (see ch. 10) is but one example amongst many. And in New Zealand, Māori religion, in desperate straits as Europeans and Christianity invaded their land and their culture, changed in a series of brilliant Māorifications of Christianity culminating, in my view, in Te Matarohanga's Io doctrine discussed in chapter 18. So if Peter's grandfather and grandmothers, and/or Peter himself, are continuing this adaptation, consciously or unconsciously, and if this adaptation makes people, Māori and Pākehā, more caring of our environment, I happily and heartily applaud. For, from a religious studies perspective, though not, I gather, from an historian's, it is brilliantly done.

20. Feminism

It is fitting that I conclude the account of my Religious Studies career by discussing the influence that feminism belatedly had on me. This influence extends into all aspects of my life, not just my personal journey and my attitude to religions. But it is certainly powerful there. And it led to my departure from the Religious Studies scene being a stormy and unhappy one.

During my teaching about Hinduism, as a counter to largely negative New Zealand attitudes to Hinduism and to India, I deliberately tried to give a favourable view. I was aware of ways in which Hinduism was used by the brahmin and kshatriya classes – priestly and ruling – to bolster their authority and keep the lower classes 'in their place'. In particular, beliefs about rebirth and karma were often blatantly used in this way, and, as I've noted, Gandhi was appalled by this and fought mightily against it. But even this I skated over lightly in my early teaching. And I was not even properly aware of the equally appalling ways in which Hinduism, in common with most religions, oppresses and devalues women.

Truth to tell, though I tell it wincing with shame, I was uncritically presenting a male version of Hinduism, and doing it in male language. The textbook we used at Stage I was titled *Man's Religions*, and for quite a while none of us staff members, all male, thought much about this. Worse, we were ourselves guilty of similar male bias and male language, using "man" for "human", "he" as a unisex pronoun, and so on – the full catastrophe, as a feminist might say.

Then, thank goodness, came a group of really fabulous feisty women Stage III and M.A. students. Very gently, considering the outrage they must have been feeling, but also very firmly, they began to straighten us out. I quickly realized how bad for women, and demeaning of them, my previous habit had been, and I began strenuously to try to mend my ways. Though it felt clumsy and long-winded at first I tried hard always to use "human" not "man" as a generic term, and to say and write "she or he" and "her or his" whenever a plural neuter pronoun, "they" or "their", was not appropriate. For I do believe that the language we use is very influential. And of course in time it came easily and naturally to me.

I also began to include in lectures, in reading suggestions, and in discussions, at all stages, material relevant to women. It was little and late, but a start. Finally, but not till 1984, we introduced a course entitled "Women and Religion" at Stage III. The very title, and a specific course concentrating on women, was an indication of how far we had to go, for of course ideally all courses at all levels should be dealing equally with women and men. Moreover there was something very bizarre, very wrong really, about an all male staff running such a course. But, as with feminist issues generally, there needed to be a period of deliberate concentration on women in religion to redress the previously overwhelming imbalance the other way. And better that we male staff did this than no one. Our feisty women students, some of them now tutoring for us and having increasing influence on the department, agreed with us on this, and were of great assistance both in alerting us to useful material and in encouraging us to have a go.

But it all made me very aware of the gender imbalance in our department – well, not even an imbalance really, since all our permanent staff members were men and there were no women to balance us. And just at this time Ann and I decided that I should retire early.

This was for other, and complex, reasons. Another study leave was due in a year or two. We were thinking of going to an African country to study Hinduism amongst Indians there. But, despite having loved my research in Fiji, I realized I no longer wanted to pry into other people's religious lives. And things started to snowball. Ray, Ann's mother, was not well, and to leave her for ten months would be neither easy nor admirable. I was increasingly unhappy about setting myself up as judge when grading students, and about posing as an expert in Hinduism since the more I learnt about it the more I realized how little I knew. And were I to take study leave I would be morally bound to stay on doing these things for several years after.

I like to say that at this juncture Bert Brownlie, the Vice Chancellor, came to me and said "Jim, if the university buys you a yacht will you take early retirement now?" And though he didn't do that, and didn't even want me to go, he had persuaded Council to offer very generous early retirement provisions in order to persuade some of us ageing staff to move on to make place for new younger staff. This included a generous 'golden handshake', but in terms of continuing regular income it meant we would drop to a third of what we were then earning. Though the boys had all finished school, and our financial commitments were therefore dwindling, I was at first nervous about what seemed to me a drastic drop.

But Ann came to the rescue again. Having seen how little people lived on in India she regarded the drop as an exciting challenge not a daunting one, and convinced me we would manage easily. So we accepted the offer, used the golden handshake to help us buy our yacht, had plenty of time to enjoy her, and adjusted to the lower income with no trouble at all. The university planned to save more than the golden handshake by paying my younger successor less than it had been paying me, so it was a win-win situation, but still very fortunate for us.

I immediately saw in my retirement a chance to appoint a woman in my place. Feminist Studies had recently been started at Canterbury, and overseas feminist scholars were making an impact on Religious Studies. The time was certainly ripe. In consultation with Feminist Studies lecturers we inserted an additional clause in the advertisement for a replacement for me. The advertisement asked for applicants for the position of lecturer in Religious Studies specializing in Hinduism, and added something like "preference will be given to candidates with expertise in the feminist study of religion".

I was delighted, for it seemed to me this ensured the appointment of a woman. Given the overwhelming male dominance not only of Canterbury University staff, but also of academics everywhere, and of academic books and articles, it seemed to me out of the question to appoint a man to teach the feminist study of religion. I also felt very strongly that the subject and the department needed a woman's perspective, and that not even the most sympathetic male could provide this. I felt so strongly about it that when it was arranged that I give a final paper to our Religious Studies Society I made it an impassioned and, I thought, unanswerable argument to support this. It sparked little discussion and no dissent, so I naively thought the day was won.

I detail this to explain why I felt so angry and betrayed by what followed. With hindsight I now feel less angry but still very sad. For male university staff at that time (1988/9), it could be said my colleagues had made a real effort and gone a long way to trying to ensure that a woman was appointed. And we actually offered the post initially to an English woman who had impeccable credentials in Hinduism, and interest in and sympathy for a feminist approach to Religious Studies. The decision to do so was unanimous.

But the best-laid plans of mice and men gang aft agley. We received a very apologetic and moving letter from this woman, saying that when the realization hit home that she would have to leave England and family and friends she found she couldn't do it. So – back to square one. And this was when the shit hit the fan. For the choice narrowed down to that between a young female scholar with good references, a good suggested outline for Hinduism courses, and good credentials in feminist study of religion, but whose main area of interest till then had been Tibetan Buddhism; and a more experienced male scholar with excellent credentials in Hinduism, including years of study and research in India, excellent linguistic credentials in Sanskrit and Hindi, good references regarding teaching and rapport with students – but, a man.

Naïvely, I was sure the clause giving preference to expertise in the feminist study of religion would make the choice of the woman a foregone conclusion. But not only was I outvoted three to one, I also felt shifty and unfair tactics were used, including a dodgy appeal to the Vice Chancellor to mediate – he had no expertise with which to judge between the candidates – and a refusal to let our women M.A. students and tutors have any part in our discussions, while admitting a lengthy criticism of the woman candidate's expertise in Tibetan Buddhism from a male M.A. student. I was appalled and outraged – perhaps unfairly as well as naively – and when the vote was taken burst from the meeting in blinding tears and wandered the grounds in despair, hating the thought of having to meet with and deal with my colleagues and erstwhile friends again.

So ended my Religious Studies career, but not my personal journey.

PART IV
Physical Monism

21. Nietzsche and Existentialism

During the final period of his ministry at Knox Church, Christchurch, Dad developed a slight slurring of speech, at first noticeable only to himself, then to us. This may have been one of the things that prompted him to move to the rural parish of Sefton, a sort of semi-retirement. The condition worsened and he consulted a doctor, who was not only an old friend but also a senior member of Knox congregation. The doctor arranged tests and discovered Dad had bulbar sclerosis, an untreatable condition that was eroding the insulation on his motor nerves and would cause his early death.

Dad had told the doctor to be frank with him whatever the outcome as he had a responsibility to his session and congregation to tell them immediately if he had to resign. Unbelievably the doctor didn't do this even though, knowing Dad so well, he must have known that both by character and by faith Dad was far better placed than most to deal with knowledge of his imminent death. Instead he rang my sister Margaret to get my phone number, presumably because I was Dad's oldest son.

To any other than a male chauvinist, my sister Alison, Dad's oldest child, would have been more appropriate for what followed. But what followed was in any case wholly inappropriate. "Oh," said Margaret, "is it bad news?" "I'm afraid so," the doctor replied, "and I need to speak to Jim." If I remember rightly he then rang and asked me to come to see him, though the interview may have been over the phone. He told me the news and – even more unbelievably – asked me to tell Mum but not Dad! Of course I didn't even consider doing this, but as it was two days before Christmas Margaret and I decided to wait till after Christmas to break the news. I then went to Sefton, went to the manse study, and told my father he was dying, not the most pleasant task I have undertaken. He, of course, immediately told Mum, then informed his session. He kept going as long as he could, and then a little longer – Margaret remembers that when he took his last service at Sefton he had to get Mum to read his sermon.

So he retired from his ministry, and he and Mum moved into a small house in Christchurch, where he slowly wasted away. His speech went first, but for a while he could still read and write. We could converse with him by speaking and he with us by writing in an increasingly shaky hand. Don Glenny, a lovely Presbyterian minister, one of many who went into the ministry inspired by Dad, said this was like having a conversation with an extremely intelligent notebook. But over a year or so that ability, and all others, eroded away as the disease wreaked havoc with the ability of his nerves to conduct signals from the brain to the rest of the body. Swallowing became difficult, breathing became difficult, movement of any sort became difficult.

Mum looked after him at home as long as possible, and he remained brave and cheerful. Then came the day, in 1969, when Sefton parish opened its new manse. Despite it being a cold wet day Dad was determined to go. He caught a cold, it turned to pneumonia so weakened was his body, and he was rushed into Princess Margaret Hospital where, a day or so later, he died.

While this was probably preferable to continuing to waste slowly away before our eyes, his timing was not ideal. My sister Hilary and her husband Ian, with their tiny baby Jamie, were living in Haast, a small remote town in South Westland. Margaret, with also tiny Kate and Sarah, was staying with them for a few days prior to bringing Hilary back to see Dad. When they got the news that Dad had died they all rushed back over Haast Pass through torrential rain, weeping bitterly. Hilary, pregnant with Jo, lay on the back seat vomiting as well as weeping.

My brother John was hastening back from Boston to see Dad, and heard the news of his death while in transit in Rome airport. He could have been home earlier, but Dad had told him not to forgo on his account a visit to Scotland en route. He says now: "In retrospect I am probably glad because my memories of Dad are all of a hale and hearty man". My brother Hugh was ski-mountaineering at the head of the Murchison Glacier and heard the news via the hut radio, too late to get back for the funeral. Despite this, he much later wrote: "Funnily enough I have an image locked in some part of my brain of Dad being carried on a stretcher into Princess Margaret Hospital, and raising an arm to you and Mum while somehow conveying to you 'Don't be too alarmed, I've had a very good innings'." Dad would be proud of you, Hugh – never let the facts get in the way of a good story.

Meanwhile, back in Christchurch, Mum and Ali and I took turns to sit by Dad's hospital bed, talking to him when he was conscious, listening in anguish to his shallow breathing through an oxygen mask when he was not. It was ghastly, but mercifully didn't last long. I was sitting sorrowfully beside him on the evening of the third day, but was due to give a lecture at

8 pm. Mum came back and we sat silently together for a while. It was clear Dad wouldn't last much longer. So what was my duty, dutiful Presbyterian son as I was? To ring and say I couldn't give the lecture because my father was dying, so that I could stay and support Mum and be with Dad at the end? Or to fulfill my commitment and go and give the lecture? I did the latter.

And what was the lecture titled? "Nietzsche and the Death of God". Numb with grief I managed somehow to stumble through it. At least my lugubrious tones and deadened voice were appropriate to the topic. When I got back to the hospital Dad had died.

Even now, through tears as I write, I don't regret this. Dad was unconscious and probably didn't know if I was there or not, and had he been able to know the situation he would undoubtedly have urged me to go, just as he had urged John to go to Scotland. I feel sad I was not there to share the grief of the final moment with Mum, but she also would have urged me to go, and maybe Alison arrived to be with her as Dad died. And surely this is a suitably macabre introduction to a chapter dealing with Nietzsche and the existentialists for all of whom death, and the void it seems to be, was central.

Nietzsche

Friedrich Nietzsche, a German philosopher born in 1844, suffered a severe mental breakdown in 1889, the cause and nature of which is still debated, and died, probably of brain cancer, in 1900. Like Hume in Scotland before him he bravely spoke out against the then near-universal European belief in the Christian God. But whereas Hume with gentle wit and irony, and meticulous arguments, suggested only that belief in God was not rationally justifiable, Nietzsche poured furious scorn on the whole of Christianity, beliefs and attitudes alike.

His most famous saying is "God is dead. And we have killed him."[1] Of course, like me, he didn't believe there had been a living Christian God who now was dead, but rather that belief in such a god was no longer possible in the light of modern scientific understanding. He acknowledged the enormity of this loss of belief, and evoked chillingly how it left humanity adrift in a vast and indifferent universe. "Since Copernicus, mankind has been rolling from the centre towards x."[2] Our beliefs about our place in the scheme of things had shifted from being the apex of creation and the centre of a creator's concern – "What is man that thou art mindful of him? ... thou hast made him little less than God"[3] – to a brief speck of conscious life on a tiny planet of an insignificant star. And he couldn't believe humans hadn't realized the enormity of this shift, but were going on as if nothing had changed. He writes of a great shadow spreading over Europe, darkening the sun, which his contemporaries had not yet even noticed.

But far from bemoaning this loss of belief he gloried in it. For he despised Christianity and its "slave mentality", its doctrine of the hopeless sinfulness of humans and its urging that we grovel before an angry god in attempts to avert his wrath. "That 'holy' ends are lacking in Christianity is my objection to its means. Only bad ends: the poisoning, slandering, denying of life, contempt for the body, the denigration and self-violation of man through the concept of sin."[4] And: "With that I have done and pronounce my judgement. I condemn Christianity, I bring against the Christian Church the most terrible charge any prosecutor has ever uttered. To me it is the extremest thinkable form of corruption … [It] has left nothing untouched by its depravity, it has made of every value a disvalue, of every truth a lie, of every kind of integrity a vileness of soul."[5]

As I mentioned in the chapter on Māori religion, he compared Christian attitudes to their God unfavourably with those of the ancient Greeks to their gods. "What … the Greeks would despise such a thing."[6] And he writes: "What sets us apart is not that we recognize no God … but that we find that which has been reverenced as God not 'godlike' but pitiable, absurd, harmful, not merely an error but a crime against life … we deny God as God … If this God of the Christians were proved to us to exist, we should know even less how to believe in him."[7] Elsewhere he writes that we reject God now not merely intellectually but as a matter of taste.

As for Christian morality and its judgemental tone, he pours equal scorn on that. "Reality shows us an enchanting wealth of types, the luxuriance of a prodigal play and change of forms: and does some pitiful journeyman moralist say at the sight of it: 'No! man ought to be different'? … He even knows how man ought to be, this bigoted wretch; he paints himself on the wall and says 'ecce homo' [behold the man]! …We others, we immoralists, have on the contrary opened wide our hearts to every kind of understanding, comprehension, approval. We do not readily deny, we seek our honour in affirming."[8]

Now, free from these false and demeaning beliefs and attitudes, we humans can with courage and dignity face up to our brief limited existence and create our own meaning and morals. In his clipped and often cryptic sayings, which infuriate many sober philosophers but which I found very stimulating, he attempted to rebuild morals on a non-supernatural basis. I certainly didn't agree with all his suggestions. Some of them are very harsh on the weak and feeble, and, much later, some were taken up by Hitler and his thugs to justify extermination of handicapped people and Jews. But they were able to do this partly because after Nietzsche's death his sister reworked his unpublished writings to support her own anti-semitism and nationalism, to both of which Nietzsche himself was strongly and explicitly opposed.[9]

But I did respond enthusiastically to his sustained attempt to find a framework for living, and for making moral decisions, based on our knowledge of the natural world rather than on beliefs about, and supposed commandments from, supernatural beings. By the time I came on Nietzsche, included a lecture on him for a while in one of our Stage I courses, and gave my 'Death of God' lecture on the eve of the death of Dad, I too was on this quest. And many of Nietzsche's pithy positive suggestions, as well as his equally pithy negative sayings about Christianity, struck a resounding echo in me.

My 'Nietzsche period' was brief and long ago, and my memory of the details of what he wrote and how it influenced me is hazy. But I do remember with gratitude how supportive it was for me at the time to read someone so passionate about basing one's life on a physical view of the universe, and so stimulating in expressing how necessary he felt this was. And I agreed, and agree now, with his basic suggestion about how to do it. We are on our own in this vast universe, and insignificant in its vastness. We have no supernatural guide and helper. We are born to die. Unless we face up to this reality, and ourselves create some purpose and value for our lives, we must despair. This is how I felt then, and still feel very strongly now.

However, I also feel I differ from Nietzsche in my attitude to this necessity. There is in Nietzsche's writing not only a rather shrill but also a rather desperate and unhappy note, as if he finds the reality he is trying to face up to rather dark and daunting. Bravely and brilliantly he tries to make the best of a bad job, but there seems not much joy in it for him, rather a grim determination. I am fortunate to have a happier nature than him, and am able to regard Nietzsche's challenge not as a fearsome fate but as an exciting and liberating opportunity.

Existentialism

Now Nietzsche was not an existentialist – he was simply himself, part of no movement, largely ignored or vilified during his lifetime, and dying embittered because of this. But he is often cited as a forerunner of existentialism, and I think rightly so. For the thing that unites the disparate group of writers called existentialists is that, like Nietzsche, they insisted we face up to what they believed was the real nature of our existence – a moment of self-awareness between the boundaries of birth and death – and ourselves make of it something of value.

Existentialism was a philosophical movement mainly located on the continent of Europe – France and Germany in particular. It was despised and ridiculed by English-speaking philosophers in whose tradition I had been trained, and whose tradition the philosophy side of our department followed. One such philosopher – Sydney Hook – characterised existentialism as a philosophy of the absurd, which appealed to people who were terribly excited by ideas but resented the discipline necessary to organize them.

I had some sympathy with this view. Existentialist writers are often frustratingly obtuse and long-winded, hinting at and circling round ideas and attitudes rather than stating them clearly and concisely. I also regard existentialism as a physically based alternative to religion, rather than as philosophy as I understand the subject (rigorous rational examination of beliefs and claims to knowledge). But religion was my subject by then and, as I still taught some philosophy as well, I straddled the divide between the two subjects, into which divide existentialism seemed to have fallen without trace in many philosophy departments. So, with my usual mixture of trepidation and determination, I offered to run an M.A. course on existentialism.

I therefore ploughed through the dense soil of existentialist writings, in particular those of the German philosopher Martin Heidegger,[10] and the French author Jean-Paul Sartre.[11] What I will now tell you is what I took out of them, not necessarily what they intended me to. Both centre their thoughts and feelings on – wait for it – nothingness. Indeed, the title of the relevant book by Sartre is, in English translation, *Being and Nothingness.*

How can you talk or write about nothingness? Well you can't, really. What the existentialists try to do is make us feel nothingness. Sartre has a simple but for me quite effective way of doing this, albeit at a superficial level. He tells how he goes into a café having arranged to meet there his friend Pierre. The café is crowded, replete with being, you might say: people, food, talk, music. But Pierre is not there, and, because Sartre expected him to be, his overwhelming impression is not of what is there but of what is not – of the absence of Pierre, the nothingness in the place where Pierre ought to be.

Apply this now to the boundaries of my individual life and consciousness, my individual 'being'. It began with birth, a mysterious happening over which I had no control, and which was the beginning of me rather than a happening to me. And it will end in death, an even darker mystery to come, and now at every moment the possibility not of an event which will happen to me, but the cessation of me (unless, of course, one believes in life after death, which Sartre and Heidegger did not, and as I do not). The world, and humans in it, existed before I was born and will exist after I die. So, like Sartre's café full of being but empty of Pierre, objectively speaking the world is full of being before my birth and after my death. But subjectively speaking, that is seen or felt while I concentrate on me, as Sartre was concentrating on Pierre, before my birth and after my death there is, for me, of me, only absence, nothingness, a void.

I spend quite a bit of time thinking about this. It is one of my forms of, or substitutes for, meditation as practised by Buddhists and Hindus. And I find it chilling, uncanny, awesome, humbling, exciting, inspiring – I could add adjectives forever and never fully express the impact it has on me.

Sartre and Heidegger both, in differing ways, think that it is above all the anxiety we feel when contemplating death that causes many of us not to spend too much time contemplating it in such a harsh light. It arouses in us a deep anxiety about life, a desperate feeling of having no control over our lives, which is more than we can handle. So either we refuse to face up to it at all, and direct our basic anxiety onto minor everyday things – food, relationships, career – over which we seem to have some control; or we seek to escape from this harsh reality by taking refuge in religious systems and beliefs which claim that death is not the end. Either way, they say, we are then living "inauthentically" (Heidegger's term) or "in bad faith" (Sartre).

But their message and intention is not negative. They go on to urge that we can and should live authentically, in good faith. And it is nothingness, the void, which is the motivation. It is this brief and threatened nature of our lives which, if faced firmly, can lead us to treasure them more intensely, and become more determined to make the most of them. For though the beginning and end of my life are essentially beyond my control, suicide excepted, what I do during my life, and above all my attitude to my life, seem within my control at least to some extent. And when I acknowledge fully to myself that death is the end, and as a result value every moment of my life, and pack as much into it as possible, then I am living authentically. Take a bow, Māui.

Stated so baldly and briefly this might seem too obvious to need saying, even trite. What the existentialist writers do is expend considerable energy and an inordinate number of words trying to get us to feel the truth of this simple analysis in the marrow of our bones and in every moment of every day. As I made clear earlier, especially in my discussion of Māui, I already felt it intensely and constantly, and had already drawn similar conclusions. So it is small wonder that, despite my frustration at their wordiness, I responded very favourably to the existentialists. Their influence on me was that of pleasure and support from finding others who had to some extent the same approach to life.

I say to some extent. As with Nietzsche, in much existentialist writing I detect a note of defiant desperation which, fortunately, I do not share, despite the chill that contemplation of cessation often sends down my spine. Māui and existentialists share the belief that facing up to death should motivate us to live more fully. But existentialists are rather grim about it, whereas Māui is excited, even delighted. Temperamentally I am with Māui on this.

Pink Floyd

Having warmed to existentialist thought because I felt it partly mirrored my own, no wonder I love Pink Floyd. Their lyrics are often what I would call morbidly existential as distinct from me who am (mostly) optimistically existential. And we need the morbid side, rubbing our noses in the inevitability of old age and death, before we can progress to the positive side. Read now these lines; better still get the records and listen to them:

And you run and you run to catch up with the sun
But it's sinking,
Racing around to come up behind you again.
The sun is the same in a relative way
But you're older,
Shorter of breath and one day closer to death.[12]

And:

The memories of a man in his old age
Are the deeds of a man in his prime.
You shuffle in the gloom of a sickroom,
And talk to yourself as you die.
For life is a short warm moment,
And death is a long cold rest.

You get your chance to try in the twinkling of an eye,
Eighty years with luck or even less.[13]

Most chilling to me, because so subtly evoking the silence of space surrounding our tiny circle of sound, is:

Icy winter wind begone, this is not your domain.
In the sky a bird was heard to cry.
Misty morning whisperings and gentle stirring sound
Belies the deathly silence that lies all around.[14]

22. Mountaineering

Paul Tillich, a theologian concerned with making the Christian faith relevant to our modern age, defined faith not in terms of what is believed, but in terms of intensity of belief and commitment. He suggests that what makes a faith religious is that it is centred on our ultimate concern, that which is most important to us, absorbs all or most of our time and energy.[1] And he has a point. It is in this sense that we say "rugby is the religion of many New Zealand men". We also say of people that they pursue goals with religious intensity, even when the goals are natural not supernatural.

This clarifies one of the many ways mountaineering has influenced my journey. For, especially in the first half of my life, mountaineering came close to being my religion, my ultimate concern. It was because of this that I thought that Yahweh wanted me to give it up. As noted in chapter 2, for several years I thought about and planned and prepared for our summer trips all year. In addition, then and for many years thereafter, I went into the mountains at every available opportunity. My excitement, both in anticipation and when on trips, was intense indeed. I can relive still my feelings when listening to Ed Hillary talking to the Calcutta Mountaineering Association en route to my first Himalayan expedition. As he showed slides of, and described, the peaks we were to attempt, I almost leapt out of my skin as the realization hit home that I was about to be let loose on Himalayan peaks, the Mecca of mountaineers.

This excitement naturally intensified another way mountaineering has enriched my journey. Mountaineering immersed me wholeheartedly in some of the most awesome and beautiful aspects of nature. This is not unique to mountaineers. Humans have always been deeply moved by mountains, indeed have often peopled their peaks with gods and goddesses and spirits. This is partly because of their aesthetic appeal. They have startling purity of line and form, austere but dramatic combinations of colour, and vibrate with the exquisite fragility of mountain flowers. Not being a poet I can't evoke this for you, but it is an enormously important part of everyone's appreciation of mountains. And it lies as a constant backdrop to a mountaineer's appreciation. Mountains gladden the eye and uplift the heart with beauty.

But there is more to it than this. For mountains, towering so high above us, arouse also awe, a mingling of fascination and fear. Fascination, because they seem able to lift us out of petty self-centred concerns; but also fear, because however much we clothe them in myth and story they are in reality indifferent to us and our concerns, and can crush us psychologically and destroy us physically. Small wonder that mountains arouse such deep feelings in most of us, and that poets and religious thinkers have so often used the imagery of mountains to express their thoughts and feelings.

All this – the non-mountaineers' reactions – is felt with greater intensity by mountaineers. If mountains are beautiful and awe-inspiring from below, then words almost fail when high amongst them. The great New Zealand mountain guide Peter Graham says of the view from Aoraki/Mt Cook[2] on his first ascent "magnificent, almost beyond description".[3] As for beauty, Freda du Faur, the first woman to ascend Aoraki, evokes it vividly: "...as the setting sun's rays pierced through the thin mist there began a series of the most wonderful colour effects ... We saw the distant mountains through a luminous curtain of softest transparency ... outlined against pale green evening sky rose peak after peak vivid with an edge of purest gold; the nearer cones were touched with violet and rose, while over Baker's Saddle drifted soft little clouds of crimson and gold, which shattered themselves into rainbow mist and vanished ... The changes of colour were so quick it was impossible to follow them – they were here and gone in a breath."[4]

Freda also comments on the awe high peaks inspire: "...this call of the mountains, sometimes friendly and of good cheer; but often eerie, wild, and full of melancholy warning."[5] And even Tom Fyfe, the iron man who led the first ascent of Aoraki, was impressed with "an almost overpowering sense of desolation and solitude".[6]

Mountaineers have these reactions more intensely because for us it is not sufficient just to look from below. From the moment Freda saw the snow-clad alps "I worshipped their beauty and was filled with a passionate longing to touch those shining snows, to climb to their heights of silence and solitude, and feel myself one with the mighty forces around me."[7]

I also was filled with this passionate longing, and from a very early age. And I too, though at a less articulate level than Freda, felt at one with the mighty physical forces around me when in the mountains. So when I encountered the spiritual monism of the Upanishads and Shankara, I had already, through mountaineering, an emotional base for the experience of unity with all. That this base had a physical not a metaphysical origin perhaps made inevitable, and certainly assisted, my eventual transition from spiritual to physical monism.

Responding to the challenge of climbing to mountain heights of silence and solitude had other benefits for me also. Life itself is a long series of challenges: to make a success of school, marriage, bringing up children, career. All these challenges are extremely complex, and not only the rules of the game but also the criteria of success or failure are slippery and obscure. The basic mountain challenge, by contrast, is much simpler. I know at the time whether I have succeeded or failed, for a peak has a definite and often beautifully sharp summit. And even if I fail, I know more clearly and immediately whether I have tried as hard as possible, for the effort required is of relatively short duration, and the mind can encompass it all and assess it. In the challenges of everyday life success, or even assessment of our efforts, is a lifetime's process.

But though it is comparatively simple, there are several strands even to the mountain challenge. The first, and simplest, is the challenge of reaching the summit. Like many things in mountaineering one can't argue for or against this desire to top a peak. Some feel it, others direct their energies elsewhere. But to those who do feel and respond to it a new dimension is added to life, and a new depth to determination.

This is the core of the mountain challenge. Because it is so simple and direct nothing else can touch it for intensity, and all other aspects of climbing depend on it. We may tell non-mountaineers, we certainly try to tell ourselves, that we are not 'peak-baggers'. We lie. Unless we deeply desire to reach that summit, and gain immense satisfaction if we do, we would not be mountaineers.

But since 'peak-baggers' has a derogatory sound I should stress that pride is not usually the dominant note on reaching a peak. "They sent me on alone the length of the rope. I gained the summit and waited for them, feeling very little, very lonely, and much inclined to cry."[8] So writes Freda du Faur of her first ascent of Aoraki. And from Freda comes also the thought that an important part of this challenge is that no-one is hurt save perhaps the mountaineers themselves. Certainly what we are challenging, a mountain, is not affected. Freda comments after her climb of Maunga-atua (Mt. Sefton): "Serene and aloof as ever, the great mountain dominated the valley, unaltered, unalterable, no matter how many defiling feet might touch its white snows."[9]

A second strand of the mountain challenge is more subtle, of longer duration, and in some ways even more deeply satisfying. It is the challenge of staying alive and, preferably, comfortable, in an indifferent environment. Carrying on our bent backs the necessities for three or four weeks, plus a luxury or two, we escape from cloistered city life where mother earth is suffocating under a dead weight of asphalt and buildings, and where the weather is shut out by the suffocating walls of these buildings. In this we hark back to conditions closer to those of early humans, and of our pre-human ancestors. Of course we are still highly artificial. Freeze-dried food in plastic bags is a far cry from the pre-historic hunter's food, and tents and primus stoves many thousands of years from caves and flickering fires. But it is significant that snowcaves, and rock bivvies and camp fires, are especially appealing. For though we are still artificial, we are much closer than usual to dependence on nature and skill. At a deep level we feel more at one with our evolutionary past, and this is profoundly satisfying.

A third strand is more complex again. It is the challenge to use the mountain to test and overcome our greatest adversary, ourselves. It is always present. For me its most acute form is in that dreadful hour of starting. My unwilling body is bullied from the sleeping bag, food is forced into it, and a hesitant foot is set in the direction of the distant summit. Then, throughout the climb, the major challenge is always myself. Even very severe pitches could be climbed by many – perhaps even by me. That is I have the physical strength and skill to make the moves. What stops me then? Fear. The fear in my gut, tiny on broad holds and gentle slopes, explodes on pitches near or beyond my previous best and takes over my entire being. The pitch may not be beyond my physical limit and it may not even be near it. But I have to overcome this fear inside me to make the move.

Yet another strand is companionship. Shared hardship and danger creates a bond not lightly broken, and once again the comparative simplicity of the situation is the key. Working together for a political party, or in a job, we are just as dependent on others. But this dependence is complex, and neither success nor failure is as obvious and intense as when the shared task is sticking to the mountain, with injury or death the probable penalty of misplaced trust. Perhaps because of this (despair and laughter in a serious situation are separated only by a frown or a smile) mountain companionship is often laced with humour in improbable circumstances. The mutual strength gained by regarding the realization of one's worst fears as irresistibly funny is to me one of the great appeals of mountaineering.

Interlaced with challenge, in all its strands, and companionship, with all its closeness and humour, are a host of simple physical pleasures inseparable from the mountain picture. There is the pure joy of fluid movement: a fit body gliding gracefully over uneven ground, artistry in balance on small holds, exhilaration of speed in a glissade. There is the way in which a dry crust after two days without food excels the finest cuisine. The Reverend William Green, after a night out near the summit of Aoraki during the first serious attempt to reach the peak, says: "We lost no time in discussing some cold duck and bread, both of which seemed excellent, though the latter was now twenty days old ..."[10] And the exquisite feeling of pure water on dry throats is better than any beer. So too the bliss of sun after storm, rest after effort, warmth after cold. These joys, though available in city life, depend on contrast if they are not to be taken for granted. Providing this contrast is one of mountaineering's important claims to wisdom. It is true this wisdom depends on the principle of beating one's head against a brick wall because it is so nice when one stops. But our conclusion should be that this is a good principle, and that the person beating the head, and not the critic, is the sane one.

Finally, note that the danger inherent in mountaineering, often criticized, has been one of its most important influences on me. It has driven home to me again and again the message of the existentialists, and heightened for me the importance of Māui's determination to live life to the full though death be its end. In mountaineering, this ultimate issue of life and death cannot be dodged. It is at least potentially there in every mountain move we make. It is not alone in this. It is potentially there in every car we drive, every road we cross, every beat of our hearts. But in cars, and on roads, and in hearts, it is dulled by familiarity and complacency. In mountaineering it is obvious, simple, compelling. The issue of life and death is sharpened to a battle between a sloping hold and the force of gravity, and the feeling this arouses is intense indeed.

Tom Fyfe gives expression to it. He and his companions have come to a huge schrund as they descend from the first ascent of Aoraki. Darkness has fallen: "...our sense of touch was all we had to rely on. One at a time we moved on, the other two endeavouring to anchor; but, judging from the holds that I myself could obtain, a slip by one would have 'done for' us all."[11] All mountaineers have experienced similar situations.

Are mountaineers, then, simply walking death wishes disguised in old clothes? Quite the contrary. It is not a death wish that is stimulated by this situation but an urgent desire to live and laugh and love. It is contrast again that is crucial. With death starkly staring at us, without its usual camouflage of insurance policies and sheltered urban living, we live in those moments with exhilarating intensity.

This near clear look at death allows Gerard Manley Hopkins to use mountaineering as a metaphor for the mind's constant and more complex battle with death and despair:

O the mind, mind has mountains; cliffs of fall
Frightful, sheer, no-man-fathomed. Hold them cheap
May who ne'er hung there. Nor does long our small
Durance deal with that steep or deep. Here! Creep,
Wretch, under a comfort serves in a whirlwind: all
Life death does end and each day dies with sleep.[12]

So, for me, mountaineering not only immersed me in nature, it also clarified and intensified the complex challenges of everyday living: survival, relationships, simple physical joys, eating and drinking, and the mysterious boundary of death. That these are aspects of all life explains why they are so important to me. That mountaineering simplifies them, providing clear concrete instances, explains why it focuses my feelings so keenly, not just my mind. At least some of the appeal of mountaineering lies in its ability to be a practice ground for life itself.

I suppose that, because of this, it could be an escape, a substitute for facing up to the complexities of everyday living, and to the need to make something worthwhile of our lives in the face of inevitable death, which are our permanent and most important challenges. But it should be of great help in accepting these challenges, and in clarifying our priorities in them. We can return from simple mountain challenges more confident when facing complex ones. We can remember how to put aside pettiness and retain humour in working with others even when the shared danger is a confusing social or political or ecological one. We can retain from abrupt mountain contrasts the ability to enjoy and be content with simple things in everyday life. And we can surely live life more fully if every day, and not for moments only on sloping holds, we live conscious of life's mysterious end in death. For I believe we find richness of life by realizing its fragility and living it hugely nonetheless.

23. Physical Monism

By the 1970's I had moved completely away from belief in the Christian God, and was deeply involved in attempts to base my attitudes and my morals on the rapidly developing scientific theories about our planet and the universe of which it is so tiny a part. So I am an atheist, that is one who does not believe in a God or gods. But increasingly I became annoyed at being labelled by what I did not believe, rather than by what I did. It seemed a capitulation to the arrogant Christian tendency to refer all things to itself.

It also betrayed a narrow western mind-set. As discussed in chapter 9, in some schools of Indian thought the distinction between theism and atheism is of very little importance. And Gautama the Buddha was essentially an atheist in that, though he didn't deny that gods and goddesses existed, he thought them totally irrelevant to his religious quest. Yet it would be odd indeed to think the essence of his teachings had been satisfactorily summed up by noting that he was an atheist.

But there was a problem. There seemed to be, in the west, no alternative label for the position at which I had, with so much angst, arrived. So I decided to invent one.

I made clear in chapter 10 that I was deeply affected by the spiritual monism (advaita/non-dualism) expounded in much Indian scripture, especially the Upanishads and the writings of Shankara. Now I began to explore whether some of the good things which spiritual monism seems to do for its adherents can be done by a physical monism, my new label. By physical monism I mean the modern scientific picture of the universe used not just for intellectual understanding, but also as a basis for emotional and moral adjustment to life.

Experiencing unity

Firstly, spiritual monism gives me a picture of my place in the scheme of things not as an isolated entity but as integral part of a vastly greater whole.

'I', an apparently individual centre of consciousness, am but a momentary manifestation of a supreme and all pervasive consciousness, Brahman. So too are all living beings surrounding me, and the universe we all live in. All is Brahman: That art Thou.

The emotional satisfaction gained can be profound. It is like a lost child finding her family, and like the belonging one feels in one's own land, but in relation to the whole exciting universe and not just a tiny portion of it. And in Indian spiritual monism this is the effect it is meant to have: in place of our experience of being an individual entity, buffeted by other separate entities, we are to experience the bliss of belonging. It should be noted, however, that the effect could be different. We could feel annihilated as an individual, insignificant and despairing before the vastness of Brahman. Indeed, Ramanuja, a theistic philosopher writing some centuries after Shankara, contends that this would be the undesirable effect of Shankara's doctrine if its claims were seriously attended to.[1]

Can physical monism match this? Well, it certainly gives a basis for a sense of the unity of all things. The sciences are dedicated to the search for a unified theory which can account for all phenomena. While they have still a long way to go in this search, a picture is emerging which does place us in the scheme of things not as isolated unrelated entities but as integral parts of a vastly greater whole. There is a basic energy, which is the same throughout the vast reaches of the universe, and which manifests itself in a fantastic variety of living and non-living forms.

Interestingly, there was for a while in the development of the sciences a parallel to the spiritual monist doctrine of maya, the belief that the diverse manifestations of Brahman are inferior, appearances only. There was a tendency, perhaps still alive amongst some physicists, to regard physics as the real science, chemistry as less ultimate, and biology, let alone psychology, as dealing with complex appearances of energy, not with energy itself. But I think this has largely gone. All is regarded as equally real, it is just that we view reality in different ways for different purposes. We need to see it all as the same energy to sense the unity pulsating through all; but we need also to see the rich diversity to sense how wonderful this unity is. Physics without biology would give a very austere picture of the universe, just as biology without physics and chemistry would not do justice to how living things are related to the rest of the universe.

So the sciences are giving an increasingly detailed basis for a sense of unity with all things. Shankara advises us to realize unity with Brahman by meditating on Upanishadic evocations of transcendental unity.

Physical monism might suggest, rather, that we study modern physics and astronomy and chemistry and biology – these at least – and then meditate on their significance for our attitudes and actions. We can sense the unity of all life through our knowledge of the common factor of cell reproduction, which links us to all forms of life, including plants. We can sense the unity between us and inorganic things through our knowledge that both are composed of the same basic atoms and molecules. And we can wonder at the scope and vastness of this unity as we contemplate the incredible picture of the universe that modern astronomy gives, a picture matching at length in the west the spaciousness of the ancient Indian mythological view. Thus we would have a basis for experiencing unity in terms of what the universe is really like. It would "not depend on the will of man, but merely on what really and unalterably exists"[2] if the modern picture of the universe is in broad outline accurate.

This modern picture has not often been used for its emotional effect in this way, but here and there one can find poets and sages hymning it; thus, Rabindranath Tagore:

> *The same stream of life that runs through my veins night and day runs through the world and dances in rhythmic measures.*
>
> *It is the same life that shoots in joy through the dust of the earth in numberless blades of grass and breaks into tumultuous waves of leaves and flowers.*
>
> *It is the same life that is rocked in the ocean-cradle of birth and death, in ebb and flow.*
>
> *I feel my limbs are made glorious by the touch of this world of life.*
>
> *And my pride is from the life-throb of ages dancing in my blood this moment.*[3]

The emotional parallel with spiritual monism is complete in that here, too, there is ambiguity. This same modern picture of the universe can result and has resulted in a feeling not of exhilarating unity but of annihilation, insignificance. Nietzsche wrote: "Since Copernicus, mankind has been rolling from the centre towards x."[4] And Steven Weinberg, a physicist, muses as he flies over the fluffy clouds and winding mountainous roads of Wyoming:

> It is very hard to realize that all this is just a tiny part of an overwhelmingly hostile universe. It is even harder to realize

> that this present universe has evolved from an unspeakably unfamiliar early condition and faces a future of endless cold or intolerable heat. The more the universe seems comprehensible, the more it also seems pointless.
>
> But if there is no solace in the fruits of our research, there is at least some consolation in the research itself. Men and women are not content to comfort themselves with tales of gods and giants, or to confine their thoughts to the daily affairs of life; they also build telescopes and satellites and accelerators, and sit at their desks for endless hours working out the meaning of the data they gather. The effort to understand the universe is one of the few things that lifts human life a little above the level of farce, and gives it some of the grace of tragedy.[5]

This contrast between Tagore and Weinberg highlights the fact that the scientific picture of the universe, in itself, is value-neutral. As a physical monist I have to use it emotionally and morally in my attempts to adjust to life. How I do this doubtless depends on many complicated factors. But more Tagores and more Weinbergs holding up for me their varying valuations would certainly be of assistance to me in deciding on, or creating, my own.

A basis for moral feeling and action

Secondly, through the sense of unity with all that it invokes, spiritual monism can give a basis for moral feeling and action. By breaking down individuality it can help break down selfishness. This has often been expressed strikingly to me by Hindu friends, one of whom was not completely convinced of the truth of spiritual monism, but still stressed its moral power: "I'm not sure if there really is a para-atma … but I can see the importance of believing there is for then one has a basis for the belief that you and I are the same substance, and thus a basis for breaking down hostility and the habit of seeing differences." This should help us to feel concern for each other: "What is the real message of the Ramayana? To show compassion and love to one another, for all are part of para-atma, and since all are of one substance, all should care for each other."[6]

Again, however, there is ambiguity in spiritual monism. I am convinced that morally it often does work in this way, extending and sustaining our concern for others. But it can, and on occasion does, result in a sophisticated selfishness: a concentration on seeking one's own bliss by withdrawal into the mystical experience of unity, indifferent to relationships with, and concern for, others.

So, morally, what about physical monism? Well, in the same way, by evoking in me a sense of unity it, too, can provide me with a basis for moral feeling and action. For example, it helps break down my narrow selfishness in two ways.

Firstly, physical monism can extend my feeling for others. Many religions have recognized the affection and concern we have for our family and/or close friends and have, in different ways according to their different frameworks, attempted to move us to extend these feelings to the whole tribal or national group, to the whole human species, and, in the Indian traditions, to all living things. The trick is to convince us we have something in common – same ancestors, same mother or father creator god, same immersion in the round of rebirth. Physical monism has an excellent basis for this extension of fellow feeling, for the sciences tell us that we share basic molecular structures with all life forms. One scientist writes:

> [We have now] enough information to evoke the inspiring spectacle of the vast range of controlled activities that constitutes the life of man and of the living world … Even if man is very different it is fundamentally important to realize he is part of the one great living world.[7]
>
> We are just able to recognize that all men are brothers. Should we not go much further and proceed on the assumption that we are of one flesh, not only with animals but with all plants, fungi and bacteria as well? … this concept is the sober scientific truth.[8]

And my Hindu friend quoted above wrote to me:

> It could be that there is a soul which leaves this body and enters another … it would be wrong just to reject this idea. But it could be that elements of another's body are in our body now – reincarnation, recycling, in this sense. There must have been billions of people since the beginning, enough to cover the whole surface of the earth. We die, decay, a plant uses the material, someone eats the plant – so in this way there is some of other people in us, and thus the central energy manifests itself in different generations. Perhaps this is how the idea of central energy helps humanity, fellow-feeling; I realize some of your grandfather may be in me and some of mine in you, and I feel that though we are not linked genetically or by ordinary family ties yet we are linked, you are my brother, and so I feel for you.
>
> It is up to society how it spreads this idea, but it could work. Some feel this is giving up religion, but I don't think so. The fundamental

principle (fellow-feeling, helping one another) is the same, as it has been in all religions. Only beliefs about this or that as god differ."[9]

Secondly, physical monism can give a basis for moral feeling and action in terms of enlightened self-interest. By revealing our interrelatedness with all parts of our environment it can convince us that if we harm one part we could well be harming ourselves. This sort of attempt to broaden our understanding of what is really in our own best interests has been used a lot in current ecological debates.

Moreover, in ways not so directly involving an overall vision of unity, the sciences can contribute to an emotional basis for morality. For example, our survival as a species has been dependent both on aggressive feelings and actions toward things threatening our group, and on feelings of affection towards, and co-operative actions with, members of our group. It is easier now, understanding better how interrelated with all people and things we are, and horrifyingly aware of the power of modern weapons to destroy our environment along with our 'enemies', to give a rational justification for encouraging co-operative, and discouraging aggressive, feelings and actions. Moreover, having both sorts of feelings set in the evolutionary picture can help us come to terms with them more realistically, understanding that, like it or not, both are deep-rooted in our nature.

As with spiritual monism, there is ambiguity here. Nothing said above prevents me from reaffirming narrow selfishness. Even more easily in a vast interrelated environment than in a small human family I could say "Never mind my fellows, I'll get what I can for myself." Physical monism is neither better nor worse off than spiritual monism in this respect, for the connection between beliefs and feelings is not like that between premisses and conclusions in valid arguments.

Consciousness is the key

Thirdly, in spiritual monism this vision of unity and the resulting basis for moral feeling and action is not something imposed from outside the believer. It is our own essential nature, consciousness, which is the key to the transforming experience. Atman, our self-luminous awareness, is Brahman, the Supreme Reality. Hence, as Shankara insists, "it does not depend on the will of man, but merely on what really and unalterably exists". Of course we do need to exercise our will to meditate on and realize this reality. This is a point sometimes stressed by spiritual monists to highlight a contrast with theistic systems, especially of the Hebraic variety, where one's transformation is believed to be dependent on something external to oneself, namely the will of a separate God, and therefore not be in one's own control.

For a physical monist also consciousness is the key to this vision of unity and this basis for morality. However, this is in a lesser, though still vital, sense.

Consciousness is the key in that it has uncovered or created this unitary picture of the universe. It is not, of course, an individual human consciousness that has done this, but the painstaking co-operative effort of countless human minds since before the dawn of history, working wonderfully through religious mythology and philosophical speculation and, at length, through more rigorous theory formulation and experimental testing.

Moreover, it is through our consciousness that we, as individuals, can learn about this scientific world picture, and sense its significance and wonder. In this we do in a sense become part of a greater consciousness; certainly we transcend our individual consciousness in that we are released from a narrow subjective view of what we are, and from a self-centred view of how we relate to other beings and things. The self-luminous core of the human personality, consciousness, is the key to a transforming experience. Used properly in combined study and meditation on its own nature, and on the nature of all things, it can throw off (at least some of) its limitations, can expand itself and realize its unity with the greater whole.

Moreover this vision of unity is not something imposed from outside (though one hopes it bears some relation to what is outside); it is created and/or appropriated by our consciousness. Thus part of Shankara's stress on the importance of consciousness is retained in physical monism. However, an important part of Shankara's view is not retained, indeed is denied. For modern science believes consciousness is but one manifestation of the basic energy, and a rare and recent one at that. Shankara believes it is the basic energy.

Wonder, awe and mystery

Fourthly, despite the intimacy and familiarity suggested by the belief that our essence is identical with Supreme Reality, spiritual monism gives its adherents a basis for a sense of wonder and awe and mystery. Brahman is immensely greater than this apparently individual speck of it that I think is me. Brahman is incomprehensible, cannot be grasped by the mind: it is that before which words turn back[10] – necessarily so since it is the whole of which we are apparent parts, and the part cannot fully comprehend the whole.

For a physical monist, what of wonder and awe and mystery? Have the sciences made them obsolete? Though at one time in the West it was thought they might, they have surely deepened our sense of mystery. Mysteries are not unanswered questions which the mind might one day answer, such as details of inter-relationships between quarks and bosons, atoms, molecules or stars. Mystery, to me, refers to a sense of wonder at the complexity of such inter-relationships, which is increased not decreased by increased knowledge of them. It refers also to our inability to give any ultimate explanation of the universal process as a whole, or even to explain why there should be anything at all, rather than nothing.

This inability is often cited as a reason for proposing an ultimate metaphysical explanation – Brahman, or Tao, or God. But these do not in any way solve or dissolve the mystery as even believers in them admit – they are mystery supreme. They simply give a name for the totality of things, and some theory about, or analogy for, the nature of their inter-relationships (e.g. Brahman – the interrelationship is of the nature of consciousness); or they add an entity to be inter-related with the rest (God with the world). And they raise the even less answerable question of how and why this supernatural entity exists rather than just physical reality, or nothing at all.

In physical monism, then, there is necessarily an element which corresponds to the 'mystery impenetrable' aspect of Shankara's Brahman. Let me give the two basic examples, the big and the small.

Consider the 'boundaries of the universe' mystery. We have enormously expanded our notion of the size of the universe, and enormously extended our knowledge of how areas remote from our own relate to other parts and to our solar system. We can postulate a universe expanding out from a theoretical centre or big bang, and even – shades of Hindu mythology – an alternatively expanding and contracting universe. But if we ask "Expanding into what? What lies beyond the boundaries of the expanding universe, or outside the contracted explosive dot of the concentrated universe?", we simply do not know how to answer, or even to imagine an answer.

Nor are we in better shape if we say there are no boundaries, for we cannot really conceive of it going on forever without end. Indeed, a basic 'meditation' for physical monists is to lie in a mountain meadow on a clear night, gazing at the stars and boggling the mind with the impossibility of imagining either an end or a forever to space.

All our explanations are relative to a limited sphere and a particular viewpoint. I can say what is outside New Zealand, but only because I place it in the context of planet Earth. I can say what is outside the Earth, but only because I have a wide but comprehensible sphere of reference, the solar system. And we can place our solar system in a galaxy, and relate our galaxy to others. But I cannot say what is outside the universe, for there is no wider sphere: 'universe' is simply a name for the totality, so there can be no wider sphere. So whether space has an end or not is not a problem which the mind might solve, but a mystery, a producer of wonder and humility. The physical monist's totality, the universe, is a mystery as much as is Brahman for Shankara, and for the same reasons. And, as with Brahman, we can take up an attitude to the universe, puny heroic specks that we are, and we can base this attitude as much as possible on what we know about the nature of inter-relationships within this totality. But we cannot explain the universe, dissolve the mystery, for there is no wider sphere in which to place it, and hence explain it.

At the other end of the scale, where the smallest sub-atomic particles dissolve into waves of energy or fields of force, so that we do not even know how to speak of or imagine them, there is also a mystery. Explanation is simply the relating of one thing or process to another. In this context it involves relating a particular thing or type to a more general thing or type. Thus we explain the characteristics of the water molecule by relating it to hydrogen and oxygen atoms which are more general, that is occur in combinations other than H_2O. We explain the difference between a hydrogen and an oxygen atom by relating them both to the structure of atoms and their differing combinations and orbits of particles smaller still. And so we go on down the fascinating trail of the physicist, hunting the elusive basic particles or forces.

Now wherever we stop, whether with the atom like some ancient Indians and Greeks, or with subatomic particles or vibrations or flashes of causal energy, like other ancient Indians and Greeks, or with highly sophisticated modern understandings of energy, we have only explained in terms of interrelationships. We can say why a hydrogen atom behaves and combines differently from an oxygen atom (because the structure, in terms of numbers and relationships of sub-atomic particles, is different). But we cannot say of our basic particles or waves or vibrations why they are as they are. We can only say that they are. Of course we can dig deeper and deeper and replace our 'ultimate' level with another: physics has been doing this with great excitement since Rutherford. But we do not remove, we only shift, the mystery. Here again we have not a problem which the human mind might solve, but simply the necessity that explanations in terms of interrelationships cannot in turn explain the whole. Before we can give such explanations we have to accept the whole, or, rather, some basic model for envisaging the whole.

Bleaker comforts but great advantages

I am suggesting, then, that so far as four basic areas crucial to adjustment to life are concerned – a sense of unity with everything, a basis for moral feeling and action, a key role for consciousness, and a sense of wonder and mystery – physical monism can function as effectively, or ineffectively, as can spiritual monism. But a huge part of the appeal of traditional religious beliefs lies, I believe, in the comforts they appear to provide in the face of the countless ills and other misfortunes that plague us in life, and, above all, in the face of the certainty of our death. Can physical monism help us here as well?

It needs to be acknowledged, firstly, that the answers physical monism gives here are bleaker, and the comforts colder, than some of those given by systems which believe death is not the end of us. But in many such systems the comforts come at a heavy price. If you live according to the precepts of the religion concerned you are promised eternal life in heaven, or a happier rebirth, or the timeless bliss of nirvana. But if you don't, eternal agony in the flames and boiling pitch of hell, or an endless cycle of rebirths into suffering, are the threatened fates. As a physical monist I am free from fear of these fates.

Secondly, facing up to the truth about impermanence and death is strong motivation to live fully, as I have explained in the discussions of Māui and of existentialism. I can understand how this might seem like making the best of a bad job, even desperation tactics, to those who feel it likely that we will carry on in some form after death. Moreover, there are times when the prospect of cessation at death seems bleak indeed, and other times when I wish I could call on a goddess or god to save me or a loved one from imminent danger. Above all, I enjoy life so intensely that I don't want it to end. But I believe that, after I die, I won't be around to regret not being alive, so this isn't a real worry. And, most of the time, I find it exciting and fulfilling to use the impending end of my life as motivation to make the most of life during the brief period of my existence.

Once again, of course, it comes down to what you believe. And modern understandings of the universe, and of life in it, lead me to believe very strongly that everything I enjoy in life –sensations, activity, thoughts and feelings – are totally dependent on the complex interactions of the atoms and molecules which make up my body and brain. It follows that when these interactions cease, and the complex structures they depend on decay into their constituent parts – as they clearly do at death – all these sensations and activities and thoughts and feelings simply cease to be. Death is not an event which will happen to me: it is the end of me. And this offers me ways of making of it something positive.

Leaving impending death aside, there are other huge advantages for me in being a physical monist. I am free from religious regulations and restrictions, free to work out for myself what is right and what is wrong, what is the best way for me to live my life as much as possible in harmony with all living beings and with the environment which we all share. It is bliss to feel this freedom, and very satisfying and exciting to use it. Maybe I feel this bliss especially intensely because of the time when I felt the yoke of Yahweh pressing heavily on me. Certainly we appreciate freedom more acutely the more intensely it contrasts with what we gain freedom from, be it cold, or effort, or restriction, or depression or some other form of misery. Perhaps people brought up with no religious shibboleths to inhibit them would not feel this freedom with quite the same intensity. So, perhaps a little bizarrely, and for this as well as other reasons, I am glad now that I went through my intense religious period.

Physical monism also gives me, at long last, a framework for understanding human life and morality which does not confuse me. When I believed we were created by a loving God I constantly anguished over how we could be so cruel to each other, and why there is so much pain and suffering from disease and decrepitude. Now that I see us as but a stage in a long evolutionary process, a process marked by fierce competition as well as by equally fierce love and loyalty to family and tribe, I still anguish over cruelty and suffering but feel I can understand it. We are a work in progress, not a finished product, and it is an unplanned spasmodic progress. This understanding does not force me to resigned acceptance of cruelty and suffering, but gives me a more informed basis from which to try to counter it, and a more realistic assessment of how difficult this task is.

These are benefits which I can explain in words. But the greatest joy to me is the feeling of blissful belonging which flows over, through and around me as I sense at a basically non-verbal level that I am a tiny but integral part of the astonishing energy of the universe. I mentioned in the chapters on Hinduism my intense experiences of unity with all during and after my immersion in Shankara's spiritual monism. These experiences are equally frequent and ecstatic now that I have them in relation to the physical universe. Tagore's poem, quoted earlier, expresses this feeling for me in relation to my unity with all living things. I feel it also, with equal intensity, in relation to the whole universe, stars, galaxies, atoms, quarks, rivers, mountains, the sea - everything. This feeling can fill me and take me over wherever I am and whatever I am doing - watching David Attenborough programmes on TV, collecting firewood and then later watching it burn, standing awed as a river pours over a huge boulder, watching our grandchildren playing in the sea, picnicking with Ann beside a lake or mountain stream, or emerging alone above the bushline on a peak in the Southern Alps. I am an integral part of everything, for all things, including me, are varying forms of one fundamental energy. As his father said to Svetaketu, "Tat twam asi (That you are)". And that, also, am I.

Whether because of my earlier immersion in Christian theology, or because of an inbuilt need which many humans share, I deeply desire a framework within which to understand myself and try to create a worthwhile life. For the reasons and feelings inadequately expressed above I much prefer my physical monism to any of the traditional religious frameworks for living, even that of my beloved Hinduism. But in a way this is an irrelevant assessment. I no longer believe in any such metaphysical systems. Even if I were unhappy in my physical monism, metaphysical comforts would no longer be available to me. So that I am very happy is fortunate indeed.

24. Papatūānuku,[1] My Mother and My Nourisher

One thing remains. Though I get great exhilaration from feeling at one with the vast physical energy of the universe, this unity is with an impersonal force. Perhaps because of my background in Christianity, where God and Jesus are thought of as personal, and perhaps also because of my enthusiastic reaction to all the personal goddesses and gods of Hinduism, I do feel a need to relate to the universe, or at least to the portion of it we call the Earth, in a more personal way.

This is where my immersion in Māori religion comes in, firstly through my teaching about it, and then through my involvement in its emotions and rituals on the greenstone trails. As mentioned in ch. 18, because it evolved in, and therefore fits so beautifully with, this land in which I live and which I love, it arouses deeper and more satisfying emotions in me than even Hinduism. And, as with Hinduism, I find it easy to be moved by and respond to Māori beliefs about, and personifications of, the natural forms and forces about me, without accepting the beliefs and personifications as literally true.

I am moved by many Māori personifications. When gazing in awe at a giant rātā or kauri tree, leaning my head against its trunk to sense its power and its age, it is natural for me to feel it as a person, as a child of Tāne, and to imagine the protective power of Tāne all around me, and his immense power of growth and renewal sustaining me. When being buffeted by ferocious winds, whether in the mountains or at sea, I find it exciting to feel it as the fury of Tāwhiri trying to avenge the separation of his beloved parents Rangi and Papa. On the cabin wall of our yacht *Karoro* Ann and I have a striking wooden carving of the face of Tangaroa – I should really say Tangaloa as we bought it in Tonga and this is the Tongan form of his name. So I have a personal name for the sea and all that it has meant and means to me in delight and in terror. Rangi I use less often. The sky is to me, as a physical monist, the unimaginable vastness of space, not a ceiling above our earth, and is therefore more difficult to imagine and relate to as a person. Besides, Tāne told us to let Rangi stand far above us, and become as a stranger to us. But he also told us to let Papa remain close to us as our nursing mother.[2] And it is to Papatūānuku that I turn most to warm up my physical monism.

Papatūānuku, also known as planet Earth, is, in a very important sense, my mother and the mother of every living thing on her, past, present and future. Because of her position in relation to the sun, and because of the substances of which she is composed and surrounded, life emerged and evolved in her seas and on her lands and in her air. By her waters and her soils and her atmosphere she sustains all her billions of children. She is indeed our mother and our nourisher. And I feel grateful every day for this chance of living on this planet, and every day I delight in her bounty and her beauty.

Is this just romantic nonsense on my part, or do I believe the Earth is itself a living organism, perhaps even a conscious one, as some versions of the Gaia theory[3] seem to suggest?

Neither. I can enter into the lives and emotions and situations of characters in a novel without believing they exist as real individual people. I can hope for them and fear for them, and even carry on imaginary conversations with them, sometimes long after reading the book. So too I can imaginatively relate to Papatūānuku as if she were a real person, can hope and fear for her, can love her, can tell her how much I love her, can thank her for all her manifold blessings to me, without believing she really is a conscious individual person. Jesus might even have been pleased with me about this, for he is reported as saying "unless you become as a little child you cannot enter the kingdom of heaven"[4], and little children frequently relate to and converse with imaginary friends.

It is hard for me to express in words how satisfying and comforting this is for me. And maybe, yet again, this comfort stems from my Christian period. Christians are urged to think of God and Jesus as personal friends, to talk to them, confide in them, love them. So be it. If Papatūānuku is, for me, a substitute for Yahweh and/or Jesus, then she is also, for me, a much more satisfying, and much less interfering and demanding, substitute than Yahweh or Jesus seemed to be for me.

But in any case, romantic nonsense or not, this imaginative personification is only a part of why I now regard myself as at home in Papatūānuku. Even though I really believe this planet is a slightly flattened sphere of inorganic matter, with a thin film of living beings on or near its surface, I love this planet passionately and, personifications aside, Papatūānuku is my preferred name for planet Earth. And when I have boggled my mind by gazing at the night sky of stars, and trying to imagine the unimaginable distances to them and between them, it is to Papatūānuku, and the extraordinary story of the emergence and evolution of her life forms, that I turn for a cosier and more imaginable entity to feel at one with. With Tagore I rejoice in the "stream of life that runs through my veins night and day",[5] all life, animal and plant and microbial. With trampers and mountaineers I am awed by the majesty and beauty of hills and valleys, and with sailors and surfers am fascinated and frightened by the power of the sea, and float in peaceful joy at its serenity on days of calm or in sheltered anchorages.

Words, words – but perhaps they at least point to the feelings I am trying to share. I am writing this on our yacht *Karoro* in a bay in Port Hardy, D'Urville Island. Bellbird Bay, as we call it, is surrounded by heavily forested hills. Day after day Ann and I wander into this forest so that its beauty and age and silence can caress and calm us, and, in Ann's case, so she can capture its perfection in pastel. And these are my thoughts and feelings.

Firstly, it is absolutely marvelous. Sunlight glances through leaf and bough and vine, creating endless patterns of light and shade, limitless shapes and forms and angles. Birds dart into my vision, then disappear from sight but not from sound as song dances back and forth between them. On yet smaller scale insects vibrate in and out of sunbeams. And, beyond sight or sound, I sense the dark and fertile underworld which sustains all this.

A hymn we used to sing asks, "... though every prospect pleases, and only man is vile?" But hang on a minute, mate. Man may often be vile but he, we, nonetheless belong here. For, secondly, I feel profoundly that I am as integral a part of this scene as are the trees and vines and birds and insects and microbes and fungi, though arguably a more complex and more troubled part. I, like all the rest, am a child of Papatūānuku. And, thirdly, as this deep certainty mingles with the beauty and the peace, my conscious complexities and confusions dissolve into the underlying pattern of life and death, of flourishing and decay, which in so unconscious and untroubled a way pervades the perfection that surrounds me.

So my long story, full of sound and fury and signifying very little, ends not with a bang but with a love-song. I love Papatūānuku. Out of her fecundity I have emerged for a brief moment as a conscious person. During this brief moment she has richly nourished me, physically, mentally and emotionally. When I die the atoms and molecules then in my body will return to Papa and her atmosphere to become parts of other living beings, or to become part of her basic substance.

After Dad died I received a sympathy card which had on it a picture of autumn leaves below a tree, and a caption saying "The leaves die, but then they nourish new life". So let it be for me. Jaharwarlal Nehru asked that after he died some of his ashes be sprinkled in Mother Ganga at Allahabad, and the rest be taken high in a plane and scattered over the fields where the peasants of India toil, so that he would become "an indistinguishable part of India".[6] Substitute Rough Creek, Arthur's Pass, where the ashes of my mother and my oldest sister were scattered, and Papatūānuku and Aotearoa/New Zealand[7], and so let it be for me. For on no sound evidence at all I believe passionately that Papatūānuku is the most beautiful planet in the universe and, on only slighter sounder grounds, that Aotearoa is the most beautiful part of Papatūānuku. I have been fortunate enough to spend a lifetime as a child, and thus an integral part, of Papatūānuku and Aotearoa. So I am heartily content.

End Notes

1. When I Was A Child

1 1 Corinthians 11. 5–6, 10.
2 Luke 14. 15–24.
3 e.g.. Leviticus 18–22 and 20.13; Romans 1. 26–27.

2. God 'Calls'

1 John 3.16.
2 Exodus 20.3.
3 Exodus 20.5.
4 Matthew 13.49–50.

4. Arguments for the Existence of God

1 William Paley, 1743–1805: *Natural Theology, or Evidences of the Existence and Attributes of the Deity.*
2 Hume, 1711–76: note especially *Dialogues Concerning Natural Religion*, edited and with introduction by Norman Kemp Smith, Thomas Nelson and Sons, London, 1935, and 2nd edition 1947.
3 *Dialogues* Pt. VIII, pp. 186–7 in Kemp Smith.
4 Kemp Smith, pp. 76–9.
5 *Dialogues* Pt. II, especially pp.149–50: Pts. III and IV; and Pt. VII, especially pp.176–7.
6 *Dialogues* Pt. VIII.
7 *Dialogues* Pt. II, especially pp. 144 and149.
8 *Dialogues* Pt. IV, especially pp. 161–2.
9 *Dialogues* Pt. V, especially pp.167–9.
10 *Dialogues* Pt. X, p.202.
11 Tertullian, 160 to about 225 A.D; *De Carne Christi*, ch. 5.

5. Arguments Against the Existence of the Christian God

1 Isaiah 55.9.
2 Job 38.4.
3 Matthew 5.44; see also Luke 6.35.
4 *The Brothers Karamazov*, trs. Constance Garnet, Everyman's Library edition, J.M. Dent and Sons, 1927, vol. I, pp.247–51.
5 *New Essays in Philosophical Theology*, ed. Antony Flew and Alasdair McIntyre, SCM Press, London, 1955.
6 *New Essays*, p. 96.

6. Theology

1 e.g. Mark 2.10.
2 Mark 10.17–18; Luke 18.18–19.
3 Matthew 12.17–18, 18.21–22, 21.1–5, 27.9–10.
4 Genesis 1.3.
5 John 1.1–5.
6 John 1.14.
7 John 14.6.
8 e.g. Matthew 5.44, 18.21–22; Luke 17.3–4.
9 Luke 10.29–37.
10 Mattthew 13.49–50; see also Mark 9.47–48.
11 Mark 11.15–17; Matthew 21.12–13.
12 Mark 15.34; Matthew 27.45. In Luke, Jesus dies a more seemly death, saying, as he is crucified, "Father forgive them; for they know not what they do" (Luke 23.34); and, at the end, crying "Father, into thy hands I commit my spirit" (Luke 23.46.).
13 Philippians 2.5–7.
14 *The Qur'an*, Sura 5.116–7.
15 Acts 2.1–4.
16 Micah 6.6–8.
17 Amos 5.21.

7. Sherpas and their Buddhism

1 Sir Edmund Hillary, *Schoolhouse in the Clouds*, Doubleday, New York, 1964.

2 For a general account of Sherpa life and religion, see Christoph van Furer-Haimendorf, *The Sherpas of Nepal*, John Murray, London, 1964.

9. Materialism, Proto-scientific Theories, and Dualism

1 Surendranath Dasgupta, *A History of Indian Philosophy* (5 vols.), Cambridge University Press, 1957.

2 Radhakrishnan and Moore, *A Source Book in Indian Philosophy*, Princeton University Press, 1957.

3 *Source Book*, pp.227–35, 247–9.

4 Matthew 19.3.

5 Dasgupta, Vol. 1, pp. 326–30; B.N. Seal, *The Positive Sciences of the Ancient Hindus*, Longmans Green and Co., London and New York, 1915 Motilal Banarsidass, Delhi, 1985, p.99.

6 Dasgupta, Vol. 1, pp. 243–58; Seal, pp. 24–43 (my account is a simplified summary of the rather complex processes outlined in these pages).

7 Dasgupta, Vol. 1, pp. 158–68; *Source Book*, pp. 280–88.

8 Dasgupta, Vol. 1, pp.258–9.

10. Advaita/non-dualism

1 For the religion of the invading Aryans, and its intermingling with the religious ideas and practices of the earlier inhabitants of India, see: *Dasgupta*, Vol. 1, chs. 2 & 3; *Source Book*, pp. 3–36; A. L. Basham, *The Wonder That Was India*, Sidgwick and Jackson, London, 1954, ch. 7, pp. 232–56.

2 See ch.18.

3 For convenience the priestly class is throughout referred to as 'brahmin' instead of 'brahman' and given a lower case 'b', to distinguish it from the universal energy Brahman.

4 *The Upanishads*, trs. and edited by Swami Nikhilananda, abridged edition, Harper Torchbooks, New York, 1964, p. 334, Chandogya Upanishad 6.12.1-3; see also Basham, pp. 250–51.

5 Sankara, *Brahmasutrabhasya*, trs. George Thibaut in *Sacred Books of the East* (*SBE*), Vol.38, Oxford University Press, London, 1896.

6 Isaiah 55.9.

7 *The Upanishads*, Nikhilananda, p.271, Taittariya Upanishad, 2,9,1.

8 *SBE*, Vol.38, p.340 (4.1.3).

9 *Religious Studies* 6, no. 1, March 1970, pp.57–68.

10 See Ramanuja's *Brahmasutrabhasya*, trs. George Thibaut, *SBE* Vol.48, Oxford University Press,

11 *SBE* Vol.38, p.164 (3.2.21) and pp. 333–7 (4.1.2).

12 *SBE* Vol.38, p.165 (3.2.21).

13 Matthew 6.4.

14 e.g. Conze, *Buddhism Its Essence and Development*, Cassirer, Oxford 1951, 3d ed. 1957 pp.43–48 *(The Four Holy Truths); A Source Book in Indian Philosophy*, pp. 273–8.

15 *A Source Book in Indian Philosophy*, pp. 289–92 (from Aggi-Vacchagotta Sutta in Majjhima Nikaya, i.483–8).

12. Ganga and Hinduism

1 Edmund Hillary, *From the Ocean to the Sky*, Hodder and Stoughton, London, 1979, pp 241–58.

2 *The Gospel of Sri Ramakrishna*, Mahedranath Gupta, trs. Swami Nikhilananda, Sri Ramakrishna Math, Chennai, vol. 2, ch. 45, pp.741–42.

3 *Gandhi, All Men Are Brothers*, compiled and edited by Krishna Kripalani, first published by Unesco in 1918, p. 76, saying 93.

4 *Hymns of the Tamil Saivite Saints*, ed. Kingsbury and Phillips, Association Press, Calcutta, 1921, p. 97.

5 Heinrich Zimmer, *Myths and Symbols in Indian Art and Civilization*, Harper Torchbooks, New York, 1962. p. 19.

6 Zimmer, *Myths and Symbols*, p.6.

7 Karl H. Potter, *Presuppositions of India's Philosophies*, 1963, reprinted Motilal

Banarsidass, Delhi, 1991, pp. 11–12.

8 *Tales and Parables of Sri Ramakrishna*, first published Sri Ramakrishna Math, Chennai, 1978, pp. 120-21, parable 40.

9 *Tales and Parables*, p.119, parable 39.

13. Early Years

1 For 'translations' of the Qu'ran into English see: *The Koran Interpreted*, A.J. Arberry, London, Allen and Unwin, 1980; and, *The Meaning of the Glorious Koran*, M. M. Pickthall, first published A.A. Knopf, New York, 1930. Both respect the Muslim view that the Qu'ran (Koran) cannot be adequately translated. My quotes, here and the one in chapter 6, follow Arberry's wording and verse numbers. Verse numbers vary in different 'translations', though not by much. I have given Pickthall's numbering in brackets, and in other 'translations' it should not be difficult to locate the verses concerned.

2 e.g. Sura 3.57-64, 198 (64–71,199).

3 e.g. Suras 2.81 (87), 3.37-56 (42–63), 5.116–7 (116–7).

4 e.g. Sura 4.169 (171).

5 Yann Martel, *Life of Pi*, Canongate, Edinburgh, 2003, chs. 17–20, 23.

6 e.g. Sura 2.226–32 (226–32).

7 Sura 4.3 (3)and 127–8 (128–9), Sura 2.241–2 (240–41).

8 Also, a frequent description of Allah is "All-forgiving, All-compassionate", e.g. Sura 2.226–32 (226).

9 e.g. Sura 2.172 (177), Sura 4.40 (36).

10 e.g. Sura 6.124 (125) and 128 (129), Sura 7.37–51 (37–53).

11 There are numerous translations of *The Analects*, and the verse numbering is not the same in all. I give the numbering of D.C. Lau's translation, Penguin Classics, 1979, but have in places paraphrased rather than quoting his exact wording.

12 *The Analects*, Bk. 17.7.

13 *The Analects*, Bk. 5.20.

14 *The Analects*, Bk. 11.26.

15 Lao Tzu, *Tao Te Ching*, trs. D. C. Lau, Penguin Books, Harmondsworth, 1963.

16 *The Complete Works of Chuang Tzu*, trs. Burton Watson, Columbia University Press, 1968.

17 *Tao Te Ching*, Bk. 1.39.

18 *Tao Te Ching*, Bk. 1.20, Bk. 2.186.

19 *Tao Te Ching*, Bk. 2.186.

20 *Tao Te Ching*, Bk.1.1.

21 *Chuang Tzu*, section 19, 'Mastering Life'.

22 *Chuang Tzu*, section 18, 'Perfect Happiness'. See also Arthur Waley, *Three Ways of Thought in Ancient China*, Allen and Unwin, London, 1939, pp. 21–2.

14. Buddhism

1 Conze, Edward, *Buddhism Its Essence and Development*, Cassirer, Oxford, 1951,3rd ed. 1957; *Buddhist Texts Through the Ages*, Cassirer, Oxford, 1954; *Buddhist Meditation*, Allen and Unwin, London, 1956.

2 Conze, *Buddhism*, p.58.

3 Conze, *Buddhist Meditation*, especially pp. 79–80, 95, 104–7.

4 *Buddhist Meditation*, pp.104–7

5 *Buddhist Meditation*, p.123.

6 *Buddhist Meditation*, pp.127–8.

7 *Buddhist Meditation*, pp.131–3

8 Conze, *Buddhist Texts Through the Ages*, pp.127–35, especially 131–2.

15. Hinduism Again

1 For a very careful discussion of Tantric ritual use of maithuna (sexual intercourse) see John Woodroffe, *Shakti and Shakta*, Pt. XXII, 'Pancatattva or Secret Ritual', especially pp. 561–81.

2 Woodroffe, p.581.

3 Woodroffe, p.566.

4 Woodroffe, p.581.

5 Woodroffe, p.561.

6 *Tales and Parables of Sri Ramakrishna*, Sri Ramakrishna Math, Chennai, 1978, Tale 40.

7 Alas, I have been unable to locate the source of this memorable phrase, but I am certain I did not make it up.

8 Rabindranath Tagore, *The Religion of Man*, Allen and Unwin, London, 1931.

9 *The Religion of Man*, pp. 18–19.

10 *The Religion of Man*, p. 144–5.

11 *Gandhi, An Autobiography*, trs. Mahadev Desai, Beacon Press paperback edition, Boston, 1957, p.327.

12 *The Collected Works of Mahatma Gandhi*, Govt. of India, New Delhi, 1958.
13 Gandhi, *All Men Are Brothers*, ed. Krishna Kripalani, Navajivan Publishing House, Amedabad, 1960, p.91.
14 *Collected Works*, Vol. 7, pp.72–3 (originally Indian Opinion, 6.7.1907). See also Jim Wilson, 'Gandhi's God – A Substitute For The British Empire', *Religion* Vol. 16, 1986, pp. 343–57.
15 *The Gandhi Reader*, ed. Homer A. Jack, AMS Press, New York, 1956, chapter 10 (pp. 235–53).
16 *The Gandhi Reader*, chapter 18, especially pp.426–37.
17 Genesis 1.29

17. Fiji: Religious Adventures

1 J. Wilson, 'Text and Context in Fijian Hinduism', *Religion*, Routledge and Kegan Paul, London and Boston, Vol. 5, 1975.
2 Rudolf Otto, *The Idea of the Holy*, trs. J.W. Harvey, OUP, New York, 1st published 1917.

18. Māori Religion

1 Antony Alpers, *Māori Myths and Tribal Legends*, Longman Paul, Auckland, 1964, pp.15–16; Te Rangi Hiroa (Peter Buck), *The Coming of the Māori* , Māori Purposes Fund Board/Whitcoulls, 1st Pub. 1949, 2nd. Ed. 1950, my copy reprinted 1982, p.434; Eric Schwimmer, *The World of the Māori* , Reed, Wellington, 1966, pp.13–14.
2 Hiroa, p. 435.
3 Hiroa, p. 435.
4 Alpers, pp.16–27; George Grey, *Polynesian Mythology*, Whitcombe and Tombs, Christchurch, 1956, pp. 1–11; Hiroa, pp.438–41; Schwimmer, pp. 15–18.
5 Alpers, pp.28–70; Grey, pp.12–44; Schwimmer, pp.24–30; Hiroa, pp.4–5, 414–15.
6 Alpers, p.62.
7 Alpers, p.70; see also Hiroa, 453.
8 Alpers, p.70; see also Hiroa, 453.
9 R.S. Oppenheim, *Māori Death Customs*, Reed, Wellington, 1973, p.41; Schwimmer, p.60.
10 Hiroa, pp.443–4, 526, 531–6; Schwimmer, pp.114–6.
11 Hiroa, p. 526.
12 Schwimmer, p.116.

19. The Greenstone Trail

1 Barry Brailsford, *Greenstone Trails*, A.H. & A.W. Reed, Wellington, 1984.
2 *Song of Waitaha; The histories of a nation*, published by Ngātapuwae Trust, 1994; printed by Wyatt and Wilson Print, Christchurch; bound by F. Cartwright and Son Ltd., Christchurch.
3 *Whispers of Waitaha*, Wharariki Publishing Company, 2006.

21. Nietzsche and Existentialism

1 *Gay Science*, section 125.
2 *Will to Power*, Bk. I.1.5.
3 Psalm 8.4.
4 *The Antichrist*, 47.
5 *The Antichrist*, 62.
6 I regret I have been unable to re-find this quote, but I did not make it up.
7 *The Antichrist*, 47.
8 *Twilight of the Idols: Morality as Anti-Nature*, 6.
9 Wikipedia article, first section.
10 Martin Heidegger, *Sein und Zeit*, 1927; English trs. *Being and Time*, London, SCM Press, 1962, and Albany State University of New York, 1966.
11 Jean-Paul Sartre, *L'Etre et Le Neant*, 1943; English trs. *Being and Nothingness*, Philosophical Library, 1956.
12 *Dark Side of the Moon*, 1973, side 1, track 4, "Time".
13 *Obscured by Clouds*, 1972, side 2, track 8 "Free Four".
14 *Ummagumma*, 1969, Record 2, side 3, track 2 "Grantchester Meadows".

22. Mountaineering

1 Paul Tillich, *Systematic Theology*, University of Chicago Press, Chicago, 1967, 1.12; and *Dynamics of Faith*, Harper and Row, New York, 1957, 1.
2 Aoraki/Mt Cook is New Zealand's highest peak.
3 Peter Graham, *Mountain Guide*, ed. John Pascoe, A.H. and A.W. Reed, Wellington, 1965, p.96.

4 Freda du Faur, *The Conquest of Mt. Cook*, Allen and Unwin, London, 1915, p.102.
5 Freda du Faur, p. 198.
6 Fyfe, T.C., *Otago Daily Times*, Feb. 21, 1895; *N.Z. Alpine Journal*, vol. II, No. 7, May 1895, p.36.
7 Freda du Faur, p. 27.
8 Freda du Faur, p. 104.
9 Freda du Faur, p. 238.
10 Green, W.S., *The High Alps of New Zealand*, London, 1883, p.262.
11 Fyfe, T.C., *N.Z. Alpine Journal*, vol.II, No. 7, May 1895, p.37.
12 Hopkins, *Gerard Manley, A Selection of His Poems and Prose*, ed. W.H. Gardner, Penguin Poets Edition, 1st pub. 1953, p.61 ("No worst, there is none. Pitched past pitch of grief ...").

23. Physical Monism

1 Ramanuja, *Brahmasutrabhasya*, 1.1.1, trs. Thibaut, Sacred Books of the East, vol. 48, p.70.
2 Shankara, *Brahmasutrabhasya*, 3.2.21, trs. Thibaut, Sacred Books of the East, vol.38, p.165.
3 Tagore, *Gitanjali*, LXIX.
4 Nietzsche, *The Will to Power*, Bk. 1, 1.5
5 Weinberg, *The First Three Minutes*, New York, Basic Books, 1977, pp. 154–5.
6 Wilson, J., 'Text and Context in Fijian Hinduism', *Religion* 5, p.106.
7 Young, J. Z., *Introduction to the Study of Man*, Oxford, Clarendon Press, 1971, pp.vi & vii.
8 Young, *Introduction to the Study of Man*, p.15.
9 See Wilson, 'Text and Context', pp.103–4.
10 e.g. *Brhadaranyaka Upanishad* IV.iv.22; *Taittiriya Upanshad* II.iv.1.

24. Papatūānuku, My Mother and My Nourisher

1 'Papatūānuku' is the Māori name for Mother Earth.
2 See, e.g. George Grey, *Polynesian Mythology*, Whitcombe and Tombs, Christchurch, 1956, p.2.
3 James Lovelock, *Gaia – A New Look at Life on Earth*, Oxford University Press, 1979.
4 Matthew 18.3.
5 Tagore, *Gitanjali*, LXIX.
6 Jaharwalal Nehru, *Will and Testament*, June 21, 1954 – accessible on internet.
7 "Aotearoa" is the Māori name for New Zealand.

www.ingramcontent.com/pod-product-compliance
Ingram Content Group UK Ltd.
Pitfield, Milton Keynes, MK11 3LW, UK
UKHW021906190726
13853UKWH00002B/539

9 789387 242647